Growth and Inflation
in the Soviet Economy

Growth and Inflation
in the Soviet Economy

Fyodor I. Kushnirsky

Westview Press
BOULDER, SAN FRANCISCO, & LONDON

Westview Special Studies on the Soviet Union

Copyright © 1989 by Westview Press, Inc.

Published in 1989 in the United States of America by Westview Press, Inc., 5500 Central Avenue, Boulder, Colorado 80301, and in the United Kingdom by Westview Press, Inc., 13 Brunswick Centre, London WC1N 1AF, England

Kushnirsky, Fyodor I.
  Growth and inflation in the Soviet economy.
    (Westview special studies on the Soviet Union and
Eastern Europe)
  Bibliography: p.
  Includes index.
    1. Industrial productivity—Soviet Union. 2. Infla-
tion (Finance)—Soviet Union. 3. Machinery industry—
Soviet Union. 4. Soviet Union—Industries—Case studies.
I. Title. II. Series.
HC340.I52K88 1989 338.0947
ISBN 0-8133-7700-5

88-36274

Printed and bound in the United States of America

The paper used in this publication meets the requirements of the American National Standard for Permanence of Paper for Printed Library Materials Z39.48-1984.

10   9   8   7   6   5   4   3   2   1

To Svetlana, Eugene and Ilya

Contents

Acknowledgements

I would like to acknowledge and thank a number of individuals for their participation in this project. At different stages of my work, I received suggestions and comments, sometimes very critical, from Abram Bergson, Joseph Berliner, Igor Birman, Erwin Blackstone, Robert Campbell, Padma Desai, David Epstein, Richard Ericson, Gerold Guensberg, Ed Hewett, Lynn Holmes, Vladimir Kontorovich, Iwan Koropeckyi, Herbert Levine, Alec Nove, Martin Shpechler, James Steiner, William Stull, Judith Thornton and Albina Tretyakova. The comments from the participants of seminars at Columbia, Temple, University of Indiana and Pennsylvania were also useful.

The project especially benefited from numerous editorial and substantive improvements made by Arnold Raphaelson. The work would have been impossible without support from Delphic Associates and without help from the staff of the Center for International Research of the U.S. Bureau of the Census. Excellent typing was done by Ruth Jackson. The index was prepared by my son Eugene. The Statistics Department of Temple University generously let me use their software and equipment, and Kem Farney and Michael McCarthy were helpful in the organization of this work.

Fyodor I. Kushnirsky

Introduction

Western students of the Soviet economy have paid considerable attention to the problem of estimating rates of Soviet economic growth. Progress made at the macrolevel has been reviewed by Ofer (1987). Most studies have been concerned with growth and inflation for specific sectors of the Soviet economy, the machine-building and metalworking (MBMW) sector being the most prominent. The estimates by Steiner (1978), Leggett (1981), and Converse (1982) discount the tempos reported for the MBMW sector because of the finding of concealed inflation there. The presence of hidden inflation was also found by Birman (1980) who analyzed the problem of too many rubles chasing too few consumer goods in the U.S.S.R. The different nature of inflationary processes in the Soviet consumer and producer-goods markets was stressed by Kushnirsky (1984).

An extended discussion of the real growth of Soviet fixed investment was initiated by Nove (1981), Cohn (1981), and Wiles (1982). The issue has been reexamined by Bergson (1987) who finds no conclusive evidence that Soviet data on real fixed investment are subject to concealed inflation, even though he does not exclude such a possibility. Hanson (1987) and Nove (1987) disagree and believe that the new criticism, expressed in the Soviet literature at both the official and unofficial levels, proves that the official data are inflated.

Western analysts have not ignored the Soviet problem of growth and productivity slowdown, either. Levine (1982) categorized the factors leading to the slowdown as exogenous, stemming from maturing economy, resulting from planning decisions and systematic. Some of these factors were further specified in a discussion by Gomulka (1985), Desai (1985), and Kontorovich (1985).

The attention paid to the estimation of Soviet real economic growth is quite understandable: Ordinary Westerners as well as their governments want to know how super is that superpower. What is less evident to an ordinary Westerner is why others estimate something that the Soviets have already calculated and published. The Soviet Union is not a less-developed country lacking sufficient resources to record, collect and process the necessary data. On the contrary, perhaps no other country has devoted so many resources to the cause of the organization, analysis, and verification of statistical information as the Soviet Union.

The Soviet national system of statistical information is organized and controlled by the State Committee on Statistics (*Goskomstat* or, formerly, *TsSU*). It collects different kinds of informational reports (*otchetnost'*) from industrial firms, collective farms and other organizations. Along with *Goskomstat*, information is collected by local authorities, republic economic and government bureaucracies, ministries, departments, State Planning Committee *(Gosplan)* and hierarchial party organs. Even more significant in numbers is the staff of industrial enterprises that compiles the information. The data are prepared by such enterprise departments as planning, technology, bookkeeping, labor and wages, and supply. Computerized data processing plays an important role at large and medium-size enterprises. In many instances, computer centers collect the information directly from the enterprise workshops.

At the same time, the reader is aware of the fact that the Soviets do not publish many essential statistical data which are not classified. The data that they do publish are frequently in a cryptic form or are otherwise distorted because of undisclosed changes in statistical methodology and definitions or the use of different prices for the same indicators in the same publications. Given these statistical puzzles, many of the published data allow for broad interpretation as well as misinterpretation. Certain types of reports, such as deflationary wholesale prices or a decline in Soviet military expenditures from 12.7 percent of the national budget in 1960 to 4.6 percent in 1986 (*Narkhoz SSSR za 70 let*, 1987, p.63), are met with skepticism. This implies a lack of respect for Soviet official statistics.

While it is difficult to summarize the attitudes of Western analysts, the majority has not accepted the official information on Soviet economic growth. But, if one believes that the Soviets publish distorted information, it is also natural to believe that, along with the data for the public view, there should be another set of books. This follows from the fact that the Soviets continue to spend tremendous resources on national statistics and have a qualified cadre, software, and hardware. Moreover, it is clear that planners and government and party authorities want access to accurate data. The true secret information could, therefore, be used to serve the planning process and the authorities, and the published information is to mislead the enemies of socialism and its friends alike.

This picture is, of course, an oversimplification. Nevertheless, the notion of the existence of two parallel sets of accounts has interesting consequences. First of all, if there are true data, there are true growth rates. A Western analyst who estimates Soviet economic growth thus needs reliable data, and the closer these data are to the secret set, the "truer" are the estimates. There is a hope that the true growth rates will sooner or later be uncovered with the gradual progress in the search for information and in estimation. There remains a problem in knowing just when one has arrived at true rates.

However, the new developments in the Soviet Union seriously challenge this stereotypical line of reasoning. Gorbachev calls for a radical reform of Soviet statistics. The fact that he does not like what he sees could undermine any belief in the existence of the true secret information. Even more important is the evidence provided by some Soviet writers who critically assess the country's economic growth. For example, the estimates by Seliunin and Khanin (1987), Val'tukh and Lavrovskii (1986), and Fal'tsman (1987) dramatically depart from the official ones. This may not be surprising in the period of *glasnost'*. What may be surprising is that the writers themselves come up with quite different estimates for the same economic indicators.

The source of the writers' information must have been the materials of *Goskomstat*. A necessary condition for being permitted to use this information is that it is pertinent to an authorized study, i.e., included in a research institute's thematic plan (*tematicheskii plan*). In this case, having an official request from the institute, one would be given access to the information "for official use" (*dlia sluzhebnogo pol'zovaniia*). Ironically, all *Goskomstat* data are termed this way, including those that are actually published. Of course, classified information requiring special clearance (*dopusk*) is another story. The estimates of the Soviet writers vary for different reasons, in particular since they may use different techniques to refine official statistics. If they were able to obtain the alternative set of true data, such variation might not happen. If Gorbachev were given data he believes true, he would not call for a radical reform of their statistics. The Soviets now find themselves in the position of Western analysts struggling to reconstruct meaningful Soviet data. While this is no news to many knowledgeable Soviet economists who simply could not speak out in the pre-Gorbachev period, Soviet statisticians would not agree with such an assessment. This is quite natural for people who do their best when they are suddenly told that they spent time and effort on something which is meaningless.

The causes of Soviet statistical problems are analyzed in this book in a broad context of issues related to the measurement of Soviet economic growth. Summarized in just a few questions, the following are discussed: What do Soviet measures of growth and inflation mean? How are their prices set? What lies behind the official measures of growth, and how could alternative estimates be obtained? How does the Soviet system of distribution, as opposed to free-market sales of goods and services, affect their estimates? If inflation exists in the Soviet economy, what mechanisms conceal it? How could planners' perceptions on quality change be used for separating real from inflationary components of growth? In answering these and other questions, we believe that the complexity of the issues could be better understood when theoretical reasoning is combined with practical estimation.

In the first, theoretical part of the book we take into account the priority of Soviet economic planning in terms of physical commodities, not in monetary aggregates. Consequently, microeconomic models and indicators are stressed. The investment process is one example. Total Soviet investment is planned on the basis of the capacities of the construction industry and the MBMW sector supplying producers' durables. Actual investment may deviate significantly from planned, but this, again, depends on whether the construction and MBMW sectors meet planning targets, rather than on any financing factors. Indicators of real growth and inflation can serve as another illustration. Inflation may always and everywhere be a monetary phenomenon; however, when it comes to transactions in the Soviet producer-goods markets, the nominal money supply is determined by the supplies and prices of material inputs. The State bank allows only those transactions that are foreseen by the national economic plan or otherwise authorized. If, for example, input prices rise, the funds appropriated to the producer will automatically increase. Hence, nominal money supply is endogenous and accommodates price changes. From this standpoint, trends in costs, not money supply, affect price inflation in the producer-goods markets.

An important feature of the growth of the Soviet economy is the emphasis on producer, not consumer goods. The importance of the MBMW sector has been stressed by the Soviet authorities because that sector induces technological change in the economy, provides machines and equipment for new construction projects, and turns out military systems and hardware. Western analysts also find the Soviet MBMW sector of primary importance. It is the most dynamic sector of the Soviet economy in terms of growth, varying product assortments, price fluctuations and quality change. It is therefore clear that the MBMW sector is paramount for the evaluation of Soviet long-term economic growth.

While growth figures are high for Soviet industry in general, they are especially impressive for the MBMW sector which has far outperformed other sectors of the economy. The official average growth rate for this sector equals 10 percent from 1960 to 1986 (*Narkhoz SSSR za 70 let*, 1987, p.130). The question widely debated in the U.S.S.R. now is whether these impressive figures actually reflect the growth of physical output. To put it differently, did the Soviet economy receive more machines and equipment as a result of this growth, and, if so, was the rate of real growth the same as the growth in value terms? This question interests both western analysts and the Soviet planners who cannot track the production of all of the goods in physical units. But why would one raise such a question in the first place? After all, output in value terms is composed of prices and physical units; if constant prices are used, then economic growth must be the same in value terms and in physical units, with an adjustment for quality improvements.

To answer this and similar questions, the procedures of Soviet measurement of output, productivity, costs and prices have been analyzed in this study. Special attention is given to the processes of planning quality improvements and pricing new technological items. An analysis of procedures and methodological instructions used in planning and pricing MBMW products may be helpful in revealing possible discrepancies between prices of new goods and their quality characteristics. Other factors important to the Soviet sellers' market are also analyzed. The analyses are based on the consideration of Soviet theoretical price models and growth and price indices. Actual trends in the MBMW output, productivity, costs, and prices are demonstrated with the use of different statistical materials.

In the second, empirical part we first take a partial approach by estimating real and inflationary growth of the branches representing the Soviet MBMW sector – the automotive industry, the electrotechnical industry and the energy and power machinery. As usual, an extended reconstruction process is required in each case. Its task is to estimate the indicators of outputs in physical units, value terms and the end-use or quality characteristics of machines and equipment. For the automotive industry, individual prices play an important role in the reconstruction process, whereas, for the electrotechnical industry and the energy and power machinery, a more aggregate approach is used. The discussion of the estimation process could have been based on these materials without actually presenting them. But, since some of the readers may specifically be interested in the reconstructed data, we feel it is necessary to present as many as possible.

To separate the real and inflationary components of growth for the three industries, the growth of output in money terms is compared with the rise of output (measured in units of quality) by specific product group. For the electrotechnical industry and energy and power machinery, single characteristics of quality are selected; for the automotive industry, there is a complex index of quality, incorporating six different characteristics of both cars and trucks. The growth and price indices obtained by product group are then averaged for each of the three industries.

In a general approach, the findings of the partial consideration for the three MBMW branches are interpreted in the light of an ongoing debate on Soviet official statistics. This debate was stirred by a 1987 article by Seliunin and Khanin (S-K) in a Soviet literary and social journal, *Novyi Mir*. There has been no lack of critical publications in the U.S.S.R. recently, and the harsh criticism of Soviet statistics by S-K would remain unnoticed but for their sensational assertion that Soviet national income did not grow about 90 times in the 1928-85 period, but only 6 to 7 times (Seliunin and Khanin, 1987, p.192). How is this possible? To answer the question, we compare several growth rates for the Soviet economy and its MBMW sector and try to understand why they significantly differ. For this purpose, the issue of the reliability of Soviet statistical information is investigated, and even greater attention is given to methodology. In particular, the S-K methodology is analyzed. Finally, the problems of statistical methodology are linked to the problems of the Soviet economic model in order to speculate whether there could be winners and losers in the Soviet statistical debate.

PART I

The Measurement of Growth and Inflation

Chapter 1
Setting Prices in Producer Goods Markets

1.1. ·Prices Used in the Soviet Economy

The price mechanism is one of the most important parts of Soviet economic planning. Not surprisingly, regulations on price setting have been both rigorous and rigid. If one attempts to comprehend the specifics of the determination of prices, one will find that there are as many price setting schemes as there are different industries and even product groups. A typical Soviet handbook on pricing would have a short theoretical part, a longer description of the methodology, and an extended list of separate chapters on price setting for fuels, energy, chemicals, machines, agricultural products, consumer goods, etc.[1]

For industrial goods, all these prices can be of two general types: wholesale or retail. All other prices are variations of these two, resulting either from the methods by which they are set or from their interpretation in planning and statistics. Unlike prices in a free-market economy, only consumer goods have both wholesale and retail prices. Consequently, most heavy-industry products are sold at wholesale prices. Wholesale prices can be of two kinds: the enterprise wholesale price or the industry wholesale price.

The enterprise wholesale price (*optovaia tsena predpriiatiia*) is the price charged by the firm. It is comprised of the product's cost, a profit markup, and, for high-quality goods, a surcharge for quality. The purpose of this price is to compensate the producer's expenses and to provide a fair rate of return. The enterprise wholesale price is the basis for all other prices used for manufactured goods in the Soviet economy. The methodological framework for the computation of the cost and profit components in the enterprise wholesale price is, as a rule, the same for all products. Within this framework the main distinction lies in pricing new products, a process described in Section 3.2.

The industry wholesale price (*optovaia tsena promyshlennosti*) is the enterprise wholesale price plus the markup for the sales organization (*snabzhenchesko-sbytovaia natsenka*) and the turnover tax (*nalog s oborota*). If a branch of industry has both the enterprise and the industry wholesale prices, the user pays the latter, i.e., the higher one, while the producer receives the enterprise wholesale price. The discrepancy is divided between the intermediary (the sales markup) and the state budget (the turnover tax). For machines and equipment, as well as for other producer goods such as chemicals, construction materials, nonferrous metals and coal, the industry wholesale price coincides with the enterprise wholesale price. For ferrous metals and timber, the industry wholesale price exceeds the enterprise wholesale price by the sales markup. For oil products, gas and electricity, the industry wholesale price includes both the sales markup and the turnover tax. The industry wholesale price of an oil product would then have the same structure as the industry wholesale price for a consumer good.

Figure 1.1 illustrates the structure of a hypothetical Soviet retail price set to equal 100 rubles. In this example, the enterprise wholesale price, as the sum of total cost and profit, equals 70 rubles. Three industry wholesale prices are shown. For a machine, it coincides with the enterprise wholesale price of 70 rubles. For a metal product, it also includes the sales markup of 6 rubles and equals 76 rubles. For a consumer good, the turnover tax of 20 rubles is added to the industry wholesale price, so that the latter amounts to 96 rubles. Finally, the retail markup of 4 rubles closes the gap between the industry wholesale and the consumer product retail price of 100 rubles.

Wholesale prices can be either permanent or temporary. Permanent prices are those officially approved by an organization responsible for a stipulated list of product groups (*nomenklatura*) and included in special price lists (*preiskurant*). *Preiskurant* is a price publication for a certain product group, with appendices for prices

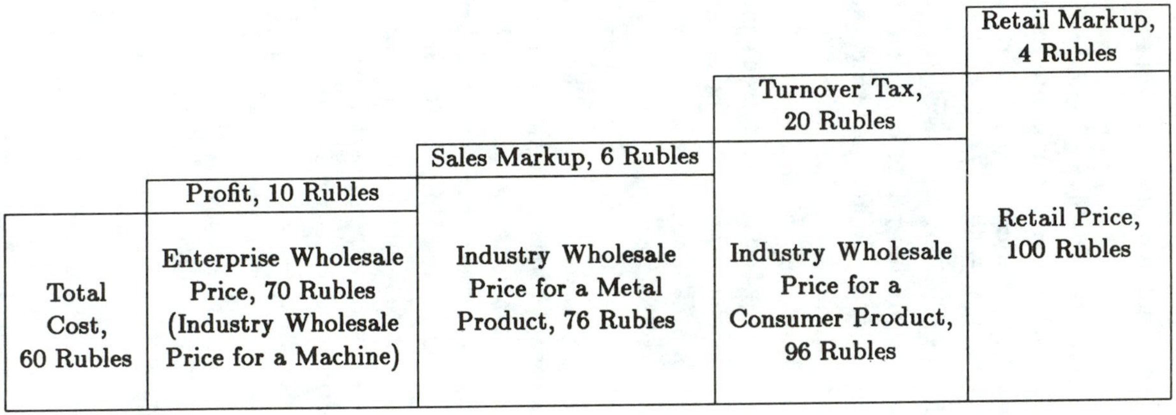

Figure 1.1. Structure of a Hypothetical Soviet Price

approved after the publication date. *Preiskurant* prices can be approved by the State Committee on Prices (*Goskomtsen*), the *goskomtsen* of the republics, U.S.S.R. ministries and departments or local authorities. The more important the product, the higher the authority approving the price. Most calculations on wholesale prices and their justification are performed by the ministries and departments, regardless of the organization issuing the corresponding *preiskurant*. *Preiskuranty* are numbered in accordance with the level of bureaucratic hierarchy which approves them. The numeration is different for wholesale and retail prices.

Preiskuranty for wholesale prices issued by the U.S.S.R. *Goskomtsen* have four-digit numbers. All products are classified according to their origin. The first two numbers correspond to the industry of origin, and the other two indicate the order of the product group within the industry. For example, ferrous metallurgy is assigned number 01, and the *preiskurant* of wholesale prices for its 25 product groups are numbered from 01-01 to 01-25. When a *preiskurant* is approved by a republic *goskomtsen* or a ministry, two additional numbers are added to the above classification. First, the fifteen Soviet republics are numbered in order of their economic importance: 01 stands for the Russian Soviet Federated Socialist Republic (R.S.F.S.R.), 02 for the Ukraine, etc. The ministries and departments follow. If a *preiskurant* is approved by province (*oblast'*) or city authorities, it is labeled, along with the above, by two letters, like "Mg" for Moscow. *Preiskuranty* of retail prices approved by the U.S.S.R. *Goskomtsen* have three-digit numbers, from 001 to 029 for food products and from 030 to I-138 for nonfood products. (The letter I stands for imports.) Along with the information on prices, a *preiskurant* contains a brief description of the goods' quality and technical characteristics.

The purpose of temporary wholesale prices is self-explanatory: they last until permanent prices are approved. The lack of reliable information on these prices creates difficulties for analysts studying Soviet pricing policies. Their effect on prices in various industries, especially in the machine-building and metalworking sector (MBMW), is usually noted rather than seriously analyzed. Soviet studies also use only *preiskurant* wholesale prices since, for planning purposes, the tendencies of these prices are considered important. In estimating inflation, however, ignoring temporary prices may yield a downward biased result. Planners have constantly changed the conditions for setting temporary prices. As a matter of fact, probably no other provision on pricing has undergone such significant alterations as temporary pricing.

Temporary pricing was established after the 1955 revision of wholesale prices. One of the goals of using temporary prices was to stimulate the producer to manufacture new products and to introduce technological change. Since the producers incur greater expenses in the first period of mastering new production, the decision had been made to reimburse them by establishing relatively high prices for newly introduced products. The stimulation of technological change by accelerating the turnover of production capital has eventually become the chief purpose of temporary pricing.

The system of incentives for a Soviet producer differs from that for his western counterpart. The Soviet producer expends money with no risk involved because the money comes from the state budget, not his pocket. Long-run potential gains in production and sales revenue are also less important to the Soviet producer for evident reasons: the Soviet's is a sellers' market, and the existence of the national economic plan guarantees the sale of a product, whether it is an old or a new one. What remains are short-run gains in the form of bonuses to designers, technologists, and managers for the introduction of new and better quality goods. Higher than usual temporary prices were supposed to be a source of such bonuses. The new system of self-sufficiency and self-financing, which is in the process of being established, is intended to introduce some market elements and thus raise the role of risk and long-run considerations in planning technological change.

Another goal of using temporary prices was to reduce the effect on *preiskurant* prices of the high costs of the initial years of production. For that purpose, a decision was made to use temporary prices for one or two years, depending on the complexity of a technology, and then to switch to permanent prices. But the implementation and duration of temporary pricing began to grow rapidly. The reason was that no explicit limitation had been imposed on the application of temporary prices. In fact, any alteration in a factory's product mix could be classified as eligible for temporary pricing. The resultant growth in the cost of machines and equipment and, consequently, industrial construction did not satisfy planners.

In 1966 the terms for using temporary prices were revised. The key test put forward was whether the product was new for the domestic market, rather than for the enterprise manufacturing it. This approach decreased the number of temporary prices significantly, to about 1,000 temporary prices approved by central authorities annually in the 1969-74 period (Koshuta and Rozenova, 1976). Also, the terms of temporary prices were reduced to between 9 and 15 months, depending on the complexity of the technology used. As before, temporary prices were to be approved by the ministries supervising the producer, after coordinating the prices with the ministry whose enterprises would be the main consumers of the product. At this time, however, the decision was made to impose mandatory registration of all temporary prices at *Goskomtsen*. This was done not only for accounting purposes, but also to give *Goskomtsen* an opportunity to verify the production costs and the grounds for classifying the products as newly manufactured.

Despite all the limitations, enterprises introducing new goods were able to raise their profits and incentive funds at a pace considered excessive. The process was especially alarming in the MBMW sector, where production costs were often reduced by 40 to 60 percent in the third or fourth year of manufacturing new machines. That led to significant discrepancies in goods profitability, measured for different industries as the ratio of profits to either capital stock or costs. The MBMW sector has always had profit rates higher than those in other industries. The 1967 price reform reduced the level of MBMW prices by more than 30 percent. Later, in the 9th five-year plan (1971-75), these prices were again reduced by an average of 14 percent. During that period, 320 *preiskuranty* out of a total of 700 were revised (Dronov, 1979). Further, the provision for setting prices of new products was changed so that the costs of the second year of production, not the first one, would be counted as the base of prices. That measure was to lower both the level of prices in general and the fluctuation of the ratio of actual to approved cost as a component of a particular price. In the 1980s it was decided to reinstate the pricing of new goods based on the cost of the first year of production because the profit rate of new goods appeared to be low (Glushkov, 1983).

All the alterations in temporary pricing demonstrate an attempt on the part of Soviet planners to achieve a greater stability in prices. While the stability of prices does not imply rigidity, flexibility is still out of question for the Soviet economy. To provide flexible prices, economic mechanisms should delegate pricing decisions to the producer. Some Soviet economists have for a long time suggested that the producer should be granted the right to set prices in economic contracts with the purchaser. This is being implemented now. Three consecutive stages in the price level were considered: (1) relatively high prices for newly introduced goods, (2) stable prices for goods being in production for several years, and (3) discounted prices for obsolescent goods (Valevich, 1979). In the past, planners could not approve such a practice. They knew that enterprise managers had no economic responsibility for the inputs they spend and could therefore not resist pressure from the producer to raise prices. This would lead to inflation in producer-goods markets. Since the consumer did not influence the level of prices at all, planners believed that permanent administrative supervision and control were the only remedy. The self-sufficiency and self-financing provisions introduced in the 12th five-year plan (1986-90) are supposed to make the producer more accountable for investment and other inputs and, consequently, to ease the planners' fears of using more flexible prices.

Another problem, related to the role of prices in planning, makes the future of flexible prices uncertain for the Soviet economy. All the aggregate indicators evaluating economic performance are estimated in prices of the national economic plan. This assumes the rigidity of prices during the whole period under consideration. Otherwise, if the indicators move in unpredictable directions, planning itself becomes meaningless. This is one of the reasons why the targets of Soviet five-year plans usually become dated by the midperiod, and annual plans deviate greatly from the relevant projections from the five-year plan. It has been suggested by planners (and in part implemented) that general revisions of prices be done prior to a five-year period in order to keep them constant during the period. But this, of course, would not add much to the flexibility of prices.

In addition to the gradual changes in temporary pricing discussed earlier, central authorities took other measures to impose stricter control over temporary pricing. One of the main provisions was the change in the basic structure of temporary prices, which was caused by the planners' intention to reduce the role of the ministries in the approval of these prices. Since permanent prices are not high enough to stimulate technological change, it was decided that the formula of temporary pricing would consist of two components; only the the markup component would be temporary.

There are other types of temporary prices. One is contract prices (*dogovornye tseny*) whose importance, as indicated above, may grow significantly in the future. Their use is, rightly or wrongly, supposed to simplify the process of the approval of new prices and to reduce the bureaucratic barriers in price documentation. Contract prices were used in the past, but not for goods in serial or mass production. They were important for pricing military hardware. The producer would be interested in contract prices for two reasons. First, a profit markup allowed in the contract price is generally greater than the average for the product group. Second, the authorities do not check the production-cost component of the contract price as carefully as they do the *preiskurant* price.

A new regulation has broadened the scope of contract prices (*Ekonomicheskaia Gazeta* 5, 1988, p.23). For the first time, they will be used for goods in serial and mass production, for a period of up to two years. In this sense, contract prices resemble general temporary prices. More accurately, the old difference between temporary prices and contract prices will disappear, and most temporary prices will be set on a contract basis, negotiated between the producer and the industrial consumer. As before, contract prices will also be used for machines manufactured by single orders (*individual'nye zakazy*) or goods produced for one-time orders (*razovye zakazy*). Contract prices could be applied to new exported goods when these do not have an approved *preiskurant* price. In all circumstances, most of the contract prices will be confined to new machines and equipment.

One who thinks that contract prices are in any way close to market prices will be mistaken. Although literally the buyer is given the authority to negotiate the price, practically its level will still be determined by the technological conditions of production. This is clear from the new regulation which requires the producer to be held responsible for keeping "price discipline" (*distsiplina tsen*) in setting contract prices. In specific terms, contract prices have to be in line with prices of other similar products. If the producer firm is caught setting unjustifiably high prices, it will be penalized, and the profit will be withheld to the state budget. The language of the regulation thus implies that the authorities do not believe in the buyer's ability or willingness to press the producer for price concessions. Otherwise, there would be no need for notorious "price discipline."

Retail prices are used for consumer goods sold to the population. Depending on the type of trader, there are state, collective farm (*kolkhoz*), or cooperative retail prices. The bulk of these are the state retail prices. They can be based on the enterprise wholesale price or the industry wholesale price. The retail price also incorporates the turnover tax and the markup for the sales organization and the retailer or for the retailer only.

Procurement prices are prices charged by collective farms and state farms (*sovkhozy*) to the state trade and cooperative organizations. The cooperative organizations are the Soviet so-called consumer cooperative societies (*potrebitel'skaia kooperatsiia*). They are not the newly permitted private cooperatives which must pay *kolkhoz* market prices. The procurement price is set by the same principle as the wholesale price for industrial goods, i.e., as the sum of total cost and a profit markup.

A good can have either a single wholesale price (*edinaia obshche-soiuznaia tsena*) or several prices differentiated by region. Goods such as machines, textiles, fabrics, footwear, and chemicals only have a single price which does not depend on the location of production or sale. When a good's price does depend on the location of sale (*poiasnaia tsena*), the varying levels of the price usually reflect the differences in the cost of transportation. This is true, for example, for cement whose price is differentiated by eight regions of the country (Zav'ialkov, 1981, p.116). For coal and iron ore, the zone prices (*zonal'nye tseny*) are used. They reflect the differences in the cost of production and are specified by basins and deposits. For example, there are 43 zones for coal and seven for iron ores (Zav'ialkov, 1981, pp. 174 and 182).

Both wholesale and retail prices have two versions – current and comparable – that may or may not coincide. A good's current price (*tekyshchaia tsena*) is the one at which it is actually sold. The good also has a comparable price (*sopostavimaia tsena*) used, in particular, for the measurement of economic growth. Initially, when the good is introduced, both prices are the same, but later on, as a result of a possible official revision, the current price can become lower or higher than the comparable price. The latter is not everlasting, either; it changes with the revision of the base year for the entire industry. Although the functions of comparable prices are similar to those of constant prices, the setting of comparable prices has some peculiarities that make them different from the western concept of constant prices. (On the meaning and the use of comparable prices see Sections 2.2 and 2.3.)

The methodology of the computation of each of the three major types of prices – enterprise wholesale, industry wholesale, and retail – is not uniform. There are variations for different products. For example, there are three ways of finding the industry wholesale price, because there are *preiskuranty* based on the enterprise wholesale price, based on both the enterprise and the industry wholesale prices, or based on the retail price. To calculate the industry wholesale price in the first case, the enterprise wholesale price, along with the sales markup and any turnover tax, should be used. In the second case, no additional computation is necessary since two parallel *preiskuranty* are approved – one for the enterprise wholesale price and another for the industry wholesale price. The third case is for consumer goods when only the retail price is approved, and the industry wholesale price is found as the difference between the retail price and the sum of the turnover tax and the retail and sales markups.

Depending on the level of aggregation, all prices can be either individual product prices or average prices. Average prices (*srednie tseny*) are computed as the weighted average for certain product items or entire product groups. The computation of average prices is an important step in the planning procedure, and it is done for both current and comparable prices. As a matter of fact, the national economic plan is based on using average prices, and individual prices are only applied in the cases of unique or distinctive products. The method of averaging affects the level of aggregate prices and, as explained in Section 2.3, plays an important role in driving up the prices of Soviet industrial goods.

1.2. Theoretical Price Models

Different goods and services are commensurable when measured in money terms. Prices, along with being a mechanism for bringing market supply and demand to equilibrium, play an important role as weights that enable us to find economic aggregates such as gross national product and its components. In the Soviet context, prices also play an important role of specifying the center's commands in the form of planned value indicators. The revision of prices consequently destroys all of the relationships established in the national economic plan. For example, this happened to the the 11th five-year plan (1981-85) as a result of the 1982 price reform, when many of the plan targets became dated. Since a complete recalculation of the plan would have been an unrealistic task, the updating of these targets took place in the annual plans that recurrently lost their connection with the five-year plan.

Pricing is one of many areas where theoretical reasoning and practical solutions seldom coincide. This is especially true in the Soviet context where, for several reasons, there has been great interest in the theory of pricing. Firstly, in the absence of market mechanisms, planners command prices, and there is an obvious need for theoretical guidelines for setting the prices of millions of goods and services produced in the Soviet economy. Secondly, Soviet pricing policies are based on the Marxist theory of value; all goods are to be exchanged according to their values that, in turn, depend on labor time spent for production. If so determined, a good's value could be used as its price. But the concept of labor value is, like the concept of opportunity cost, merely an abstraction because only "socially necessary" (*obshchestvenno neobkhodimyi*) labor is accepted as the good's value. (Not surprisingly, Soviet political economists have produced numerous volumes in an attempt to make the labor value concept operational.) Thirdly, with the introduction of optimal programming, a belief arose in the Soviet Union that, finally, there was the solution to the problem of price formation. The shadow prices resultant from the solution of a linear programming problem for the entire economy would provide prices once their scale is set. Consequently, research in optimization theory and applications was stimulated, with the advancement of the theory outstripping the development of applications.

All the theoretical approaches to price setting in the Soviet economy are based on the cost-plus-profit principle. The chief difference among the variety of theoretical models is related to incorporating the profit component in the price, a difficult task even when the cost component is known. Several major conceptual models are distinguished by Soviet political economists:

1. A value model of price (*stoimostnaia kontseptsiia*) which is the closest to the Marxist idea of value. In this approach, the profit markup is added to the good's cost as a proportion of wages thus underlining labor primacy:

$$p_i = c_i + mw_i \tag{1.1}$$

where p_i, c_i, and w_i = price, total production cost, and labor cost, respectively, for the ith good; $m = \pi/W$ = marginal profit markup defined as the ratio of normative (i.e., targeted) profit π for the economy as a whole to the total wage bill W paid in the production sphere. The idea behind this approach is that equal work creates equal value added in all industries, with a consequently equal profit multiplier.

As an example of computation, suppose that the cost c_i of producing a good equals 1,000 rubles, including a labor cost w_i of 240 rubles. The targeted annual profit π for the economy is 153 billion rubles, and the production-sphere annual wages W are 180 billion rubles. Then the marginal profit markup equals

$$m = \frac{153}{180} = .85,$$

and the good's price is

$$p = 1000 + .85(240) = 1204.$$

As follows from this example, the good's profit rate is equal to 20.4 percent $\left(\frac{204}{1000} \cdot 100\right)$. It is evident from formula (1.1) that the equality of the marginal profit markups does not mean the equality of the profit rates for all goods. The rate will depend upon the relationship between a good's total cost and its wage component. Labor-intensive goods will, *ceteris paribus*, receive a higher profit rate.

The decisions of Soviet planners do not follow the recommendations of their political economists. Planners have rejected the value model of price since it undermines the role of investment in fixed and working capital. Given this model, firms are encouraged to keep their rate of technical substitution low. By doing so, they would raise the proportion of wages in total cost and, as a result, the profit component and the price itself. Conversely, an innovative firm investing more heavily in its production capital and reducing manual work will be punished.

This approach would also send a false signal about society's cost of production. For example, suppose that two fabrics are manufactured, one from natural and the other from synthetic fibers. Assuming costs and wages equal, formula (1.1) would command the same price for both. But, indeed, the price of a natural fabric should have been higher since it takes more capital to produce than a synthetic fabric. By not taking into account the cost of investment, formula (1.1) undercalculates the actual production cost for the natural fabric. Thus, equal prices commanded by formula (1.1) would lead to a high profitability of the production of the synthetic fabric and will depress the production of the natural fabric.

2. An average-cost model of price (*kontseptsiia usrednennoi stoimosti*) in which profit is incorporated in the price as a proportion of production cost:

$$p_i = (1 + m)c_i \tag{1.2}$$

where p_i and total c_i = price and total production cost, respectively, for the ith good; $m = \pi/C$ = marginal profit markup defined as the ratio of normative (i.e., targeted) profit π for the economy as a whole to total cost C of the country's material production.

As an example of this computation, suppose that production cost c_i for a good is the same as in the first example, above, i.e., equals 1,000 rubles, as well as the same is the targeted annual profit for the economy π of 153 billion rubles. Further, suppose that the total cost of the country's material production C is 1,020 billion rubles. The marginal profit markup is then equal to

$$m = \frac{153}{1020} = .15,$$

and the good's price equals

$$p = (1 + .15)1000 = 1150,$$

with the profit rate of 15 percent ($\frac{150}{1000} \cdot 100$). Hence, changing the model of price has lowered the good's profit rate as compared to 20.4 percent in the first example.

The average-cost model has an advantage over the value model of price since, as follows from formula (1.2), it provides the same profit rate for all goods when measured as a proportion of production cost. However, if investment cost were added as it should have been, the profit rate would vary, and firms with capital-intensive production would receive the lowest rates. If the value model of price redistributes profits in favor of labor-intensive industries, the average-cost model does so in favor of both labor and material-intensive industries. By acquiring expensive material inputs, a firm can boost its costs and, as a result, its profits and prices.

3. A production model of price (*kontseptsiia tseny proizvodstva*) was introduced in an attempt to reflect the investment cost more adequately. In this approach, profit is incorporated in the good's price proportionally to capital spent in the production process:

$$p_i = c_i + mk_i, \tag{1.3}$$

where p_i, c_i, and k_i = price, total production cost, and capital expenditure, respectively, for the ith good; $m = \pi/K$ = marginal profit markup defined as the ratio of normative (i.e., targeted) profit π for the economy as a whole to total production capital stock K used in the economy. Capital expenditure k_i per unit of good is defined as follows: $k_i = K_i/Q_i$, where K_i and Q_i = capital expenditure required for the production of the ith good and its total physical output, respectively. Capital stock K_i used in the production of the ith good is a part of the firm's amortized fixed capital and working capital.

As an example of computation, suppose that, as in the previous two examples, the good's production cost c_i equals 1,000 rubles, and the targeted annual profit for the economy π is 153 billion rubles. Further, suppose that the economy's production capital stock K equals 1,377 billion rubles, and that annual capital expenditure for the good's production is 166,500 rubles, while 100 physical units of good are manufactured. Then the marginal profit markup equals

$$m = \frac{153}{1377} = .111,$$

capital expenditure per unit of good is

$$k = \frac{166500}{100} = 1665,$$

and the good's price is

$$p = 1000 + .111(1665) = 1185,$$

with the profit rate of 18.5 percent over production cost $(\frac{185}{1000} \cdot 100)$.

The production model of price should have satisfied planners since, in this case, according to formula (1.3) the price accounts for both the costs of material and labor inputs (component c_i) and capital input (component k_i). Although this is nominally true, the roles of components differ. While operational cost is included directly, capital expenditure is included through the marginal profit multiplier. As a result, the higher the capital expenditure, the higher the firm's profit and the price charged for the good. Hence, this model redistributes profits in the economy in favor of capital-intensive industries, because profit is a return to capital provided to firms without cost to them. It is even possible to imagine a firm with manual technology that would receive no profit at all if formula (1.3) were used.

The production model of price had become popular during the 1965 economic reform which stressed the importance of a firm's paying for its capital stock. The main objection to its use during that time was not caused by the bias mentioned above, but instead was the result of rather technical factors. Formula (1.3) requires dividing capital expenditures of the firm among all of the goods manufactured, which is hard to do for a multiproduct technological process. In other words, it is difficult to calculate component k_i in formula (1.3) reliably for separate products.

4.   A modified production model of price (*kontseptsiia modifitsirovannoi stoimosti*) was used during the 1967 price reform as a practical alternative to the technical difficulties of calculating the profit component in the production model of price. The format of computation resembles the one for the average-cost model of price, but the profit multiplier is determined as in the case of the production model of price:

$$p_i = (1 + m)c_i, \tag{1.4}$$

where p_i and c_i = price and total production cost, respectively, for the ith good; $m = \pi/K$ = marginal profit markup defined as the ratio of normative (i.e., targeted) profit π for the economy as a whole to total production capital stock K in the economy.

For this computation, suppose that all the data are as in the previous example, i.e., production cost c_i for a good is 1,000 rubles, the targeted annual profit for the economy π is 153 billion rubles, and the economy's production capital stock K is 1,377 billion rubles. Then the marginal profit markup equals

$$m = \frac{153}{1377} = .111,$$

and the good's price is

$$p = (1 + .111)1000 = 1111,$$

with the profit rate of 11.1 percent with respect to production cost $(\frac{111}{1000} \cdot 100)$.

By substituting cost for capital expenditure as the basis for finding the profit component of the price, the modified production model overcomes the technical difficulties of the production model of price and thus eases the computation process. At the same time, however, it redistributes profits in favor of material-intensive and labor-intensive industries and, in this sense, leads to biased results. Hence, the model is similar to the average-cost model in which the marginal profit markup is also applied to the production cost. But, since these profit markups are defined differently in the two models, they result in different prices, and, from the standpoint of the firm, a greater multiplier leads to a better price. And, given the multiplier, in both cases inflating costs is a clear-cut way to generate a higher profit component in the price.

5. A net-value model of price (*kontseptsiia chistoi produktsii*) is a practical, not political economic, solution to the problem of incorporating the profit component in the price. (To maintain the same level of generalization as for the other models discussed, it is presented here as a single model although profit-rate differentials exist for different industries). This approach was used during the 1982 price reform, and ever since it has become the chief tool for pricing new products. The idea behind this approach (reflected in the model's name) is to divide the targeted lump-sum profit among different manufactures in accordance with their values added:

$$p_i = c_i + m(c_i - g_i), \qquad (1.5)$$

where p_i, c_i, and g_i = price, total production cost, and the cost of material inputs, respectively, for the ith product; $m = \pi/(C - G)$ = marginal profit markup defined as the ratio of normative (i.e., targeted) profit π for the economy as a whole to the difference between the economy's total production cost C and the cost of material inputs G. This difference exceeds wages by the depreciation allowance and the cost of other labor-related items.

The intent of formula (1.5) is clear: to reduce the opportunity for inflating prices by buying expensive material inputs. Eliminating the cost of material inputs as a determinant for the profit component of the price indeed gives this approach an edge over that used in the 1967 price reform. On the other hand, even though the profit component is found as a proportion of cost net of material inputs, full production cost is also used in the pricing formula directly. As a result, the firm can raise its profit by initially inflating and further reducing all elements of its costs, not only wages. The new model may not be bias-free either since, as formula (1.5) shows, it redistributes profits in the economy in favor of labor-intensive industries, with a high value-added component in their price, despite the fact of taking into account depreciation. Although it is exactly what the planners intended, technologies based on manual work will be in a better situation than those with high rates of technical substitution.

While all of the theoretical price models considered above are biased, there may be no ideal model which is bias-free. This illustrates the fact that it is impossible to suggest a general formula of pricing which would work equally well for all goods and under all circumstances. And, while these models are concerned with incorporating a profit markup in the good's price, what about cost?

Although the use of production cost as the base for prices has a theoretical justification in the Marxist theory of value, one should not overestimate the role of this theory in planning. A reference to Marx and Lenin has been a standard requirement, but it was in the nature of a ritual. Pragmatic considerations usually prevail, given the constraints within which planners operate, and no planner seeks Marxist recommendations when solving real-life problems. Put differently, if Soviet prices continue to be based on production cost, it is not for ideological reasons. The main reason is because cost, in retrospect, is one of the most verifiable indicators upon which prices have been built in the Soviet economy. As will be shown in Chapter 4, there have been numerous attempts to build prices of new machines on the basis of their characteristics such as productivity, durability, or operational expenses. Those attempts failed in the past since it was hard for planners to verify the producer's projections of these characteristics, which are intrinsically imprecise. Despite this reality, there is a resurgent interest in pricing on the basis of "objective" technical characteristics whose specifics are discussed in Section 3.2.

The problem of reliability of cost as the base of price should be put in a proper perspective, too. First, the concern is not with absolute reliability, but it is instead with relative reliability, in comparison with other indicators. Second, the planned cost used in setting new prices is much less trustworthy than the actual cost reported by a firm at the end of every time period. Third, even when actual cost truly reflects the firm's expenditures, the firm may not operate at minimum cost. Fourth, there exists a problem of management's hiding reserves for the purpose of further cost reduction, a practice which is both a temptation in order to report success in meeting plan targets and a necessity in a condition of these targets being taut and frequently unrealistic.

There are also methodological problems in using cost as the base for pricing. As indicated above, only "socially necessary" cost must be taken into account. This means that if, for example, a firm wastes inputs, the resultant high cost must not be compensated by accordingly raising the price. On the other hand, a firm can have low average cost due to its favorable location or access to better inputs. This firm's low cost cannot serve as the base of price either, since it will deprive most of the firms operating in less favorable conditions of a "normal" profit markup. There is a consensus in the Soviet economic literature that the cost component of price should not be based on costs that are too high or too low. Yet this process of ignoring outlier cost situations does not address the questions of what level of cost is to be considered "socially necessary" and what prices are to correspond to that level.

With the advancement of linear programming, the question of price setting has been answered at a purely theoretical level: prices should be built on the basis of the shadow prices (of the optimal program) that minimize total cost and thus approximate the marginal opportunity costs of the inputs involved. All inputs in the optimal program would then receive prices sufficient to cover production expenses. The scale of prices would be determined by the marginal good, i.e., one for the highest-cost producer among those that are still included in the program. Profit received by the producers would then range from zero for the marginal good to the highest for the most lucrative good. Following the principle that all normally-operating firms make about the same profit, planners will then withhold any abnormal profits in the form of fixed or rental payments.

There are difficulties in implementing the optimal-programming approach. One of them is that, if the profit rate is determined by a firm having the highest cost, all others will enjoy an easy life – an unacceptable situation from the planners' perspective. Planners prefer to set prices which would press the majority of firms to reduce their costs and to raise efficiency. This corresponds to a well-known "mobilizing" effect of Soviet economic planning based on imposing taut plan targets. According to the planners' philosophy, even if these targets are not attainable, tautness per se results in a better over-all result than would have been achieved otherwise. (Interestingly enough, in the process of shifting greater decision making power to enterprises, planners want them to operate on the basis of norms but also impose levels of these norms that would still be "mobilizing".)

It may be fair to conclude that, when firms do not operate at minimum cost and hide their reserves, the optimization approach has no advantages over the planners' setting prices on the basis of the analysis of individual firm's and product's costs. Solving a linear-programming problem in this case would result in a rather mechanistic scheme for price setting and, probably, in a higher scale of prices. Finally, even if optimal prices could be found on this basis, in a very short time they would cease to be the best prices because of changes in costs due to the dynamic changes in production and consumption. Since the bulk of Soviet wholesale prices last for at least five years, the linear-programming solution may turn out to be nonoperational or at least unrealistically costly.

Though the notion that the planners' approach to setting prices on the basis of cost analysis may be rational, there remains the question of what cost measure should be the basis of prices. Three types of costs can be computed for each good in the Soviet economy: individual, regional average, or product-group average. Which measure reflects costs as socially necessary? There is no consensus on this point. As indicated above, individual enterprise's cost cannot be used as the base for prices since, in this case, all expenditures including unreasonable ones would be reimbursed. Averaging reduces the impact of fluctuations in individual costs from the conditions of an "average" technological process. But, from the planners' perspective, average cost as measured in statistics would just mirror the status quo for a region or a product group. They therefore view average cost only as a starting point for the computation of a generally lower planned, or normative average cost.

To do the averaging for any good's production cost, they select a group of firms whose technology is viewed as "typical" for the good. The procedures for the selection are not exactly specified.

Since certain normative parameters are used in these procedures, the resultant cost is also termed normative. Although, at the first glance, these procedures can only be subjective, the selection of typical conditions of production may not be difficult at all for many Soviet manufactures. The reason is that the degree of monopolization is high, and in many instances a good is turned out by only one firm. This is especially true for a variety of machines and equipment. Moreover, hundreds of ministerial project institutes and design bureaus are involved in this process, and this helps in the analyses of technological processes and costs involved. The institutes are also charged with creating and updating the normatives. Unfortunately, these normatives are based on the information obtained from production firms that are not interested in revealing their reserves.

1.3. Prices for MBMW Products

Different prices are computed and used for different purposes in the Soviet MBMW sector. In some cases, these prices are specific to this sector, but, in most others, they are typical for Soviet producer-goods markets. As explained in Section 1.1, all of the prices used for Soviet manufactured products are either versions or derivatives of the three types of prices – enterprise wholesale price, industry wholesale price, and retail price. General principles of setting these prices also apply to the MBMW sector. However, while prices are literally the same, they have to meet certain requirements caused by the fact that the MBMW sector is associated with technological change in the Soviet economy. Along with the justification of prices, the producer has also to justify economic benefit from manufacturing and using MBMW goods, a process described in Chapter 3.

The enterprise wholesale price is the price charged by the firm. It is comprised of the product's cost, a profit markup, and a surcharge for high-quality machines and equipment. The enterprise wholesale price is the basis for all other prices, and the price models discussed in Section 1.2 are pertinent to this type of price. The industry wholesale price is the enterprise wholesale price plus the markup for the sales organization and the turnover tax. If a branch of industry has both, the user pays the higher industry wholesale price while the seller receives the lower enterprise wholesale price. Machines, equipment, and other MBMW products may only have the enterprise wholesale price or, when categorized as consumer goods, both the enterprise wholesale price and the retail price. The retail price will incorporate the enterprise wholesale price, turnover tax, and the markups for the sales organization and the retailer. Soviet consumers pay retail prices on such MBMW goods as cars, motorcycles, bicycles, refrigerators, television sets, radios, home appliances and hardware.

Depending on the term of validity, MBMW wholesale prices can be either permanent or temporary. Permanent prices (*postoiannye tseny*) are approved for an unspecified time period, until the next revision of the price list (*preiskurant*). There is one type of permanent prices specific to the MBMW sector that has several values, each with a specified term of validity. These are stepwise prices (*stupenchatye tseny*) which generally demonstrate a pattern of decline so that at first the producer makes above-normal, then normal, and finally below-normal profits. Initially viewed as a device for stimulating higher turnover of machines and equipment, stepwise prices lost their importance because it is generally difficult to forecast the rate of a price decline that would be compatible with the change in costs. Yet Gorbachev's economic reform once again stirred an interest in stepwise prices.

Several types of temporary prices are used in the MBMW sector. Among these, there are temporary prices (*vremennye tseny*) per se, single-order (*edinichnyi zakaz*) prices, one-time order (*razovyi zakaz*) prices, and prototype-product (*opytnyi obrazets*) prices. Temporary prices are used for newly introduced original machines and equipment for up to two years of mass production, after which they should be replaced by permanent prices. Single-order prices are used for unique and complex machines and equipment that are not intended for mass production. In Soviet practice, single-order prices have been approved by the authorities in a process similar to the way they approve prices of goods that are serially produced. One-time order prices are used for a single product or a series of products that are not repeatedly turned out in two consecutive years. Although it is easy to confuse single orders and one-time orders, they are distinguished by the type of products involved. While single-order products are usually viewed as unique, one-time orders are placed for parts, instruments, and goods for nonproductive use, research and development (R&D), and decentralized investments. Prototype-product prices are used for new goods that are destined for mass production but remain in the R&D stage. Setting prototype-product prices is a process similar to the one-time order prices. One-time order prices are set by an agreement between the producer and the user and thus are termed contract prices (*dogovornye tseny*). As discussed in Section 1.1, the scope of the application of contract prices will grow in the Soviet economy. The new legislation on the state enterprise makes them the chief conduit for pricing new machines and equipment. Although it may now be easier for the producer to get the contract prices approved, much more is required before contract prices become the first market-oriented prices for Soviet producer goods.

Soviet authorities are especially concerned with the justification of and setting MBMW prices because the sector's products – machines, equipment, and instruments – are supposed to introduce technological change in the Soviet economy. When referring to the MBMW sector, one usually means enterprises of the Soviet MBMW ministries that are responsible for most of the sector's production. There are also two other groups – MBMW firms of other ministries, and MBMW shops of non-MBMW firms – that are especially important as users of MBMW equipment. For example, those MBMW shops of non-MBMW firms used 45 percent of the country's metal-cutting equipment and provided some five to six million jobs in 1980 (Kheinman, 1981, p.30). For this reason, the authorities at all levels – central, ministerial, republic, and local – are involved in pricing MBMW products.

There is another reason for the importance of prices in the MBMW sector: the broad product assortment can make planning in physical units impossible. In this respect, the sector can roughly be divided into two parts – one, manufacturing machines, and another, manufacturing instruments. (This division does not necessarily coincide with branch-of-industry lines; for example, the electrotechnical industry turns out both machines and instruments). Production plans for most machines and equipment are compiled in both physical and monetary units, but planning of instrument production is carried out in value terms only. Planners want to make sure that prices do not distort the flows and estimates of real product, especially when physical output measures are unavailable. As will be discussed in Chapter 9, some Soviet economists believe that price fluctuations have seriously affected the MBMW sector's growth rates. The case studies in Part 2 will also demonstrate the complexity of problems involved in the analysis of growth in this sector.

To illustrate how a MBMW wholesale price is determined, two examples are presented below. The methodology is based on the net-value model of price accepted in 1982 and discussed in Section 1.2. Since the computation scheme depends on how many firms produce the same good, the first example illustrates the case of a hypothetical good manufactured by only one firm. The second example pertains to a situation in which a good is manufactured by several firms and, therefore, a weighting procedure is used. To simplify the matter, the case is illustrated with an example of two producers.

Table 1.1 provides the information for a good manufactured by one firm. The data are arranged in accordance with the steps of the computation of the wholesale price within the framework of Soviet product-cost accounting. There is, however, a difference between price computation and accounting. Since planned cost is used as the base of price setting, the numbers in Table 1.1 could have been different from the actual costs of producing the good. Most items in Table 1.1 are the components of production cost. Among the biggest expenditures are those for raw materials, semifinished and finished parts, and fuels and energy. In aggregate, they result in the direct material cost of 19,500 rubles. There are also some indirect material costs divided among other cost items, such as the preparation and mastering of production, service and maintenance of equipment, shop management and overhead, plant management and overhead, and miscellaneous production expenditures. The sum of these items and wages and social insurance withholdings for production workers is the production cost of 28,600 rubles. The sum of production and sale and distribution costs is the total cost of 30,100 rubles. All of the costs reported are unit costs, or average costs per unit of output.

To find the profit markup of the price, a special normative is given in Table 1.1. As explained in Section 1.2, in order to discourage firms from manufacturing material-intensive goods to inflate their profits, the profit component is now computed as a proportion of costs other than those of material inputs. The formula used is as follows:

Table 1.1. Computation of the Wholesale Price for a Good
            Produced by One Firm

Indicator	Value
Raw Materials, Rubles	10,000
Semifinished and Finished Parts Bought, Rubles	8,000
Fuels and Energy, Rubles	1,500
Direct Material Cost, Rubles	19,500
Wages and Social Insurance Withholdings for Production Workers, Rubles	2,250
Preparation and Mastering of Production, Rubles	1,000
Service and Maintenance of Equipment, Rubles	2,250
Shop Management Cost and Overhead, Rubles	1,800
Plant Management Cost and Overhead, Rubles	1,500
Miscellaneous Production Expenditures, Rubles	550
Production Cost, Rubles	28,600
Sale and Distribution Cost, Rubles	1,500
Total Cost, Rubles	30,100
Total Cost less Direct Material Cost, Rubles	10,600
Ratio of Profit to Total Cost less Direct Material Cost, Percent	35
Normative Profit, Rubles	3,710
Wholesale Price, Rubles	33,810

$$\pi_i = m_i(c_i - g_i), \qquad (1.6)$$

where π_i, c_i, g_i = profit, total cost, and direct material cost of the ith product, respectively, and m_i = profit markup as a proportion of total cost less material cost. The difference between formulas (1.5) and (1.6) is that, in the theoretical net-value model of price, the normative marginal profit markup is assumed to be the same for all goods whereas, in reality and in formula (1.6), it depends on a specific product group. Using the marginal profit markup of 35 percent from Table 1.1 and applying formula (1.6) yields

$$\pi_i = .35(30100 - 19500) = 3710.$$

This is the good's normative profit which, added to total cost of 30,100 rubles, results in the wholesale price of 33,810 rubles.

When a good is manufactured by more than one producer, the example considered in Table 1.1 is not applicable. Instead, a weighting procedure is usually used. Its purpose is to average the unit cost among producers and, as a result, to determine the normative profit of the firms involved. Table 1.2 illustrates the case for two firms. Cost items play the key role in this example, as they did in Table 1.1. They are combined in Table 1.2 into three aggregate groups – direct material cost, wages and social insurance withholdings for production workers, and other cost items. (One can see from Table 1.1 that direct material cost consists of the cost of raw materials, parts bought, and fuel and energy, while the group of other cost items includes everything from the preparation of production to sale and distribution.)

As shown in Table 1.2, the good's total cost equals 1,150 rubles for firm A and 1,400 rubles for firm B. Cost to be included in the wholesale price is found as a weighted average:

$$c = \frac{c_1 q_1 + c_2 q_2}{q_1 + q_2}, \qquad (1.7)$$

where c, c_1, and c_2 = cost included in the wholesale price, cost for firm A, and cost for firm B, respectively; q_1 and q_2 = quantity of product manufactured by firm A and by firm B, respectively. Inserting the numbers from Table 1.2 in formula (1.7) yields:

$$c = \frac{1150(12000) + 1400(8000)}{12000 + 8000} = 1250,$$

i.e., the average total cost shown for both firms in Table 1.2.

Normative profit should also be incorporated in the wholesale price as an average component. According to formula (1.6), normative profit is the marginal profit markup times the difference between total cost and the cost of material inputs. The last difference can be computed as the weighted average:

$$c - g = \frac{(c_1 - g_1)q_1 + (c_2 - g_2)q_2}{q_1 + q_2}, \qquad (1.8)$$

Table 1.2.   Computation of the Wholesale Price for a Good
             Produced by Two Firms

	Value	
Indicator	Firm A	Firm B
Quantity of Product Manufactured	12,000	8,000
Direct Material Cost, Rubles	750	875
Wages and Social Insurance Withholdings for Production Workers, Rubles	100	180
Other Cost Items, Rubles	300	345
Total Cost, Rubles	1,150	1,400
Average Total Cost, Rubles	1,250	1,250
Total Cost less Direct Material Cost, Rubles	400	525
Average Total Cost less Direct Material Cost, Rubles	450	450
Ratio of Profit to Total Cost less Direct Material Cost, Percent	40	40
Normative Profit, Rubles	180	180
Wholesale Price, Rubles	1,430	1,430

where $c-g$, c_1-g_1, and c_2-g_2 = average cost less direct material cost and similar costs for firm A and firm B, respectively; q_1 and q_2 = quantity of good manufactured by firm A and firm B, respectively. From Table 1.2, $c_1-g_1 = 1150-750 = 400$ and $c_2-g_2 = 1400-875 = 525$ so that, inserting in formula (1.8),

$$c-g = \frac{400(12000) + 525(8000)}{12000 + 8000} = 450.$$

Using the marginal profit markup of 40 percent from Table 1.2 and formula (1.6), normative profit is

$$\pi = .4(450) = 180,$$

and the wholesale price equals

$$p = 1250 + 180 = 1430,$$

which is the final result shown in Table 1.2 for both firms.

In reality, setting Soviet wholesale prices is not as simple as it would appear from the mechanistic computation in Tables 1.1 and 1.2. As discussed in Section 1.2, firms with backward and advanced technologies are excluded from the averaging procedure. In most cases, firms producing a small proportion of total good's output are not counted, either. Yet what is the threshold for viewing the proportion as sufficient? No standard procedures exist, and decisions are made on the basis of individual considerations.

The example in Table 1.2 also gives rise to the following question: What should the producer, in this case firm B, do if it barely does or does not make a profit? Its total cost of 1,400 rubles exceeds the average cost of 1,250 rubles while the wholesale price is based on the latter. In the Soviet case, the firm will not necessarily be a loser, its likely fate in a free market. Soviet planners will accept the firm's larger than average costs if there is a justification of this. If, for example, firm B pays for the same work higher wages than firm A, most likely the firm would not be allowed to do so without an acceptable reason. Thus, a firm's location in a northern or eastern region, with significantly higher-than-average wage rates, might be the case. But if firm B's production is included in the national economic plan and costs are approved, it will be entitled to a special subsidy on top of the wholesale price. As a result, firm B's charging a de facto higher price will nullify the effects of averaging in Table 1.2. This may, however, change with the advancement of self-sufficiency (*khozraschet*) and self-financing in Soviet industry. The new provisions are designed to stimulate the producer and reduce subsidies, due to a formula that will work so that lower subsidies are reflected in a greater material incentive fund for the producer.

Chapter 2
Output and Growth

2.1. The Measurement of Production

Production targets are specified in Soviet five-year and annual plans. The main indicators of the five-year production plan are as follows: growth rates for either the normative net value of output (NVO) or the gross value of output (GVO) in comparable prices; output in physical units, with emphasis on products for exports; growth rates for the proportion of goods in a high-quality category or another indicator of product quality change. These indicators are specified for the entire five-year period and, since the 1970s, in annual terms. Most targets of the annual plan are supposed to be set at the level of annual target projections in the five-year plan. The growth rates for the NVO and GVO and the proportion of goods in the high-quality category are especially stressed. Output in physical terms is planned in a more detailed nomenclature than in five-year plans, as is sales revenue in current wholesale prices. In order to control the meeting of delivery targets, the data on product nomenclature and the assortment and list of potential buyers are also targeted in annual plans.

In theory, enterprises working under the new conditions of self-sufficiency and self-financing are now given the authority to approve their own five-year plans (*Ekonomicheskaia Gazeta* 28, 1987, p.12). At the same time, they must be guided by the centrally assigned control figures, state orders, long-term economic normatives and ceilings on centralized investment and material inputs. Production plan targets in physical units will be included in the package of state orders (*gosudarstvennye zakazy*). Only goods that are important for solving national and social problems, technological programs, and defense have to be selected for the state orders. The classification of goods according to importance, however, allows broad interpretation. In addition to physical production, there will also be centralized planning of outputs in money terms. But the targets for outputs in money terms are specified by control figures (*kontrol'nye tsifry*) which will be less obligatory than the state orders.

Generally, all the targets are planned at three levels – national, ministerial or regional, and the production firm. The intrinsic importance of a particular product determines the level of planning. The term "national economic plan" refers to the highest level, where outputs are planned by the State Planning Committee *(Gosplan)* and approved by the Supreme Soviet. According to the official explanation, goods are included in the national economic plan if they are valuable for the country's economic growth, technological change, standard of living, and defense, i.e., the same types that now will be included in the state orders. If goods are designated for a particular industry or for interindustry needs, their production has to be planned by the ministry responsible for the delivery. The list of products planned at the national, ministerial, and regional levels, i.e., by *Gosplan*, ministries, or by republic Council of Ministers, included some 40,000 items in the early 1980s (Pokropivnyi, et al., 1982, p.171). Goods used as inputs in technological processes of local importance or sold to local consumers are planned by producing firms and local authorities. In some industries, the proportion of goods planned by the firms that manufacture them is higher than in others, but on the average these goods account for 10 to 25 percent of the value of industrial output (Pokropivnyi, et al., 1982, p.171). An important difference in production planning brought about by the new economic mechanism will be the reduction in the number of goods planned centrally. Thus, according to *Gosplan* sources, about 600 types of products were included in the state orders in 1988, compared to 2,800 types in 1987 (Reut, 1988, p.4).

Physical and monetary measures of output both affect the level of prices in the Soviet economy and depend upon the individual prices set. Physical output is measured in units such as pieces, metric tons, meters, and square or cubic meters. In addition, using "standard" or "basic" units makes different items commensurable within certain product groups, e.g., standard fuel, standard can, or 15-horse-power tractor. The importance of the choice of physical indicators for planning is a recurrent theme which was stressed by the 1979 resolution of the Central Committee and the Council of Ministers. The resolution charged *Gosplan* and the relevant ministries with finding a proper system of physical indicators, in particular for machines and equipment, which would reflect their efficiency, productivity, capacity, durability, and other qualities that could serve as a reliable basis for pricing new products. In 1987 a new instruction requires taking the social and ecological characteristics of machines into consideration.

An industry's GVO (*tovarnaia produktsiia*) is the sum of GVOs for its firms. A firm's GVO includes the values of: 1) finished products sold to outside users and to the firm's own capital-construction and nonproductive units, such as medical care, day care, and housing services provided to employees; 2) semifinished goods sold to the outside users only; and 3) contract work for outside users and for the firm's own nonproductive units. For finished products, the GVO is found by multiplying wholesale prices and physical quantities. The wholesale price is set so that it covers all costs and includes a normative profit markup. If a particular product is manufactured by more than one firm, the unit costs included in the price are the weighted average of the firms. (Examples of calculation are provided in Section 2.2.) Each product's GVO is computed in both current and comparable wholesale prices. As indicated in Section 1.1, these prices coincide when they are first set and until the current price is revised. The GVO in comparable prices is used for intertemporal comparisons and for the measurement of economic growth. It is also used as the basis for finding aggregate values of output for the industry as a whole, its branches, republic economies, and provincial regions (*oblast'*).

The GVO in current prices is needed for the calculation of the enterprise's sales revenue. Sales revenue *(realizovannaia produktsiia)* is defined as the GVO in current prices plus inventories at the beginning of a time period less inventories at the end. In this process, only those changes in the firm's inventories that are related to the components of the GVO listed above are included. At the end of the 1970s, sales revenue lost its importance as one of the firm's overall success indicators, but it has become instrumental in the evaluation of the success in meeting delivery targets. Consequently, total sales revenue is now less important than its components, i.e., sales of specific goods to specific customers scheduled by the delivery plan. The GVO in current prices is used in the process of the computation of production costs and profits.

The normative NVO (*normativnaia chistaia produktsiia*) is a part of the GVO that measures a firm's own contribution to the product's value; in a way, it is similar to the western concept of value added. Two methods of finding the normative NVO exist: aggregate and detailed. In the aggregate method, the NVO is calculated by estimating the cost of material inputs and subtracting it from the firm's GVO. In the detailed method, the NVO is calculated on the basis of special normatives of net output (NNO) for all individual goods. The NNO separates the wage and profit components from the good's wholesale price. While the GVO is the product of output in physical units and the wholesale price, the NVO is the product of output in physical units and the NNO value. The NNOs for individual goods are approved and revised simultaneously with the revisions of wholesale prices. The principle of the determination of the NNO is similar to the setting of comparable wholesale prices. The difference is that, when a product's wholesale price is revised for reasons other than a change in unit labor cost (e.g., substitution of raw materials or increases in material input prices), its NNO is not altered.

The relationship between the two value indicators is illustrated for the Soviet MBMW sector in Figure 2.1 where the percentages of different components in the sector's GVO are given for 1986. As shown, the MBMW sector's GVO can be subdivided into material expenditures (69 percent) and the NVO (31 percent). One can also see from Figure 2.1 that the concept of the NVO is indeed close to a conventional macroeconomic concept of value added. The depreciation of 7 percent accounts for the difference in the two concepts since it is not counted in the NVO but is a component of the value added. Because of this relationship, the GVO can alternatively be

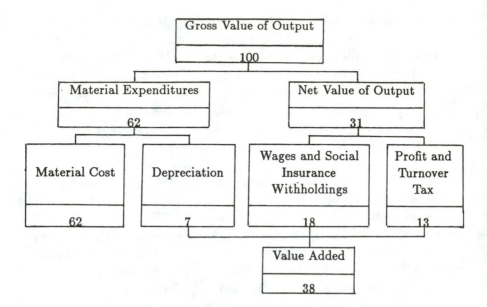

Figure 2.1. Breakdown of the 1986 Value of Output for the Soviet
MBMW Sector

divided into intermediate product, or material cost of 62 percent,
plus a value added of 38 percent.

The concept of the NVO used in Figure 2.1 is not normative
NVO. The former is obtained by direct computation of the relevant
components of production costs and profit. This is not difficult to
do for a particular firm or, on this basis, for a branch of industry
and the economy as a whole. But the normative NVO specifies the
level of individual products for which some items of production cost
cannot easily be broken down into material costs and value added.
Miscellaneous, unspecified expenditures and overhead are examples.
There is no operational scheme in the Soviet economy that would
allow more detailed accounting of such expenditures. For this reason,
and for the sake of simplicity, planners accept a normative approach
to the NVO rather than a direct calculation.

Every good produced in the Soviet economy must have its approved NNO as well as its price. In the computation of the NNO,
three components are classified. The first component includes wages

and social insurance withholdings for production workers; it is isolated from the product cost in the same way and in the same amount as in the case of the wholesale price. The second, profit component is also treated similarly. (Some complications arise when a product is turned out by more than one firm; they will be discussed later.) But the third component of the NNO – the wages and social insurance withholdings for management and maintenance personnel – does not have one counterpart in the wholesale price. Instead of collecting all the relevant expenditures from several cost items, there is a calculation of special coefficients linking these expenditures for the good to those for the firm as a whole. This practice is illustrated below.

If the NNOs are properly calculated, the sum of the normative NVOs for all goods manufactured by a firm would be equal to the firm's NVO, directly computed. But, when it comes to a branch of industry or the economy as a whole, an additional element must be considered. In Figure 2.1, the NVO includes both profit and turnover tax levied on consumer goods. While profit is a part of the wholesale price of the enterprise, turnover tax is not. Therefore, the MBMW sector's NVO, if calculated, would be less than the NVO in Figure 2.1 by the value of turnover tax. Strictly speaking, the NVO that is used by the Soviets for finding their national income does not include turnover tax either. This tax is only added to the NVO in industry wholesale prices at the last step of its computation.

What follows are examples of the computation of the GVO, NNO, and normative NVO. Table 2.1 illustrates the computation of the GVO for a hypothetical machine-building firm that turns out good 1 and good 2 and performs a contract work for an outside user. Although the computation is self-explanatory, several comments may be helpful. First, the current and comparable prices coincide for good 1 but differ for good 2. That difference could result from a reduction in the wholesale price that would not affect the comparable price if the base year for comparable prices did not change. Second, the contract work done by the firm is measured in money terms only. When the contract is signed, the wholesale price is calculated under a cost accounting scheme demonstrated in Table 1.1 of Section 1.2. As a rule, this is done on an individual basis for each type of work, and no weighting procedures are applied. The difference between the contract work's value in comparable prices of 550 thousand rubles and its value in current prices of 600 thousand rubles may have occurred because of a rise in the wholesale price with no effect on the comparable price. The totals in Table 2.1 represent the firm's GVOs in current and comparable prices.

Table 2.1. Computation of the Gross Value of Output for a Machine-Building Firm

Product	Output in Physical Units	Price, Rubles		Gross Value of Output, Thousands of Rubles	
		Current	Comparable	In Current Prices	In Comparable Prices
Good 1	800	600	600	480	480
Good 2	1,500	940	1,100	1,410	1,650
Contract Work	—	—	—	600	550
Total	2,300	—	–	2,490	2,680

The procedure for the computation of the NNO for a good manufactured by two firms is illustrated in Table 2.2. As explained above, a good's NNO is the sum of wages and normative profit. The wage component is in two parts – wages for production workers and wages for management and maintenance personnel. The first is calculated from the good's cost accounts. The normative profit component could have been determined by a method demonstrated in Tables 1.1 and 1.2 of Section 1.3. The only difficulty in the determination of the NNOs is finding each good's portion of lump-sum wages paid to the firm's management and maintenance personnel. With the introduction of the normative approach, it was decided to use the ratio of wages paid to management and maintenance personnel to wages paid to production workers for the firm as a whole for all goods manufactured by the firm. If there is only one producer, this allows the computation of the NNO's wage component as follows:

$$w = (1 + m)w^p \qquad (2.1)$$

and

$$m = \frac{W - W^p}{W^p}, \tag{2.2}$$

where w and w^p = good's wages and social insurance withholdings and good's wages for production workers, respectively; W and W^p = total wage bill of the firm and wages paid to the firm's production workers, respectively; the difference $W - W^p$ = wages paid to the firm's management and maintenance personnel; and m = ratio of wages for management and maintenance personnel to wages for production workers for the firm.

Since, in this example, the good is manufactured by two firms, using formulas (2.1) and (2.2) and the information in Table 2.2 will lead to the outcomes:

$$m_1 = \frac{6400 - 2000}{2000} = 2.2, \qquad w_1 = (1 + 2.2)500 = 1600$$

and

$$m_2 = \frac{4950 - 1800}{1800} = 1.75, \qquad w_2 = (1 + 1.75)800 = 2200.$$

But, because there could be only one wage component in a given product's NNO, an averaging procedure is used at the next step, in the same way as for the cost component of the wholesale price in Section 1.3:

$$w = \frac{w_1 q_1 + w_2 q_2}{q_1 + q_2} \tag{2.3}$$

where w, w_1, and w_2 = total wages and social insurance withholding included in the good's NNO, and the same wages and withholdings for firm A and firm B, respectively; q_1 and q_2 = quantity of the good manufactured by firm A and by firm B, respectively.

Inserting the results of computation for w_1 and w_2 and the quantities from Table 2.2 for q_1 and q_2 in formula (2.3) yields

$$w = \frac{1600(130) + 2200(70)}{130 + 70} = 1810,$$

Table 2.2. Computation of the Norm of Net Output for a Product
Manufactured by Two Firms

Indicator	Firm A	Firm B
Quantity of Product Manufactured, Physical Units	130	70
Good's Wages and Social Insurance Withholdings for Production Workers, Rubles	500	800
Total Wage Bill of the Firm, Thousands of Rubles	6,400	4,950
Wages Paid to the Firm's Production Workers, Thousands of Rubles	2,000	1,800
Ratio of Wages Paid to Management and Maintenance Personnel to Wages Paid to Production Workers for the Firm	2.2	1.7
Good's Wages and Social Insurance Withholdings for Management and Maintenance Personnel, Rubles	1,100	1,400
Good's Total Wages and Social Insurance Withholdings, Rubles	1,600	2,200
Average Good's Total Wages and Social Insurance Withholdings, Rubles	1,810	1,810
Normative Profit, Rubles	1,370	1,370
Normative of Net Output, Rubles	3,180	3,180

which clears the way for finding the NNO:

$$r = w + \pi, \tag{2.4}$$

where r, w, and π = good's NNO, wage, and profit component, respectively. If the profit component is not known, it can be found with the use of an averaging procedure or a targeted normative profit rate as explained in the example in Table 1.2 of Section 1.3. In both cases, profit is a certain proportion of total cost net of the cost of material inputs. It is assumed as given in Table 2.2, so that

$$r = 1810 + 1370 = 3180.$$

This result means that the NNO component in the good's whole-sale price equals 3,180 rubles, and the difference between the good's wholesale price and the NNO's value is the cost of material inputs.

Before illustrating the computation of the normative NVO for a firm, the specifics of accounting for the contract work should be noted. As mentioned above, the computation of the NNO for the contract work is performed on an individual basis, with no weighting procedure used. Further, the NNO for contract work is found at the final step, after finding the normative NVO, not the other way around. The normative NVO is obtained simply by summing the wage and profit components, as in the example of two goods, above. The ratio of the contract work's normative NVO to its GVO in comparable prices is then termed its NNO. An example of the computation of the normative NVO is in Table 2.3. It is an extension of the example in Table 2.1, with the same initial information for goods 1 and 2 and contract work.

2.2. Soviet Measures of Growth and Productivity

An economy grows by ascending from one phase to the next in a process measured by the values of certain economic indicators. The Soviet and western concepts both view economic growth as rising output of the economy, but output is measured differently. In the western national income and product accounts, the measure reflects the market value of final goods and services produced by the economy. In the Soviet context, some paid economic activities fail to contribute to the value of national product, and, according to Marxist classification, those services are excluded. Since only material goods become components of the national product, the product originates in the "material" sectors of the economy. These sectors either produce tangible goods (industry, agriculture, forestry, and construction) or raise their value in the process of marketing and shipping (business communications and freight transport) and packing and wrapping (wholesale and, in part, retail trade). The format for the computation of output is, again, the same. In both cases, gross output is found as a weighted aggregate quantity. At this point, similarity ends because of the different meaning of quantities and because quite different types of prices are used. In the western case, there are two equivalent approaches. In the first, current values are directly deflated by the base-period market prices; in the second approach, the same results are obtained by the deflation of values using price indices.

Table 2.3. Computation of the Normative Net Value of Output for a Firm

Product	Output, Physical Units	Normative of Net Output, Rubles	Gross Value of Output in Comparable Prices, Thousands of Rubles	Normative Net Value of Output, Thousands of Rubles	Proportion of NVO in GVO in Comparable Prices, Percent
Good 1	800	250	480	200	41.7
Good 2	1,500	314	1,650	471	28.5
Contract Work	–	.48	550	264	48.0
Total	2,300	–	2,680	935	34.9

When the Soviets measure economic growth at the level of a branch of industry or for the industry as a whole, they first find gross values of output (GVO – *tovarnaia produktsiia*) for individual firms and production associations. As explained in Section 2.1, the GVO counts all finished and semifinished products and parts and contract work. The so-called factory (*zavodskoi*) or association (*ob'edinencheskii*) methods are used in the computation. The factory method is used for an individual firm that is not a part of a production association, though there are many exceptions. The idea of these methods is to exclude from the calculation of the GVO those products and parts that are intended for intra-firm or intra-association production consumption. Once applied, a method chosen for a given product is used in further computation at all levels, including the level of the national economy.

To measure economic growth, the output growth index (*index fizicheskogo ob'ema*) is used in the Soviet economy. In this index, each firm's GVO is expressed in comparable prices. The formula is as follows:

$$I^q = \Sigma p_i^c q_{it} / \Sigma p_i^c q_{it}, \qquad (2.5)$$

where I^q = output growth index for a given firm or production association; q_{it} and q_{io} = physical output of the ith product in the current t and the base year 0, respectively; and p_i^c = comparable price for the ith product. The expressions in the numerator and the denominator of formula (2.5) are the firm's GVO in the current and the base year, respectively. To apply this method to a branch of industry, the GVOs for all of its firms and production associations are determined and summed for the current and the base years in formula (2.5). For the industry as a whole, the summation is then performed for all its branches.

The comparable prices used in formula (2.5) are the Soviet counterpart of the western concept of constant-dollar or base-year prices. For each product, they are obtained from an official price list (*preiskurant*) valid for the base year chosen for comparable prices. Therefore, if newly introduced products were ignored, index (2.5) would be a conventional, base-year weighted (or Laspeyres) index. However, incorporating goods introduced after the base year distorts that format. Since the new goods have no base-year comparable price, the first price officially approved will be taken by the Soviets as comparable and will be traced back to the base year; the comparable price is considered as existing in the year when the good itself did not exist. As a result, the weights in formula (2.5) are not fixed; they change over time as some weights are added with the introduction of new goods and as some are deleted with the discontinuation of old goods.

If prices for a new item's product group are revised after the base year with no change in comparable prices, the item's comparable price will be its first *preiskurant* price times a multiplier which is the ratio of an analogue's comparable price to its revised price. For example, suppose that product 1 is an analogue for a new product 2, and that the comparable price for product 1 is 110 rubles while its revised price is 100 rubles. Also suppose that the wholesale price approved for product 2 is 150 rubles. Then product 2's comparable price will be

$$p_2^c = 150 \cdot \frac{110}{100} = 165.$$

The concept of comparable prices is crucial to understanding the peculiarities of Soviet measures of economic growth and productivity. Here are some historic facts. Although the Soviets used 1926-27 prices as constant for intertemporal calculations in the 1930s and the 1940s, the comparable-price approach to index construction became popular in the 1950s and the 1960s. For a short time, 1952 comparable prices were used for industry, until they were replaced by 1955 prices. A major change brought about by the 1967 price reform required another change in the base year. In the period that followed the reform, 1967 prices were used as comparable prices in industry, along with 1969 prices for construction and 1965 prices for agriculture; 1965 prices were also used for the balance of the national economy as well as indicators such as gross social product and national income. When the 1976 annual and 1976-80 five-year plans were drafted, there was a switch to 1975 comparable prices for industry and construction and to 1973 prices for agricultural output, gross social product, and national income. In that case, as is usual when the industry's and gross social product's prices do not coincide, industry's GVO was recalculated from 1975 into 1973 prices. Finally, since the 1982 price reform significantly changed the level of industrial prices and new *preiskuranty* were introduced for industrial products, 1982 prices have become comparable prices for industry, until the new revision in the price base (which will take place in 1990).

For most manufactured goods, individual prices are used as comparable prices. But, as discussed in Chapter 1, individual prices cannot be used in national economic planning; instead, average comparable prices are calculated for product groups. They are computed as weighted average prices for each nomenclature item in a product group. The ministries prepare a nomenclature list for industrial goods and coordinate it with *Gosplan* and the State Committee on Material and Technical Supply (*Gossnab*). For planning purposes, both average comparable and current prices are calculated. This is done by dividing the GVO in comparable and in current prices, respectively, by output in physical units:

$$\bar{p} = \sum p_j q_j / \sum q_j, \tag{2.6}$$

where $\bar{p}$ and p_j = average comparable (or current) price of a given nomenclature item and individual comparable (or current) price of the jth good in the nomenclature item, respectively, and q_j = output of the jth good.

Contemporaneity is generally not required in formula (2.6) so that, depending on the purpose, outputs of different periods may be used as weights. For example, the following formula was applied for the calculation of a nomeclature group's price change caused by the 1982 price reform:

$$\overline{J} = \overline{p}_{82}/\overline{p}_s,$$

$\overline{J}$ = index of average price for a nomenclature item measuring the effect of the 1982 price change; $\overline{p}_{82}$ = average price for a nomenclature group in the 1982 *preiskurant* weighted by the 1980 output, and $\overline{p}_s$ = average price for the nomenclature group in the pre-1982 *preiskurant* weighted by the 1980 output. Weighting was performed as follows:

$$\overline{p}_{j82} = \Sigma p_{j82} q_{j80} / \Sigma q_{j80}$$

and

$$\overline{p}_s = \Sigma p_{js} q_{j80} / \Sigma q_{j80},$$

where p_{j82} and p_{js} = price of the jth good in the 1982 and pre-1982 *preiskurant*, respectively; and q_{j80} = output of the jth good in 1980.

Permanent *preiskurant* prices are not the only type of prices that can be used as comparable. If a new good's *preiskurant* price has not been approved, one of the temporary prices mentioned in Section 1.1 can, if approved, be used instead. If there is no price for a good to be manufactured in a planned period, a conditional price (*uslovnaia tsena*) is computed and used as the comparable price. When a *preiskurant* price is approved, it substitutes as the comparable price. Hence, a good's comparable price may change between changes in the base year for comparable prices.

Since comparable prices are used in planning as the weighted average prices for each nomenclature group, they can rise even if individual goods prices do not change. This happens as a result of changes in the weights in formula (2.6) when, for instance, a gradual shift to more expensive items takes place. According to Soviet sources, in the 1976-80 five-year period the average comparable price of chemical products rose by 10 to 26 percent (Krylov and Kanunnikov, 1977, p.65). Planners complained that at least one third of the producers surpassing plan targets could have done so because of the increases in average comparable prices (Krylov and Kanunnikov, 1977, p.65). In other words, the Soviet producer surpasses plan targets in value terms by both turning out more of physical products and by switching to more expensive items.

It follows, then, that the way of using comparable prices for the computation of growth and price indices differs from a constant-weight approach of Laspeyres or Paasche indices. Constant weights exist in Soviet growth indices only at the outset of a new base year. At that time, prices of existing products are fixed as comparable. As explained above, new goods enter the growth index with their current, not base-year weights, and the set of weights is constantly altered, as some goods are added and others are discontinued. In addition, weights can be amended for individual products as a result of a substitution of temporary prices by permanent prices or of a price revision for the relevant product group. Table 2.4 illustrates several cases. The base-year prices of all goods in Table 2.4 are their comparable prices for the base as well as the current year, which is the case until there is a switch to a new base year. Thus, despite a rise in good 1's price from seven to eight rubles and a decline in good 3's price from 10 to nine rubles, their current-year comparable prices coincide with the base-year prices. Still, a change in the set of comparable prices does occur since good 5 is introduced to replace good 4, which, according to Table 2.4, had a lower price. Despite the fact that goods 4 and 5 could be similar, good 5 will be included in the growth index (2.5) with its newly approved price of six rubles, not with good 4's comparable price of three rubles. (On the relationship between product price and quality change see Section 4.3.) Using formula (2.5), the output growth index is

$$I^q = (22 \cdot 7 + 16 \cdot 4 + 8 \cdot 10 + 30 \cdot 6)/(20 \cdot 7 + 15 \cdot 4 + 8 \cdot 10 + 50 \cdot 3) = 111.2,$$

i.e., the value of output increases by 11.2 percent.

Table 2.4. Information for the Computation of the Growth Index

Good	Base Year		Current Year		
	Quantity, Physical Units	Comparable Price, Rubles	Quantity, Physical Units	Current Price, Rubles	Comparable Price, Rubles
1	20	7	22	8	7
2	15	4	16	4	4
3	8	10	8	9	10
4	50	3	–	–	–
5	–	–	30	6	6

Since the base year for comparable prices periodically changes, the Soviets use chain indices for intertemporal comparisons when longer time periods are involved. Overlapping, which is required for smoothing, is provided for each period by measuring the output of the base year in both new comparable prices and comparable prices of the previous base. For example, to find industrial growth from 1960 to 1985, the following chain index would be needed:

$$I_{85/60} = \frac{I_{67/55}}{I_{60/55}} \cdot I_{75/67} \cdot I_{82/75} \cdot I_{85/82},$$

since the base years in that period were 1955, 1967, 1975, and 1982.

Growth rates for the Soviet economy as a whole and its industries need not coincide with growth rates for firms and production associations. The difference may be attributed to the fact that the firm's GVO has to be evaluated in terms of success in its meeting delivery contracts. This is done to improve the production of goods and services and to stress the priority of indicators in physical terms over indicators in value terms. Accordingly, a firm's actual sales revenue is reduced by the total value of goods that were not delivered to at least one buyer, without regard to overdeliveries to other buyers. For example, suppose that a firm's planned GVO in comparable prices equals one million rubles, actual sales revenue is 1,035 thousand rubles, and the firm's failure to deliver on one of the contracts is equal to 25 thousand rubles. (Since the firm actually surpassed the plan target by 35 thousand rubles, there must have been an overdelivery of 60 thousand rubles on other contracts.) Then the firm's output growth index will be

$$I^q = \frac{1035 - 25}{1000} = 1.01,$$

with a growth rate of only one percent after accounting for underdelivery. For the industry as a whole, however, there are no discounts of deliveries, and the actual GVO of the current year will be taken into account.

The problems of measuring economic growth and productivity are closely interrelated. Generally, there are two different types of measures of productivity. The first includes the measures of partial productivity that relate output to one input, such as labor or capital. The second includes the measures of multifactor productivity that relate output to a given combination of inputs. Labor productivity is one of the traditional partial productivity measures, while measuring multifactor productivity is a relatively recent phenomenon.[2] The computation format and the meaning of these western concepts of productivity only in part coincide with those used in the Soviet economy.

Labor productivity, as measured by the Bureau of Labor Statistics (BLS) of the U.S. Department of Labor, is the real output-to-hours paid ratio. Output and labor hours are direct aggregates and are not weighted when this ratio is calculated. In the Soviet economy, this measure of labor productivity is not used even though hours worked are estimated for industry. Instead, the average product of labor is measured as the output-to-employment ratio (*vyrabotka na odnogo rabotnika*) and is used as the official measure. (It is not difficult to transform this ratio into an hourly measure taking into account that so far there have been no overtime pay or significant layoffs in Soviet industry, and part-time work is negligible.)

Multifactor productivity is defined as the ratio of output to a combined input measure. In the BLS approach, the combined input measure is a weighted sum of labor and capital. The weights are the proportional shares of output that each factor contributes during a given time period. The two inputs will then be combined in terms of their total cost, each as a proportion of total value of output. The

formula for the growth of multifactor productivity used by the BLS
is as follows:

$$r^m = r^q - (s^\ell \cdot r^h + s^k \cdot r^k), \tag{2.7}$$

where r^m, r^q, r^h, and r^k = percentage change in multifactor productivity, output, hours worked, and capital services, respectively,
and s^ℓ and s^k = share of labor and capital, respectively, in the total
value of output ($s^\ell + s^k$=1). The shares of labor and capital are
averaged by the BLS for the given and previous years (Grossman,
1984). Practically, the labor share of total output is found as the
wages-to-output ratio, and the capital share is then one minus the
labor share.

Despite the shortcomings of formula (2.7) as the definition of
multifactor productivity, it is used for the U.S. economy. Comparative calculations could therefore be interesting. They are performed
below for the U.S. private business sector and for Soviet industry
and the MBMW sector. The information for the U.S. private business sector for the 1966-85 period is in Table 2.5. Inserting the data
in formula (2.7) yields:

$$r^m = 2.85 - (.68 \cdot 1.45 + .32 \cdot 3.22) = .83,$$

i.e., the average annual growth rate of multifactor productivity in
the U.S. private business sector was .83 percent from 1965 to 1985.
The official average rate of multifactor productivity growth in the
U.S. private business sector is equal to 1.5 percent for the 1948-81
period (Grossman, 1984, p.418).

Table 2.6 reports the information for the computation of multifactor productivity for Soviet industry and the MBMW sector in
the 1966-85 period. Inserting the information from Table 2.6 in formula (2.7) results in the following average annual growth rates of
multifactor productivity for Soviet industry

$$r^m = 6.01 - (.2 \cdot 1.45 + .8 \cdot 7.04) = .09$$

and for the MBMW sector

$$r^m = 9.32 - (.25 \cdot 2.23 + .75 \cdot 9.06) = 1.97,$$

Table 2.5. Information for the Computation of Multifactor Productivity for the U.S. Private Business Sector in the 1966-85 Period

Indicator	Value
Output, Average Annual Growth Rate	2.85
Labor Hours, Average Annual Growth Rate	1.45
Capital Services, Average Annual Growth Rate	3.22
Average Labor Share of Total Value of Output	.68
Average Capital Share of Total Value of Output	.32

Source: *Statistical Abstract of the United States* (1986, pp. 400 and 447).

i.e., the average growth rates of multifactor productivity in Soviet industry and in the MBMW sector from 1965 to 1986 were .09 percent and 1.97 percent, respectively.

Interpreting these results, one may say that the growth rate of multifactor productivity was negligible in Soviet industry as a whole, but was impressive, about two percent, in the MBMW sector. The difference between the two is understandable, given the widespread belief that technological change is primarily confined to the MBMW sector in the U.S.S.R. Another important contributing element could be the relationship between multifactor productivity and prices. Soviet industry is a conglomerate of branches in which prices have increased at different rates, with the rises for the MBMW sector probably being among the highest. Under these conditions, if the output growth rates are generally affected by prices, the distortion would be the greatest for MBMW products. Hence, as in other similar cases, the reliability of these productivity estimates rests upon the reliability of Soviet official statistics. (Some of the new challenges to Soviet official statistics are discussed in Chapter 9.)

In measuring labor input in Table 2.6, total employment or, more accurately, the number of employees is used for the Soviet case, instead of hours worked or paid. (Although, as indicated above, hours worked are estimated for the Soviet industry, the number of employees is used in the Soviet measure of labor productivity.) Labor productivity is the only such measure recognized in the Soviet Union, in

Table 2.6. Information for the Computation of Multifactor
Productivity for Soviet Industry and the MBMW
Sector in the 1966-85 Period

Indicator	Industry	MBMW Sector
Output, Average Annual Growth Rate	6.01	9.32
Employment, Average Annual Growth Rate	1.45	2.23
Capital Stock, Average Annual Growth Rate	7.04	9.06
Average Labor Share of Total Value of Output	.20	.25
Average Capital Share of Total Value of Output	.80	.75

Source: *Narkhoz SSSR* (*za 70 let*, pp. 131, 141, and 144; 1980,
pp. 115, 135, and 141).

accordance with the Marxist theory of value. The average measure of
productivity can be based either on the gross value of output (GVO)
or on the net value of output (NVO). When the GVO is used, it is
expressed in comparable prices. Thus, according to Soviet official
statistics, average annual growth rates for the GVO-to-employment
ratio were 4.5 percent for industry and 6.8 percent for the MBMW
sector in the 1966-86 period (*Narkhoz SSSR za 70 let*, p.141 and
1980, p.135). The difference between the two measures is compatible with the results that would have followed from Table 2.6. Since
the Soviets have switched to the computation of labor productivity
on the basis of the NVO, there will be methodological changes for
that indicator. (Some methodological issues in the calculation of the
NVO are discussed in Section 2.1.)

   In the planning calculations, there are actual and planned types
of labor productivity. Planned labor productivity can be estimated
as the ratio of normative (desired) output to planned employment.
However, this direct computation is seldom performed. Instead,
planned labor productivity is determined on the basis of productivity actually achieved in the previous period and the targeted increase
in productivity:

$$l_{t+1}^{p} = v_{t+1}^{p} \cdot l_t,$$
$$(2.8)$$

where l^p_{t+1} and l_t = labor productivity planned for the period $t+1$ and labor productivity achieved in the current period t, respectively, and v^p_{t+1} = planned index of productivity increase for the period $t+1$.

As the planned period eventually expires and turns into the accounting period, planned productivity l^p_{t+1} is used as the value to be compared to the level of productivity l_{t+1} actually achieved. The index $v_{t+1} = l_{t+1}/l^p_{t+1}$ then determines success in meeting the plan target for productivity growth, this time both planned and actual productivity being contemporaneous. When actual productivities for different periods are to be compared, the index of productivity growth is used:

$$v_t = \frac{\sum p^c_i q_{it}}{\sum L_{it}} \Big/ \frac{\sum p^c_i q_{io}}{\sum L_{io}}, \tag{2.9}$$

where p^c_i = comparable price of the ith good valid for both the current period t and the base period 0; q_{it} and q_{io} = quantity of the ith good manufactured in the current period t and the base period 0, respectively; and L_{it} and L_{io} = employment in production of the ith good in the current period t and the base period 0, respectively. Expression $\sum p^c_i q_{it}$ in formula (2.9) is the value of output in comparable prices for a given firm, branch or the whole industry in period t, and $\sum L_{it}$ is the corresponding total employment.

The following identity maintains the relationship between the growth in the value of output and labor productivity:

$$r^q = r^\ell + r^L + r^\ell r^L, \tag{2.10}$$

where r^q, r^ℓ, and r^L = growth rate of output, labor productivity, and employment, respectively. For example, suppose that in the current period labor productivity grows by three percent and employment by four percent. Then

$$r^q = .03 + .04 + .03(.04) = .071,$$

i.e., output rises by 7.1 percent. In simplified planning calculations, the cross-product term on the right-hand side of identify (2.10) is usually ignored; in that case, the result in this example would be seven percent.

2.3. The Methodology of Building Soviet Price and Growth Indices

The principle of computing price and growth indices used by the Soviets could be termed the comparable-price principle. By the definition of the method, the indices based on this principle report neither inflation nor deflation for a new good, ignoring its actual price.[3] An illustration of the comparable-price principle is the annual wholesale price index computed by TsSU for every industrial ministry and branch of industry. It is measured as the ratio of this year's sales valued in current prices to these sales valued in prices of the previous year, i.e., by a format is a Paasche price index:

$$I_t^c = \Sigma_1^n p_{it} q_{it} / \Sigma_1^n p_{it-1} q_{it}, \qquad (2.11)$$

where I_t^c = current-year weighted price index in year t; p_{it} and p_{it-1} = price of product i in year t and $t-1$, respectively; q_{it} = quantity of product i sold in year t.

The index is intended to include all goods manufactured by a ministry in the current year, so that the numerator of the expression (2.11) is the actual value of the ministry's sales revenue. Since targets for manufacturing new goods are obligatory in Soviet plans, some of the goods counted in the numerator must be new. Such goods will be included in the denominator of expression (2.11) in accordance with the comparable-price principle, i.e., with their current-year prices. It is clear then that index (2.11) will deviate from 1 only if there are current-year changes in the prices of goods manufactured in both the previous and current years. Does this index hide inflation? The method of calculation itself does not provide the answer because, theoretically, it could hide deflation as well. What is clear is that index (2.11) does not target measuring inflation but, instead, traces the price changes of those goods whose production has already been established. This task is considered important by planners, whose goal is to force the ministries and their enterprises to reduce production costs and wholesale prices. Another goal of using the index is to project price levels by commodity groups for the planned period. With this purpose, index (2.11) is combined with the following:

$$I_{t+1}^f = \left(\Sigma_1^m p_{jt} q_{jt+1} - R \right) / \Sigma_1^m p_{jt} q_{jt+1}, \qquad (2.12)$$

where I_{t+1}^f = forecast index of planned prices in year $t+1$; p_{jt} = price of product j in year t; q_{jt+1} = quantity of product j planned for sale in year $t+1$; R = targeted total price reduction for the product group.

Index (2.12) is important not only for tracing prices, but also for the entire planning process. On the one hand, since planning authorities are interested in restraining price growth, they would like to reduce the prices as much as possible. On the other hand, if the planned sum of reduction R in formula (2.12) is too high, this will adversely affect plan targets in money terms. A balance should therefore be maintained. In procedure (2.12), only the level of current-year prices is taken into consideration. From the planners' perspective, this means that, if new goods are introduced in the planned period, their prices may be temporarily high but properly justified by the producer. The relation of new prices to goods produced in the previous year is not viewed as important at this step. Index (2.12) reflects this point. When new goods and their prices shift from the planned to the current year, planners will start pressuring the producer in the direction of price reduction, using the magic R in procedure (2.12).

The example that follows illustrates procedures (2.11) and (2.12). Suppose that goods 1, 2, and 3 of the same product group were manufactured in the base year, and that goods 1, 2, and 4 will be produced in both the current and planned years, with good 4 replacing good 3. Also suppose that the base-year prices, current-year prices, and quantities produced are as given in Table 2.7. Finally, the targeted total reduction in the wholesale price equals 16.

Applying formula (2.11) to the information in Table 2.7 yields the following value of the current-year weighted price index

$$I_t^c = (5 \cdot 8 + 7 \cdot 34 + 18 \cdot 3)/(6 \cdot 8 + 7 \cdot 34 + 18 \cdot 3) = .98, \quad (2.13)$$

i.e., there is a decline of two percent in the price level of the current year. This computation is based on the comparable-price principle so that the price for good 4 is assumed the same in both the base and current periods and the termination of good 3 is ignored. The forecast index of planned prices (2.12) equals

$$I_{t+1}^f = (5 \cdot 11 + 7 \cdot 38 + 18 \cdot 5 - 16)/(5 \cdot 11 + 7 \cdot 38 + 18 \cdot 5) = .96.$$

Table 2.7. Prices and Output in Base, Current, and Planned
Periods

| Good | Base Period | | Current Period | | Planned Period |
	Price	Quantity	Price	Quantity	Quantity
1	6	18	5	8	11
2	7	10	7	34	38
3	9	2	–	–	–
4	–	–	18	3	5

This result means that the planning authorities impose an overall
reduction in planned prices of four percent relative to the status
quo situation for this group of products. Planners will most likely
analyze production costs for all the goods and will specify where the
reductions are to be made.

It is possible to imagine a situation in which the treatment of
good 4 in procedure (2.13) is erroneous, for instance, when it substitutes good 3 whose price is only half of good 4's but whose quality
supposedly is the same. If so, then the proper estimate should have
been

$$I^{c'} = (5 \cdot 8 + 7 \cdot 34 + 18 \cdot 3)/(6 \cdot 8 + 7 \cdot 34 + 9 \cdot 3) = 1.06. \quad (2.14)$$

Since goods 3 and 4 are directly comparable, i.e., have the same
quality characteristics, it is logical to use the price of good 3, instead of the price of good 4, for the base year, which is done in the
denominator of (2.14). This brings about an increase of six percent
in the price level of the commodity group, instead of a decline of two
percent shown in estimate (2.13). Of the two methods, (2.13) and
(2.14), the planners would prefer the former, or the official version.
Two probable reasons could be given.

First, the current-year data are included in all plan documents
as an anticipated achievement of planned targets (*ozhidaemoe vypol-
nenie plana*). This information is the base of the plan because all
planning calculations start with the analysis of the achieved level of
economic indicators. However, since these data are computed in the
first quarter but also cover the rest of the year, they are almost as
much projections as the plan itself. According to planning principles

in the U.S.S.R., negative trends such as the growth of the material expenditures-to-output ratio or capital-to-output ratio are seldom included in plans even if they are inevitable. Price growth is treated almost the same way; as a rule, it is not included in plans. Moreover, price increases, other than those resultant from official price reforms and revisions, cannot be justified even for the current year. Second, since planning authorities are well aware that enterprises frequently hide reserves, they would prefer, of the two possible current-year indices in the above example, a lower rather than a higher one. Why? Because the higher the current value of the index, the easier it is to lower it next year. For example, the next year's price increase of two percent would be considered as an improvement if compared to this year's increase of four percent. Therefore, to report achievements, the ministries will *ceteris paribus* have to reduce planned prices by a greater proportion when they are confronted with the current-year price index of .98, not 1.06. It should be stressed again that the difference in the two indices is the result of the methodologies applied, not the substance.

The comparable-price principle in building Soviet price and growth indices makes them different from conventional western indices. Thus, if the same information and the same formulas were used in both cases, the computation would produce different estimates. The Soviet State Committee on Statistics (*Goskomstat*) does not actually measure inflation with the indices it computes but traces the movement of prices for goods that have already been established in production. Even with the introduction of the system of self-sufficiency and self-financing, the Soviet producer will still have limited authority to alter approved prices. This means that the Soviet wholesale price indices reflect price revisions undertaken by the authorities chiefly for price reductions. That is why these indices usually exhibit a monotonic pattern of decline. Whereas, as discussed earlier, tracing established prices is viewed as important, no price or growth indices built on sample information are used in Soviet economic planning. Instead, price indices that count all items in a given product group are used for year-to-year comparisons of output values in current and base-year prices.

According to price-index theory, a change in a market basket makes only a technical difference, when one switches from a base to a current-year index, or vice versa. Yet the Soviet situation is unique in this respect. This results from the fact that changes in product assortment are not dictated by the consumer and, therefore, do not reflect consumer preferences. Only the producer and planning and managing authorities have influence over the composition of product mix. Although Soviet industrial enterprises operate under considerable restrictions, loopholes allow them to produce more expensive items instead of less expensive ones. The ministries, too, are interested in surpassing the plan, and this depends, among other things, on prices. But what if prices are fixed? Then it is possible to play on weights in the price index, i.e., on product mix. This is well known, but the consequences for building price indices have not been assessed.

When a free-market consumer switches from less to more expensive items, it is inferred that he or she is better off because of an increased real income (assuming that both cheap and expensive goods are equally accessible). For a Soviet consumer, however, one examines the basket that is under control of the seller, not the purchaser. Suppose that the Soviet producer alters the product mix without affecting the list of prices, in such a way that the number of more expensive products increases while the number of less expensive items decreases. As a result, the purchaser's basket of inputs becomes more costly. For a purchaser of inputs in a free-market economy, rising input prices usually mean lower marginal product of a dollar's worth of an input. Consequently, a good deal of input substitutions would occur. The Soviet purchaser of inputs does not have similar options. First, cheaper inputs disappear due to the input producer's alterations in product mix. Second, the Soviet purchaser receives inputs through the supply system and cannot shop around. But even if he could, would he? The answer, under given conditions, is no. Since the purchaser's budget is adjusted to meet increases in input costs, rising prices do not affect the purchaser whose isocost curve does not change its position. Hence, the optimum decisions in terms of the firm's production function and the manager's bonus function are not affected.

Evidently, both the base-year and the current-year weighted price indices in general work better when the change in prices is greater and the change in quantities produced is smaller. When prices are fixed, any fluctuation in the market basket is not reflected in either the Laspeyres or the Paasche index. While the indices may be indifferent, the Soviet managers are not. Returning to the example in Table 2.7, suppose that only goods 1 and 2 are manufactured. Then good 1's price is lowered from six to five rubles, and the output is lowered from 18 to eight physical units. The good 2's price remains unchanged, and its output grows from 10 to 34 units. To see whether the producer is better or worse off as a result of changing product mix, we will define the index of average price as follows:

$$\bar{I}_t = \frac{\sum_1^n p_{it}q_{it}}{\sum_1^n q_{it}} \Big/ \frac{\sum_1^m p_{io}q_{io}}{\sum_1^m q_{io}}, \qquad (2.15)$$

where $\bar{I}_t$ = index of average price measured in year t; p_{it} and p_{io} = price of product i in current year t and base year 0, respectively; q_{it} and q_{io} = quantity of product i manufactured in year t and 0 respectively. The list of products does not need to coincide for years t and 0; in general, $n \neq m$.

According to formula (2.15), the index of average price for the first two products in Table 2.7 equals

$$\bar{I}_t = \left(\frac{5 \cdot 8 + 7 \cdot 34}{8 + 34} \Big/ \frac{6 \cdot 18 + 7 \cdot 10}{18 + 10} \right) = 1.04.$$

Hence, there is a *ceteris paribus* increase of four percent in the average price of the group of two products. This example illustrates the well-known fact that the average price of a product group can grow even when individual prices are constant and some are reduced. Such average price growth takes place in the Soviet economy independently of the process of the introduction of new products. Soviet planners have paid much attention to this phenomenon and have required that detailed calculations of all the changes in product mix be performed by enterprises, ministries, and industrial departments of *Gosplan*. All the ministries are required to compute and submit information on average annual prices by product group.

There could be theoretical reservations to the use of the index of average price (2.15). Ignoring the difference in the number of goods in the base and the given year sets, it could be rewritten equivalently as

$$\bar{I}_t = \frac{\sum p_{it}q_{it}}{\sum p_{io}q_{io}} \Big/ \frac{\sum q_{it}}{\sum q_{io}} = V_t/Q_t, \tag{2.15'}$$

where V_t = index of the growth of output in money terms in year t and Q_t = index of the growth of output in physical units in year t. Index V_t of the growth of output in money terms rises as the result of the rise in both prices and real output. The problem of breaking down this index into its basic components, one of which is the measure of the price change while the other is the measure of the quantity change, is the index number problem. Two procedures may be used, depending on whether base or current year weights are used. In the first case, when the base-year quantities are used as weights in the price index, it compares the cost of the base-year bundle in the base and current years. Index V_t can be split into a product of the Laspeyres price and the Paasche quantity indices:

$$V_t = \frac{\sum p_{it}q_{it}}{\sum p_{io}q_{io}} = \frac{\sum p_{it}q_{io}}{\sum p_{io}q_{io}} \cdot \frac{\sum p_{it}q_{it}}{\sum p_{it}q_{io}} = I_t^L \cdot G_t^P, \tag{2.16}$$

where $I_t^L = \frac{\sum p_{it}q_{io}}{\sum p_{io}q_{io}}$ = Laspeyres price index in year t, and $G_t^L = \frac{\sum p_{it}q_{it}}{\sum p_{it}q_{io}}$ = Paasche quantity index in year t. In the second case, when the current-year quantities are used as weights in the price index, the latter compares the cost of the current-year bundle in the base and current years. Index V_t can accordingly be split into a product of the Paasche price and the Laspeyres quantity indices:

$$V_t = \frac{\sum p_{it}q_{it}}{\sum p_{io}q_{io}} = \frac{\sum p_{it}q_{it}}{\sum p_{io}q_{it}} \cdot \frac{\sum p_{io}q_{it}}{\sum p_{io}q_{io}} = I_t^P \cdot G_t^L, \tag{2.16'}$$

where $I_t^P = \frac{\sum p_{it}q_{it}}{\sum p_{io}q_{it}}$ = Paasche price index in year t, and $G_t^L = \frac{\sum p_{io}q_{it}}{\sum p_{io}q_{io}}$ = Laspeyres quantity index in year t.

Although expressions (2.16) and (2.16') provide the same answer for index V_t, the price and growth indices in the two expressions generally do not coincide. If so, then neither of the two types of indices is a theoretical solution to the problem of the decomposition of index V_t. For example, it has been argued that the price indices explain both changes in prices and, in part, changes in quantities. The reason is that, in a market with consumers freely choosing, any price changes will be met by an appropriate adjustment in quantities. The Laspeyres price index thus overestimates the price change with reference to the base-year quantities, and the Paasche index underestimates the price change with reference to the current-year quantities. According to the "method of limits" of Keynes,

$$I_t^P \leq I_t^T \leq I_t^L, \tag{2.17}$$

where I_t^T = unknown "true" price index (Afriat, 1977, p.43). Formula (2.17) is an empirical, rather than analytical relationship. It is always possible to build an example when the Laspeyres index would report a lower price change than the Paasche index. Yet, due to the mentioned adjustments in quantities, the relationship is a fact of life. To correct for the deficiencies of the two price indices, Fisher suggested an "ideal" index

$$I_t^F = \sqrt{I_t^L \cdot I_t^P},$$

where I_t^F = Fisher "ideal" index which is the geometric mean of the Laspeyres and Paasche indices (Fisher, 1927, p.482).

From this it is apparent that, in spite of fixed base or given-year quantities, the conventional price indices are not free of the effect of change in these quantities. This is important for the Soviet case where one may even go further and challenge the whole assumption of the irrelevance of the change in quantities to the growth of prices. Neither the Laspeyres nor the Paasche index would report a price change when there is no change in prices, but there is a change in the composition of the bundle of goods. If there is an increase in the number of more expensive items in a given year, this will reasonably be interpreted as a growth in income, not prices. Yet such reasonableness implies the consumer's free choice, i.e., equal access to both less and more expensive items, which is not the case in the Soviet sellers' market. As a matter of fact, the monopoly of the seller in the market is now openly admitted by the Soviet authorities.

The following example will be useful to illustrate why the application of the conventional indices may lead to erroneous results in the Soviet case. The information is in Table 2.8. Suppose that 100 liters of grade A milk is sold at the price of 50 kopecks per liter in year -1. Further, suppose that grade B milk whose quality does not differ from grade A's is introduced in year 0, and both are sold in quantities of 90 and 10 liters, respectively. The price of grade B milk is 70 kopecks per liter. Finally, there is a reciprocal switch in the quantities of the two grades of milk in year 1, with no change in prices.

Goods such as grade A and grade B milk that possess the same quality characteristics are usually termed directly comparable. In this case, according to the practice of the U.S. Bureau of Labor Statistics, the base-year price for the new specification is set equal to the base-year price for the old specification. If so, then applying the Paasche formula to year 0,

$$I_0^P = \frac{.5(90) + .7(10)}{.5(100)} = 1.04,$$

Table 2.8. Information for the Computation of the Price Index for Milk (Rubles for Prices, Liters for Quantities)

Grade	Year -1		Year 0		Year 1	
	Price	Quantity	Price	Quantity	Price	Quantity
A	.5	100	.5	90	.5	10
B		–	.7	10	.7	90

i.e., there is a four percent increase in the milk price in year 0 relative to year -1. Two different results can be obtained for year 1 depending on what year, -1 or 0, is taken as the base. Considering year 0 as the base, both the Laspeyres and Paasche indices are identically equal to one since the change occurs not in prices but in quantities:

$$I_{1(0)}^L = \frac{.5(90) + .7(10)}{.5(90) + .7(10)} = 1$$

and

$$I^P_{1(0)} = \frac{.5(10) + .7(90)}{.5(10) + .7(90)} = 1.$$

However, using year -1 as the base for year 1, the Paasche index is

$$I^P_{1(-1)} = \frac{.5(10) + .7(90)}{.5(100)} = 1.36.$$

Hence, in this case, an overall 36 percent increase in the milk price is reported from year -1 to year 1 while, with changing base years gradually, there will only be a four percent increase from year -1 to year 0 and no change from year 0 to year 1.

This inconsistency can be removed by the use of the index of average price (2.15). Applying formula (2.15) to the data in Table 2.8 for years 0 and 1, the index is

$$\overline{I}_{0(-1)} = \frac{.5(90) + .7(10)}{100}/(.5) = 1.04$$

and

$$\overline{I}_{1(0)} = \frac{.5(10) + .7(90)}{100}/\frac{.5(90) + .7(10)}{100} = 1.31,$$

and the overall price growth can be obtained either as a chain index

$$\overline{I}_{1(-1)} = 1.04(1.31) = 1.36$$

or by the direct comparison of average prices in years -1 and 1.

The rationale for using the index of average price in this example is subject to the interpretation of the change in quantities occurring between years 0 and 1. If 100 liters of milk of either of the two grades were available for the Soviet consumers, their switching to a reciprocal combination of the milk grades in the market basket could be interpreted as the result of the change in income and preferences. In other words, an implicit assumption of the accessibility of goods made for a free market would also be valid for the Soviet market. Consequently, a case could be made favoring the use of the conventional indices and against the index of average price. But, on the other hand, if the cheaper grade milk disappears from the store shelves (which was the practice of the 1970s), the consumer has no choice but to buy the more expensive grade. With the supply of milk fixed at 100 liters while demand is almost perfectly inelastic, the seller can decide what price to charge. Therefore, as long as the decision to increase the sale of a more expensive item is made by the producer, not the consumer, it should be interpreted as inflationary. The conventional price indices do not reflect this phenomenon. But the index of average price does, so it has an advantage over the conventional indices in the Soviet context. This should be the case as long as the seller's monopoly in the market is not replaced by the consumer's sovereignty.

This example demonstrates one possible effect of the introduction of new goods on inflationary growth; such growth occurs when a good's price increase outstrips any quality change. The comparable-price principle of computing Soviet price and quantity indices is not actually intended to compare the characteristics of new specifications with the base-year ones. Instead, the new specifications are treated as if they cause no price increases at all. This gives rise to reservations, even though, theoretically, they may be unreasonable, given the Soviets' specific methods for setting new prices.

A procedure linking new specifications with the existing ones would work consistently if the prices of the new specifications were corrected to the extent of any improvement in their quality. But this is done by the Soviets in the process of setting new prices, not in the process of building indices. Since they control prices, it is logical that they would set prices to account for goods quality improvements. Consequently, the Soviet approach could be divided into two independent procedures: setting prices on the basis of goods quality change and then building price or quantity indices without consideration of quality change. This is the approach used for Soviet machines and equipment. As explained in Section 3.2, when a new machine is introduced, several of its technical characteristics are used as the basis of setting its price. If this procedure works when applied, new prices will enter the price index already adjusted for quality change, and no further adjustment will be needed. If, however, the procedure exaggerates actual quality improvements, it will result in inflationary growth which will not be recorded by official Soviet price indices.

Within the framework of the conventional price indices, it is possible to adjust prices for goods quality change. However, it is impossible to do so when the improvement is accompanied by the rise in average prices due to the type of substitution explained above. To reflect both developments, the index of average price adjusted for quality can be defined as follows:

$$\bar{I}_t^r = \frac{\sum_1^n p_{it} q_{it}}{\sum_1^n r_{it} q_{it}} \Big/ \frac{\sum_1^m p_{io} q_{io}}{\sum_1^m r_{io} q_{io}}, \tag{2.18}$$

where $\bar{I}_t^r$ = index of average price adjusted for quality measured in year t; p_{it} and p_{io} = price of good i in current year t and base year 0, respectively; q_{it} and q_{io} = quantity of good i manufactured in year t and 0, respectively; r_{it} and r_{io} = index or parameter of quality chosen in year t and 0, respectively.

To illustrate the use of index (2.18), suppose that the industry has manufactured two machines (1 and 2), with the prices and quantities given in Table 2.7. Also suppose that both machines had the same productivity of 10 physical units in the base period and that the first machine increases its productivity to 11 units in the current period. Given this information, the index of average price adjusted for productivity change equals

$$\bar{I}_t^r = (\frac{5 \cdot 8 + 7 \cdot 34}{11 \cdot 8 + 10 \cdot 34} \Big/ \frac{6 \cdot 18 + 7 \cdot 10}{10 \cdot 18 + 10 \cdot 10}) = 1.02.$$

The index of average price for this group of two goods computed on page 62 amounts to 1.04; when the index is adjusted for productivity change, it equals 1.02. The growth of two percent in this case can be interpreted as the measure of price inflation.

Adjustment for quality change is a difficult problem in general, and some of the practical solutions will be considered in Chapters 6 through 8. The linking procedure usually ignores the price increase for a good whose quality has changed and replaces it by the actual price increase of other, unchanged items in the same product group. Since prices of Soviet industrial goods rise chiefly for new items but remain stable for existing ones, the linking procedure would report no price change, under an assumption that new items bring about quality improvements. As a result, the linking procedure would leave the price index constant, as also does the Soviet index based on the comparable-price principle. Hence, the linking procedure is equivalent to the Soviet procedure of building price indices when the quality characteristics of new specifications justify their price increases. However, there may be doubts about such a justification. Then one way to combine the output growth in money terms with the change in goods quality is to use the index of average price adjusted for quality.

Chapter 3
Pricing New Machines and Equipment

3.1. Prices as a Means of Stimulating Technological Change

The role of prices as an active tool of economic policy in the Soviet Union has increased in the last two decades. That development was the result of the 1965 economic reform which made sales revenue and profit the sources for covering production expenditures. In Soviet publications on prices, the following quotation from Marx has become fashionable since 1965: "By relative reduction of prices I understand such state of things when the absolute cost of the mass of machines in use increases but not to a degree in which their mass and efficiency grow" (Zav'ialkov, 1981, p.202). As usual, Marx's thought is used in this case *a posteriori*, not *a priori*. In other words, the Soviets do not look into his writings for suggestions, but instead they choose a practical, suitable course of action. The ritual, however, requires an ideological justification, and it is the task of political economists to find an appropriate passage from Marx to justify their policies.

The above quotation has been used in particular to justify the approach to pricing new machines when a price increase is allowed, provided that it will be more than offset by improvements in the machine's productivity or other essential characteristics of quality. This is not to say that planners would be happy with continued price increases for machines and equipment. Yet they realize that the producer will not introduce new goods of better quality without material incentives. Higher prices are thus used in this case to cover high expenses of the initial period of production and to provide the appropriate incentive funds. There have generally been three tools for stimulating quality improvements of new machines: 1) temporary prices at a level generally exceeding that for permanent prices, 2) higher than otherwise permissible costs of production that are incorporated in prices, and 3) a surcharge for quality improvements.

Temporary prices (discussed in Section 1.1) have been charged by the Soviet producers since the 1950s. Their two chief purposes are to reimburse the producer for the high costs of the starting period of production and to insulate permanent prices from the effects of these high costs. Along with the task of stimulating technological change, planners intended to reduce the burden of growing input costs on users or, more accurately, on the state budget reimbursing them. But the tasks are contradictory: while stimulating technological change requires higher prices for new machines and equipment, the remedy for rising costs is to reduce prices. Since even *Goskomtsen* cannot have its cake and eat it, too, it has repeatedly switched its priorities from one task to another. The several instructions on pricing new machines and equipment issued in 1969, 1974, 1982, and 1987 are an illustration.

The first, 1969 instruction started the tug of war. At that time the initiative was on the side of the stimulating approach, and it was decided to count the high costs of the first year of production as the base for new wholesale prices. Then the second, 1974 instruction pulled in the opposite direction by providing that the costs of the second year or, in the case of complex technology, even the third year should become the base of prices for new machines and equipment. The 1982 instruction once again declared that the costs of the first year were to be counted; the stimulating approach thus became the winner. This attitude was reenforced in 1987.

The decision to base prices on the costs in the second or third year of production was not supposed to jeopardize the idea of stimulating quality improvement. The rationale was that, since permanent wholesale prices are set for many years, they should be "progressive", i.e., should be based on gradually declining rather than on high initial costs. In the mid-1970s Soviet writers pointed to many examples of abnormal profits made by producers as a result of falling costs after the first several years of manufacturing new goods. The intent was not to penalize the producer or to hurt the process of technological change. It was to suggest sources other than prices to cover initially high production costs. The question raised in the discussions therefore was: Should prices of should special funds compensate for the high expenses of producing novel goods?

Conversely, in the 1980s examples of the opposite kind have been cited. Thus, according to *Goskomtsen,* many MBMW firms were hurt by low profit rates for new products (Glushkov, 1983). *Goskomtsen* inspected those firms and found that the average profit rate for machines manufactured for a period less than three years was lower than for machines with longer terms of production. A part of the reason was that the high costs of the first and the second years of production were supposed to be covered by a special fund for science and technology (*EFRNT*). In fact, they were not. The fund was sufficient to pay only for research and development of new models. It did not cover the starting costs of production, when quantities manufactured were generally small, technology was not sufficiently tested and adjusted, and workers needed on-the-job training. In short, the fund did not provide room for maneuvering on the part of the producer.

The developments showed that using special funds, instead of adjusting new prices, was ill-fated. Soviet production firms were not interested in having their regular expenditures covered by the *EFRNT* because, when more expenses are excluded from actual costs, the result is a reduction in planned costs. When planned costs are reduced, the price, sales revenue, profit and incentive funds are also reduced. Hence, the 1982 decision to count costs at the outset of production should have pleased MBMW producers. The switch in the pricing policy was driven by an attempt to warrant that a new product's profit would not be lower than that for older ones.

As a result of this ruling, in 1982 the average profit rate for new machines rose to 15.4 percent; for the first time it appeared to be higher than the average 14.6 percent (Rozenova, 1984). Moreover, for goods introduced in 1982, the rate was even higher, i.e., 15.9 percent. Planners were also happy about reducing the average profit rate for machines and equipment manufactured for longer than ten years to 14 percent. Although all these rates form a desirable trend for planners, the above numbers reveal low absolute discrepancies. The firm would still be on the safe side by manufacturing a machine for as long as ten years.

A 1983 development in pricing new machines and equipment in the Soviet economy reflected new priorities in Soviet pricing policies and could have far reaching consequences for the level of prices in the country. The new rule for price setting states that, if a new machine might be manufactured at lower material or labor costs than those for an older machine, the relevant cost reduction would not be reflected in the new price. The new price equals the old price; the difference in costs will be viewed as a producer's surplus. The actual cost of a new machine will be lower than that counted as the base of its price, and the profit markup will accordingly be higher than projected. If inputs are saved, the producer will not have to worry about the quality requirement, that is, the characteristics of the new machine could be the same as those of the existing ones. Thus, the conservation of material inputs, especially metals and energy, has become a new goal of pricing. In some instances that task may now be even more important than the long-term goal of quality improvement.

To an extent, this new approach to pricing reflects the general trend in Soviet planning, away from indicators in money terms toward conventional indicators in physical units. Applied to the case of setting new prices, this means that planners would rather lose in their fight against rising prices in order to win in terms of saving real metals, energy, or labor. One can conclude from this that, until the goal of conserving inputs is reassessed, a relatively liberal approach to cost-plus pricing will be followed in the Soviet economy. This may result in the acceleration of price inflation, a problem Soviet planners will probably have to encounter in the early 1990s.

An active search for more adequate pricing policies could not ignore the procedures for awarding a special surcharge for quality, analyzed in Section 3.3. The changes were directed toward two aims: 1) to make the requirements for receiving the surcharge tougher and, at the same time, 2) to raise the surcharge for novel or improved machines and equipment. The first change could have been expected as a reaction to the progressive growth of applications for the surcharge on the part of MBMW firms since the mid-1970s. The second change has been especially stressed in the 1980s in order to stimulate technological change. Given the priority for new technology, it was decided in 1982 to increase the surcharge for the improvements in technology from new machines up to 30 percent of their wholesale price.

The surcharge has not always depended on the economic benefit from the production and use of a new machine. In the past the benefit was computed as the difference between the so-called upper price limit and the projected wholesale price. The upper price limit indicates the ceiling for the new price computed on the basis of the analogous machine's price and the improvements in the parameters of the new machine. This approach, pursued for a long time with varying rigor, has been criticized for allowing the project institutes and the producers to set high upper price limits for new goods and to elevate planned costs to that level. As the planners' response, the instruction issued in 1982 specified that the upper price limit had to be computed on the same cost-plus principle as prices. In that case, real-life testing rejected a well intentioned but unrealistic method, and planners returned to the old approach that they could trust. However, the scope of limit pricing once again increased with the approval of a new instruction in 1987 (Instruction, 1987, pp. 15-16).

The Soviet stress on technological change has been accompanied by the understanding that this process is a two-way street and that stimuli had to be created for both the producer and the user of the new machine. The role of the pricing mechanism in this process is to divide the economic benefit from the new technology between the producer and the user. The surcharge for quality, on the one hand, and price discounts for obsolescent products, on the other, are supposed to create incentives and disincentives, respectively, for the producer. Improvements in new machines and relative price reductions per unit of machine's productivity, capacity, or other characteristics are supposed to create incentives for the user. The workings of the new incentives are discussed in Section 3.3.

3.2. Models for Pricing New Machines and Equipment

Theoretical justification for pricing new products in the Soviet economy is provided by a principle stated as "equal price for equal effect." It means that, if two goods are substitutes, their prices must be proportional to their efficiency, i.e.,

$$p_1 = p_0 \frac{r_1}{r_0},$$

(3.1)

where p_1 and p_0 = price of the new and old good, respectively, r_1 and r_0 = quality index of the new and old good, respectively. For example, if the heat capacity of coal is 4,000 kilocalories per kilogram and of natural gas is 8,800 kilocalories per cubic meter and if the coal price equals 10 rubles per metric ton, the price of natural gas should be

$$p_1 = 10\frac{8800}{4000} = 22.$$

In this example, fuel quality is expressed in terms of heat capacity, and the substitution effect results in the natural gas price of 22 rubles per 1,000 cubic meters. If a good's quality index reflects its marginal utility, then the principle of equal price for equal effect would be equivalent to utility maximization for a given level of expenditure.

For new machines and equipment several characteristics are usually taken into account, and the principle of equal price for equal effect is expressed in the form

$$p_1 = p_0 k + d, \tag{3.2}$$

where p_1 and p_0 = price of the new and old machine, respectively; k = multiplier combining the ratios of the productivity and durability of one machine to another, and d = additional effect from the user's saving on operational expenses and investment. Formula (3.2) was specified by the 1982 instruction in the form

$$p_1 = p_0 \cdot \frac{Q_1}{Q_2} \cdot \frac{1/T_0 + e}{1/T_1 + e} + \frac{(O_0 - O_1) - e(I_1 - I_0)}{1/T_1 + e}, \tag{3.3}$$

where p_1 and p_0 = price of the new and old machine, respectively; Q_1 and Q_2 = annual output with the use of the new and old machine, respectively; T_1 and T_0 = durability of the new and old machine, respectively; O_1 and O_2 = annual operational expenses with the use of the new and old machine, respectively; I_1 and I_0 = capital investment in the new and old machine, respectively, and e = normative coefficient of efficiency of Soviet investment defined as the reciprocal of the average normative term during which industrial investment should pay off (since at present $e=.15$, the average term for industrial investment to pay off is considered to be about seven

Table 3.1. Information for the Computation of the Price of a New
Machine

Indicator	Old Machine	New Machine
Price, Rubles	10,000	–
Annual Productivity (Output), Rubles	1,000	1,200
Durability, Years	8	10
Annual Operational Expenses, Rubles	6,000	4,000
Investment, Rubles	8,000	20,000
Normative Coefficient of Efficiency	.15	.15

years). To illustrate the use of formula (3.3), a hypothetical example
is presented in Table 3.1.

Inserting the data from Table 3.1 into formula (3.3) yields

$$p_1 = 10000 \cdot \frac{1200}{1000} \cdot \frac{1/8 + .15}{1/10 + .15}$$

$$+ \frac{(6000 - 4000) - .15(20000 - 8000)}{1/10 + .15} = 14000.$$

Hence, according to the principle of equal price for equal effect, the
price of the new machine should be 14,000 rubles, i.e., 1.4 times that
of the older one. Yet, for the reasons explained below, this could not
be the actual price which is intended to stimulate the industrial consumer to use the new machine rather than to be indifferent between
the new and the old ones.

Although formulas (3.2) and (3.3) are supposed to specify the
principle introduced by formula (3.1), there is no direct correspon-
dence between them. To implement formula (3.1) properly, one term
should have been used on the right-hand side in formulas (3.2) or
(3.3), not two. Since 1974, when the idea of pricing new machines
on the basis of their technical characteristics was clearly specified,
until 1982, when a new instruction was issued, formula (3.3) was
used for the determination of the upper price limit (*verkhnii predel
tseny*). The idea of the upper price limit was to indicate the price

at which the user would be indifferent between the new and the old machines. Thus, if the new machine's price is greater than p_1 in formula (3.3), the user is presumably better off with the older machine, and, if it is lower than p_1, the user is better off with the new machine. Therefore, p_1 is a fair price, and at this price there will be neither gain nor loss for the user.

Assuming that the upper price limit could play the role for which it was designed, multiplying it by a number less than one would make the user better off with the new machine. This idea was implemented by the computation of the so-called limit price (*limitnaia tsena*) whose level was to be set 15 percent to 20 percent below the upper price limit. The role of the limit price was to serve as the first approximation for the prices of new MBMW products. But, since planners could not and did not trust the parameters of new machines – productivity, durability, and operational expenses – reported by the producer, this approach was not used consistently. Instead, the lower price limit (*nizhnii predel tseny*), computed on the cost-plus-profit principle, was primarily used as the basis for new prices. In theory, the lower price limit makes the producer indifferent between the new and the old machines since it provides a rate of return for the new machine equal to that for the old one.

Prior to issuing the 1982 instruction, there were methodological differences in setting prices for different MBMW products depending on classification into three general groups: 1) products intended to substitute for older ones and, therefore, with an analogue among those being manufactured; 2) products intended to diversify rather than substitute for existing ones, and most likely have an analogue and 3) original products for the domestic market that have no analogue. Analogues have been used for setting prices for the first two categories of new machines. Formula (3.3) for the upper price limit is based on the comparison of the characteristics of a new machine with those of an analogue. For the third group, with no relevant comparison, the cost-plus-profit approach has mostly been used. To an extent, the difference in the two approaches was eliminated by the 1982 instruction that reinstated the cost-plus principle for all three groups. That was done by standardizing procedures for the computation of the limit price, which would be compared with the upper price limit but not based on it.

The version of the limit price defined in 1982 was the good old sum of planned cost and normative profit. It had to be calculated several times at different stages of the design of a new machine, in order to improve the accuracy of calculation. The chief task at each of these stages was to specify and estimate all the items of production cost. Thus, at the stages of formulating the problem (*tekhnicheskoe zadanie*), framing the proposal (*tekhnicheskoe pred-lozhenie*), and formulating the draft specification (*eskiznyi proekt*), a rough estimate of all cost items had to be made. Then, at the stages of technical specification (*tekhnicheskii proekt*) and product design (*rabochii proekt*), the level of production cost was supposed to be justified more accurately. Upon approval, the final estimate becomes the normative, or planned cost. But, to arrive at normative cost, production technology should first be designed and tested, and detailed norms for spending on material and labor inputs should be created. Those norms (by the items of specification and types of inputs) become the basis for the calculation of normative cost. To be approved, the norms should be "progressive," i.e., foresee gradual reductions in the use of material and labor inputs.

Normative profit is found with the use of a normative profit rate (*rentabel'nost'*) specified as a percentage of production cost less the cost of material inputs. The formula works so that normative profit grows in direct proportion to a good's labor cost. As a rule, the normative profit rate is the same for all goods within a product group. According to a 1982 provision, profit received from the production of a new good was not to be lower than that from the good it substitutes. If the normative profit rate is not sufficient to meet this condition for a given good, but the potential benefit from its production is considered as satisfactory, an exceptional profit rate can be set higher than the average for the product group.

Although from 1982 to 1987 the limit price was set as cost plus normative profit, it was also required that its level would be compared with the price of the good's analogue when there was one. The good's characteristics taken into consideration and the whole procedure were similar to those used for the computation of the upper price limit. But this procedure was now used only for the purpose of justifying the limit price, not computing it, as it was before 1982. Depending on the character of an improvement that the new machine brought about, several different formulas were applied. In the case where the new machine could improve the productivity or durability of the older machine, the following formula was used to check whether the improvement would justify the limit price computed beforehand on the cost-plus-profit basis:

$$L \leq .85 \left(p_0 \cdot \frac{Q_1}{Q_0} \cdot \frac{1/T_0 + e}{1/T_1 + e} \right) \tag{3.4}$$

where L, Q_1, and $T_1 = $ limit price, annual productivity, and durability of the new machine, respectively; p_0, Q_0, and $T_0 = $ price, annual productivity, and durability of an analogue, respectively; and $e = $ normative coefficient of efficiency of investment.

The ratio $\frac{Q_1}{Q_0}$ in formula (3.4) indicates the productivity growth for the new machine relative to the older one, and the ratio $\frac{1/T_0 + e}{1/T_1 + e}$ indicates the growth of the new machine's durability corrected by the normative coefficient of efficiency. The empirical multiplier .85 is chosen in formula (3.4) arbitrarily to ensure a relative price reduction for the new machine, i.e., a price reduction adjusted for the improvements in productivity and durability. As formula (3.4) shows, an adjustment is made by multiplying the old machine's price by two coefficients accounting for productivity and durability growth. To illustrate the use of formula (3.4), a hypothetical example is considered in Table 3.2. Inserting the data from Table 3.2 into the right-hand expression of formula (3.4) yields

$$.85 \left(100 \cdot \frac{6500}{5000} \cdot \frac{1/5 + .15}{1/7 + .15} \right) = 132,$$

and, since $115 \leq 132$, inequality (3.4) holds. This result means that the new machine's limit price of 115 rubles, which was presumably found independently on the cost-plus-profit basis, is justified since it is less than 132 rubles, i.e., the upper bound of the price that could be set in accordance with the improvements in the machine's productivity and durability.

Along with the growth in productivity and durability, the new machine may reduce the user's operational costs. In this case, the following inequality had to be applied:

Table 3.2. Information for the Test of the Justification of the
Limit Price

Indicator	Old Machine	New Machine
Limit Price, Rubles	—	115
Wholesale Price, Rubles	100	—
Annual Productivity (Output), Rubles	5,000	6,500
Durability, Years	5	7
Coefficient of Efficiency of Investment	.15	.15

$$L \le .85 \left(p_0 \cdot \frac{Q_1}{Q_2} \cdot \frac{1/T_0 + e}{1/T_1 + e} + .9 \frac{O_0 - O_1}{1/T_0 + e} \right) \qquad (3.5)$$

where, in addition to notation in formula (3.4), O_1 and O_0 = the user's annual operational expenses for the new and old machine, respectively. In this case, an additional normative coefficient of .9 is used to further reduce the allowable limit for the new price. To illustrate the use of formula (3.5), suppose that, along with the information in Table 3.2, user's annual operational expenses are 7,500 rubles for the new machine and 8,000 rubles for the older one. The right-hand expression in formula (3.5) then equals

$$.85 \left(100 \cdot \frac{6500}{5000} \cdot \frac{1/5 + .15}{1/7 + .15} + .9 \frac{8000 - 7500}{1/7 + .15} \right) = 1438,$$

which means that inequality (3.5) holds since the actual limit price is only 115 rubles. Although such a big difference would mean a good sign from the authorities' standpoint, it makes one suspicious. Indeed, the message from formula (3.5) is that the limit price could be justified even if it were found at the level of 1,438 rubles, in which case the improvements in the good's characteristics may sound too good to be true.

Comparing this result with the example illustrating the use of formula (3.4), one can notice a leap in the upper bound of the limit price from 132 to 1,438 rubles. It occurred because this time, along with the good's price corrected for improvements, there is the second term in formula (3.5) expressing the user's potential saving on operational expenses. At the same time, such a saving, from 8,000 down to 7,500 rubles in total annual operational expenses, cannot be viewed as significant, especially since the new machine might have been tested under ideal technological conditions. This, as the Soviet press reports, is frequently the case. But, aside from the reliability of the data, the question is in the methodology that allows such results to happen.

Apparently the effect observed is caused by the way in which the three factors – productivity, durability, and operational expenses – are introduced in formula (3.5). While the improvements in the first two factors only correct the analogue's price, the third one is introduced as an additive component. Moreover, this component is divided by a small number in order to convert the annual saving on operational expenses into the saving over the entire life of the new machine. Consequently, the saving factor overwhelms the effects of durability and productivity improvements on the limit price. For this reason, the procedure implemented by formula (3.5) is inconsistent. Without challenging the whole approach to the finding of the limit price, it is possible to make formula (3.5) consistent with procedure (3.4) by correcting it, for example, as follows:

$$L \leq .85 \left(p_0 \cdot \frac{Q_1}{Q_0} \cdot \frac{1/T_0 + e}{1/T_1 + e} \cdot \frac{O_0}{O_1} \right) \tag{3.6}$$

where an additional multiplier $\frac{O_0}{O_1}$ is the reciprocal of the proportion in which the new machine reduces annual operational expenses. Using the same information as in the example, above, the right-hand expression in formula (3.6) can then be found as

$$.85 \left(100 \cdot \frac{6500}{5000} \cdot \frac{1/5 + .15}{1/7 + .15} \cdot \frac{8000}{7500} \right) = 141,$$

and the inequality in formula (3.6) is $115 \leq 141$. Hence, in this case the constraint on the limit price equals a more realistic 141 rather than 1,438 rubles as before.

The 1982 instruction also specified that, if it were possible to compute a comprehensive index of a machine's quality improvement, the constraint for the limit price could be found alternatively with an inequality

$$L \leq .85(p_0 \cdot r), \tag{3.7}$$

where r = index of an overall improvement in the machine's quality. Inequality (3.7) is a logical condition requiring that the new machine's limit price may rise up to the level of the older machine's price times the index of the overall quality improvement. As in all the above cases, the multiplier of .85 mandates a relative price reduction, in order to ensure that a part of the benefit from the new machine is passed on to the user.

As indicated above, these inequalities were applied for checking whether the new good's limit price was justified, in the case when an analogue that had already been established in production was available. In any event, the limit price itself was computed on the cost-plus-profit principle. However, the instruction on pricing new machines and equipment issued by *Goskomtsen* in 1987 has restored the procedures for the computation of the limit price on the basis of the upper price limit, even though the instruction was prudently called "temporary" (Instruction, 1987, pp. 15-6). Along with limit prices, the instruction also covers the setting of both contract and *preiskurant* wholesale prices. According to the 1987 instruction, the principles for setting new prices should be as follows: (1) find a cost-to-benefit ratio for the new machine as lower than for the old one, (2) justify the relationship between the prices of the two machines, (3) use a normative approach to setting *preiskurant* prices by comparing the machine's price and its technical characteristics, and (4) stimulate the efficient use of the new machines that introduce new technologies for conserving material inputs and for improving product quality. Some of these principles (e.g., justifying a new machine's price on the basis of its technical characteristics) are actually being implemented in setting new prices; others are the usual planners' mobilizing rhetoric, this time with respect to the role of prices (*mobilizuiushchaia funktsiia tseny*).

The 1987 instruction does not bring any changes in the classification of new machines or the characteristics that are to be considered in price computations. New machines can either substitute for existing ones and thus produce the same type of goods or enhance the abilities of the existing machines to meet certain new demands (*razvitie parametricheskogo riada*). The characteristics of a new machine that have to be considered in the process of the comparison with an analogue are productivity (capacity, load capacity, etc.), reliability, durability and operational costs, including the cost of labor, raw materials and fuels. The analogue must be a product of similar functional characteristics at the level of the best domestic or foreign models.

There will be three consecutive stages of pricing new machines and equipment: setting limit prices, setting contract prices, and setting *preiskurant* prices. Limit prices (*limitnye tseny*) have to be computed and justified at the early stages of a new product design (*tekhnicheskoe zadanie* or *tekhnicheskii proekt*). If new products are designed for serial production, contract prices are approved for them for the period of mastering (*osvoenie*) their technology but for no longer than two years. The list of these products has to be approved by *Goskomtsen*. Contract prices are also to be set for new products manufactured in accordance with single orders (*individual'nye zakazy*). All *preiskurant* prices should be approved prior to the beginning of serial production, along with technological and normative documentation (standards, technical specifications and the like).

The limit price is found as a combination of the old machine's (analogue's) price and the benefit from the use of the new machine

$$L = p_0 + mB, \tag{3.8}$$

where L and p_0 = limit price of the new machine and price of the analogue, respectively; B = benefit from the use of the new machine; and m = proportion of the benefit included in the price and thus accruing to the producer (the instruction specifies it as equal to .7). As a rule, p_0 must be a *preiskurant* wholesale price, a requirement which leaves the question of a foreign analogue up in the air. To correct for possible obsolescence of the analogue when designing and testing the new model, p_0 in formula (3.8) could be multiplied by a coefficient of .9.

The benefit in formula (3.8) is found as

$$B = p_0(m^g m^d - 1) + \Delta O + \Delta I + \Delta R, \tag{3.9}$$

where p_0 = price of the analogue; m^g and m^d = index of the output growth and index of the durability change, respectively, resulting from the use of the new machine; $\Delta O, \Delta I$, and ΔR = change in the user's operational expenses, in the relevant capital investment, and in the combined benefit from the improvements in the good's quality and social and ecological parameters, respectively. The following approach is recommended for the computation of the variables in formula (3.9):

The index of the output growth resulting from the switch from the old to the new machine is defined as

$$m^g = \frac{Q_1}{Q_0}, \tag{3.10}$$

where Q_0 and Q_1 = value of the annual output with the use of the old and the new machine, respectively. The index of the durability change is defined as the ratio

$$m^d = \frac{1/T_0 + e}{1/T_1 + e}, \tag{3.11}$$

where T_0 and T_1 = estimated durability of the old and the new machine, respectively; e = normative coefficient of efficiency of investment which equals .15. The change in user's operational expenses

$$\Delta O = \frac{O_0 - O_1}{1/T_1 + e}, \tag{3.12}$$

where O_0 and O_1 = user's operational expenses with the old and new machine, respectively. The change in user's capital investment

$$\Delta I = \frac{e(I_0 - I_1)}{1/T_1 + e}, \tag{3.13}$$

where I_0 and I_1 = investment in the technology with the use of the old and the new machine, respectively. The change in the combined benefit from improvements in goods quality and social and ecological parameters appears to be a judgmental component rather than an observed variable; in such a case, an expert estimate (*ekspertnaia otsenka*) is usually used, and it would be confined to special types of machines and equipment.

To illustrate the use of the new methodology, an example is considered in Table 3.3; most of the data are from the two previous examples. A simplifying assumption is that there are no improvements in the parameters summarized by the term of combined benefit ΔR in formula (3.9). Using formulas (3.10)-(3.13), the variables needed for the computation of the benefit derived from switching from the old to the new machine:

The index of the output growth

Table 3.3. Information for the Computation of the Limit Price

Indicator	Old Machine	New Machine
Wholesale Price, Rubles	100	—
Annual Productivity (Output), Rubles	5,000	6,500
Annual Operational Expenses, Rubles	8,000	7,500
Investment, Rubles	10,000	12,000
Durability, Years	6	7
Coefficient of Efficiency of Investment	15	15

$$m^g = \frac{6500}{5000} = 1.3.$$

The index of the durability change

$$m^d = \frac{1/5 + .15}{1/7 + .15} = 1.2.$$

The change in user's operational expenses

$$\Delta O = \frac{8000 - 7500}{1/7 + .15} = 1707.$$

The change in user's capital investment

$$\Delta I = \frac{.15(10000 - 12000)}{1/7 + .15} = -1024.$$

As the result, the benefit from the use of the new machine can be estimated with formula (3.9):

$$B = 100(1.3 \cdot 1.2 - 1) + 1707 - 1024 = 739,$$

and the limit price, from formula (3.8),

$$L = .9(100) + .7(739) = 607 \text{ rubles,}$$

where the price of the old machine is multiplied by 0.9, to compensate for a possible obsolescence of the old model in the process of designing the new one.

The 1987 instruction further specifies that, if there is no analogue available and it is impossible to calculate the benefit from switching to the new machine, the limit price should be determined on the cost-plus-profit principle. The computation must be based on the normatives for spending on material and labor inputs and the normative rate of profitability. The latter is now allowed to be as high as 1.5 times the profit rate for other machines or equipment in the same product group.

It is difficult to see how the empirical formulas suggested by the new instruction for pricing new machines and equipment would be taken seriously by planners. Beyond an open question of justification, the results of computation are unstable and, in particular, are sensitive to errors in the data. For instance, should the actual operational expenses of using the new machine be 7,600 rubles, instead of 7,500 rubles as in the above example, recalculation with formula (3.9) yields the "true" value of the limit price of 369 rubles. Hence, as a result of a one percent understatement in operational expenses, this would-be limit price is overstated by more than 64 percent ($607 \div 369$).

Not surprisingly, the computation of *preiskurant* prices for new machines and equipment will not be based on the previously defined limit prices. The only relationship with the limit prices stressed in the 1987 instruction is that the *preiskurant* price must not exceed the level of the "actual" limit price (i.e., the one corrected by the actual benefit obtained from using the new machine in the period when contract prices are applied). The following vague formula for the *preiskurant* price is suggested:

$$p = p^m \cdot M \pm S, \tag{3.14}$$

where p = *preiskurant* price of the new machine; p^m = normative price per unit of the main technical parameter of the machine; M = value of the main technical parameter of the new machine; S = surcharges (discounts) for other technical and quality characteristics. The main technical parameter in this case is the machine's productivity, capacity, or power. For the example in Table 3.3, that would be the annual output with the use of the new machine. The role of the surcharge for machine's quality is discussed in Section 3.3.

The method suggested by formula (3.14) has not been used before for pricing new machines other than those extending the abilities of, not substituting for the existing ones. It needs to be tested. Though the computation of the limit price considers several characteristics of the new machine, the *preiskurant* price will be found on the basis of only one. Moreover, the value of the machine's main parameter may vary widely, and this adds to the ambiguity of price setting on that basis. It is likely, therefore, that the cost-plus-profit principle will still be important for the underpinning of the new approach. The tug of war between pricing new machines on the basis of their technical characteristics and the cost-plus-profit formula thus continues.

3.3 The Surcharge for Quality

In trying to improve product quality and to introduce new technology, much attention is paid in the Soviet economy to the mechanism of surcharges for high quality (*pooshchritel'naia nadbavka*) and discounts for poor quality (*skidka*). The surcharge for quality is usually awarded to those goods certified as in the high-quality category. The mandatory certification of most civilian manufactures began in the Soviet economy in 1972. Before that, only goods eligible for the special "seal of quality" (*znak kachestva*) introduced in 1967 had to be certified. Numerous attempts were made to find a formula that would determine the magnitude of the surcharge in direct proportion to the efficiency of new technology. Methodological instructions issued by *Goskomtsen* first specified the formula of computation and then modified it on the basis of ongoing experience. Such instructions were issued in 1969, 1974, and 1979. The 1979 instruction was amended for the MBMW sector by the 1982 and 1987 instructions for setting wholesale prices of new machines and equipment and by several recent resolutions of the Central Committee and Council of Ministers on the acceleration of technological change.

The purpose of all these instructions is to specify the constraints and the criteria for the computation of the surcharge for quality. The constraints have been imposed in different forms, most recently as a combination of two parameters – normative profit and economic benefit from the new machine's use. As in all similar cases discussed above, normative profit differs from actual profit in that it is the planned or targeted profit which can differ from the profit incorporated in the product's price. The benefit is intended to measure the potential gain from improved productivity, durability or lower operational costs that are expected to result from the use of the new machine.

The concept of the benefit as it is measured is controversial and is still a subject of debate in the Soviet economic literature. The most commonly used instruction for estimating the benefit from new machines and equipment was issued in 1977 by the State Committee on Science and Technology ($GNTK$), *Gosplan* and the Academy of Sciences, in lieu of the 1962 instruction. According to the 1977 instruction, the benefit from a new technological process could be found in the form

$$B = (f_1 - f_0)Q_1, \tag{3.15}$$

where B, f_1, and Q_1 = annual benefit, annual full production expenditures per unit of good, and annual output with the use of the new technology, respectively, and f_0 = annual full production expenditures per unit of good manufactured with the use of the old technology. Annual full production expenditures, in turn, are found with the formula

$$f = c + \frac{eI}{Q}, \tag{3.16}$$

where f and c = annual full production expenditures and average total cost per unit of good, respectively; I = investment in the technological process; and e = normative coefficient of efficiency of investment which, according to the 1977 instruction, equals .15.

To illustrate the use of formulas (3.15) and (3.16), Table 3.4 contains the information for the computation of the annual benefit from the use of a hypothetical new technological process. According to formulas (3.8) and (3.9),

$$f_0 = 10, \qquad f_1 = 6 + \frac{.15(1000000)}{60000} = 8.5,$$

$$B = (10 - 8.5)60000 = 90000,$$

Table 3.4. Information for the Computation of the Benefit from a
New Technological Process

Characteristics	Technological Process	
	Old	New
Annual Average Total Cost, Rubles	10	6
Annual Output, Rubles or		
Physical Units	50,000	60,000
Investment, Rubles	0	1,000,000
Coefficient of Efficiency	.15	.15

i.e., the user's annual economic benefit from the new technological
process is estimated to be 90,000 rubles.

Formula (3.15) only outlines the general principle for the determination of the economic benefit from the use of a new technology.
It was specified for new machines and equipment by the 1977 instruction as follows:

$$B = p_0 \cdot \frac{Q_1}{Q_0} \cdot \frac{1/T_0 + e}{1/T_1 + e} + \frac{(O_0 - O_1) - e(I_1 - I_0)}{1/T_1 + e} - p_1, \quad (3.17)$$

where B, Q_1, O_1, p_1, T_1, and I_1 = annual economic benefit, output,
operational expenses, product price, durability, and investment associated with the use of the new machine, respectively; Q_0, O_0, p_0, T_0,
and I_0 = annual output, operational expenses, product price, durability, and investment for the older machine, respectively; and e =
normative coefficient of efficiency of investment in new technology
that equals .15.

In formula (3.17), the annual benefit is net benefit obtained by
subtracting the new machine's price from the combined benefit from
its use. The ratios on the right-hand side in formula (3.17) are similar
to those in formula (3.3) and in formulas (3.10)-(3.13). Table 3.5
contains the information for the computation of the annual benefit
according to formula (3.17). Inserting the data from Table 3.5 into
formula (3.17) yields

Table 3.5. Information for the Computation of the Benefit for a
New Machine

| | Machine | |
Characteristic	Old Machine	New Machine
Price, Rubles	500	700
Annual Productivity (Output), Rubles		
or Physical Units	200	300
Annual Operational Expenses, Rubles	40,000	28,000
Durability, Years	8	10
Investment, Rubles	100,000	160,000
Coefficient of Efficiency	.15	.15

$$B = 500 \cdot \frac{300}{200} \cdot \frac{1/8 + .15}{1/10 + .15}$$

$$+ \frac{(40000 - 28000) - .15(160000 - 100000)}{1/10 + .15} - 700 = 12125.$$

This means that the benefit from using the new machine is estimated
to equal 12,125 rubles. But, although it is considered as an annual
effect, it is not. From analyzing formula (3.17) one could infer that,
while the first term is measured on an annual basis, the second is on
the basis of the machine's lifetime. As a result of this inconsistency,
the second term will generally outweigh the first in forming the total
effect in formula (3.17).

Thus, in our example, the new machine's productivity is one
and a half times that of the older one, and its durability increases
from eight to ten years, but the combined gross benefit (prior to the
subtraction of the new machine's price) for the user shown by the
first term only equals 825 rubles, as can be checked from the above
computation. The second term, i.e., the projected user's saving in
operational expenses, is treated much more favorably. If the present-
value formula were correctly applied, the future savings would be
discounted, and the result of the annual saving of 12,000 rubles in

operational expenses would not appear so impressive when related to the initial one-time increase in investment of 60,000 rubles (see Table 3.5). But, instead, formula (3.17) sharply discounts the cost of investment by only accounting for what would have been its annual equivalent if it were evenly spread over the machine's lifetime. In addition, the difference between the user's saving on expenses and the annual equivalent of investment is significantly increased by applying the multiplier $\frac{1}{1/T_1 + e}$, which is equal to the lifetime of the new machine corrected by the coefficient of efficiency.

It is also interesting to apply formulas (3.9)-(3.13) for the computation of the user's benefit, suggested by the 1987 instruction, to the information in Table 3.5 and to compare the results. Combining the computation with formulas (3.9)-(3.13) in one step,

$$B = 500 \left(\frac{300}{200} \cdot \frac{1/8 + .15}{1/10 + .15} - 1 \right) + \frac{40000 - 28000}{1/10 + .15}$$

$$+ \frac{.15(100000 - 160000)}{1/10 + .15} = 12325,$$

i.e., this approach yields the benefit of 12,325 rubles. The result is 200 rubles greater than the one received with formula (3.17). This is not a coincidence. If the term ΔR that estimates the user's benefit from additional improvements in goods quality and social and ecological parameters is ignored in formula (3.9), the methods implemented in formulas (3.9)-(3.13) and (3.17) are actually the same. The only difference lies in finding the net benefit. In formula (3.17) this is done by subtracting the new machine's price, but in formula (3.9), by subtracting the old machine's price (since 1 is subtracted in the parentheses on the right-hand side). The difference between the two prices in Table (3.5) equals 200 rubles, and this explains the difference between the two estimates of benefits obtained above. Thus, the 1987 instruction virtually repeats the 1977 instruction on the computation of the benefit from the use of new machines and equipment. In other words, the creativity of the authors of the 1987 instruction does not go beyond the addition of a generally unobservable term ΔR in formula (3.9).

According to the 1979 instruction of *Goskomsten*, the ceiling on the surcharge for quality depends upon the ratio of the benefit to the wholesale price, that is, the benefit per ruble of the new machine's price. Before that, the 1974 instruction recommended that the surcharge be computed on the basis of the ratio of the machine's upper price limit to its lower price limit, determined as explained in Section 3.2. Since this ratio was unreliable, planners rarely determined actual surcharge on its basis. The switch to the benefit-to-wholesale price ratio was based on the hope that it would better reflect the advantages of using novel technologies. But the reliability of the ratio is a function of the reliability of both of its elements. As demonstrated in this and the previous sections, the new product's upper price limit and the economic benefit are computed on the same principle. Hence, if one is unreliable, so is the other. Based on this reasoning, we can expect that the substitution of only one of these variables by a more reliable variable will hardly improve the ratio that determines the size of the surcharge.

What is the real life evidence? Table 3.6 illustrates the benefit-to-wholesale price ratio for twelve groups of electrotechnical equipment. For each product group, there are two percentages in Table 3.6 – minimum and maximum. They show the lowest and the highest value of the benefit-to-wholesale price ratio, respectively, so that the ratios for all other products will lie within the given intervals. For example, there are some goods in the power transformers group for which this ratio equals 10 percent, and there are some goods for which it equals 140 percent. (It is not known, however, how many goods were surveyed in each category.) If the pricing principles were applied similarly to all goods, and if the information on the economic benefit were reliable, the ratio would characterize the degree of efficiency of new machines. This could be true for goods within one product group, since pricing policies are more unified among them than among different groups. But when it comes to intergroup comparisons, various types of benefits are encountered, and complications of commensurability arise. For this reason, for example, the comparison of the maximum benefit-to-price ratio of 2,300 percent for electric welding equipment with that of 140 percent for power transformers does not necessarily mean that the efficiency of the best products in the first group is more than sixteen times that in the second group.

Table 3.6. The Economic Benefit-to-Wholesale Price Ratio for Electrotechnical Equipment

Product Group	Ratio, Percent	
	Minimum	Maximum
Power Transformers	10	140
High-Voltage Equipment	10	160
Electric Bulbs	10	170
Small Electrical Machines	10	240
Turbogenerators and Hydrogenerators	10	260
Low-Voltage Equipment	5	330
Condensers	10	330
Electrolighting Fittings	10	370
Cable Products	20	470
Electroinsulating Products	10	500
Power Transformers	20	520
Electric Welding Equipment	30	2,300

Source: Shalimov, 1981, p.54.

The surcharge for quality is generally computed as a percentage of normative profit, within the interval of 50 to 125 percent. The specifics of the computation formula are in Table 3.7. The benefit-to-wholesale price ratio is used as the criterion. The minimum amount of the surcharge is 50 percent of the normative profit for the new machine. It is awarded when the benefit-to-wholesale price ratio equals 15 percent. For the higher values of the ratio, the surcharge rises in accordance with the percentages indicated for different intervals in the third column of Table 3.7. Thus, if the B/p ratio equals 25 percent, i.e., 10 percentage points above the lower bound of 15 percent, then the surcharge is to be 52 percent of the normative profit $(50+.20\cdot10)$. The calculation of the surcharge for quality is illustrated below; the information is in Table 3.8.

The sequence of calculations is as follows:

1. The percentage of the benefit-to-wholesale price:

$$B/p = \frac{8500}{10000} \cdot 100 = 85.$$

2. Surcharge as a percentage of normative profit:

$$s = 65 + 10(.35) = 68.5.$$

3. Normative profit Π:

$$\Pi = \frac{mp}{100} = \frac{15(10000)}{100} = 1,500$$

4. The value of the surcharge S:

$$S = \frac{s\Pi}{100} = \frac{68.5(1500)}{100} = 1028,$$

i.e., the surcharge for quality amounts to 1,028 rubles in this example. If approved by the pricing authorities, this surcharge will be added to the new machine's wholesale price. Hence, as long as the surcharge is valid, the price charged will be 11,028 rubles.

Beyond normative profit there has been another constraint on the surcharge for quality. It is the value of the benefit from using the new machine. Thus, the surcharge should not exceed 70 percent of that benefit. Table 3.9 demonstrates the evolution of the role of the constraints on the surcharge for quality from 1969, where S = surcharge for quality. As one can see from Table 3.9, the emphasis on the constraints has changed with the intention to raise the amount of the surcharge. From 1969 to 1979, the upper bound grew from 50 percent to 125 percent of normative profit, that is, it could even exceed the profit itself, and from 30 to 70 percent of the economic benefit. With the two constraints, an important question is: which one is binding? Since profit is included in the good's price on the basis of a normative approach, with the normative equal for all goods in the product group, there may be no link between profit and the actual economic benefit from the new good. But, since profit is much more verifiable than the benefit, planners believed that the profit constraint could better regulate the rise of the surcharge.

Table 3.7. The Formula for the Computation of the Surcharge for Quality

Ratio of the Benefit to Wholesale Price, B/p, Percent	Surcharge as Percentage of Normative Profit	
	for Lower Bound of the Interval	for Each Additional Percentage Point
15 - 35	50	.20
35 - 55	54	.25
55 - 75	59	.30
75 - 95	65	.35
95 - 115	72	.45
115 - 135	81	.60
135 - 155	93	.75
155 - 175	108	.85
175 up	125	—

Source: Kraiukhin, 1987, p.396.

Table 3.8. The Information for the Computation of the Surcharge for Quality

Variable	Value
Wholesale Price p, Rubles	10,000
Benefit from the New Machine B, Rubles	8,500
Normative Profitability m, Percent	15

For this reason, the first constraint in Table 3.9 (normative profit), rather than the second (economic benefit), proved to be binding for

Table 3.9. Constraints on the Surcharge for Quality

Year of Imposing	Constraint	
	Normative Profit Π	Economic Benefit B
1969	$S \leq .5\Pi$	$.3B \leq S \leq .5B$
1974	$.2\Pi \leq S \leq \Pi$	$S \leq .5B$
1979	$.5\Pi \leq S \leq 1.25\Pi$	$S \leq .7B$

Source: Shalimov (1981, p.80).

most of the time. For example, from 1969 to 1973 the size of the surcharge for electrotechnical products approached the ceiling by the normative profit constraint, while the ratio of the surcharge to economic benefit was equal to only 5 percent. With the profit constraint raised to 100 percent in the 1974-79 period, the magnitude of the surcharge grew to 6 to 8 percent of the benefit. Finally, with the surcharge ceiling approaching 125 percent of normal profit according to the 1979 instruction, the surcharge-to-benefit ratio rose to 10 to 12 percent. This level is much lower than the new ceiling of 70 percent. Certainly the idea of the two constraints did not work when only one was binding.

Since the purpose is stimulating technological change, the whole idea of the surcharge makes sense only if it is affected by the economic benefit from the new technology. Therefore it is understandable that planners wanted to increase the role of economic benefit in the computation of the surcharge. At the same time, as discussed above, they did not want the surcharge to be inflated by inflated projections of the benefit. When the attempts to find a formula that would meet both requirements failed, only the profit constraint was applied. However, the critical state of the quality of new machines finally forced planners to turn their backs on the problem of reliability and to allow the setting of the surcharge on the basis of economic benefit, with less emphasis on the profit constraint. Thus, the ceiling on the surcharge of up to 70 percent of the benefit can now be approved for new goods that implement an invention, substitute for an imported analogue or are included in the national economic plan and therefore viewed as important. Until 1986 the surcharge for other high-quality products that did not fall in the above categories could equal half of the economic benefit but not in excess of 30 percent of the product's price. Since 1986 a new regulation governs the value of the surcharge. The maximum surcharge (30 percent of the wholesale price) could only be awarded to machines and equipment whose productivity and durability are at least 1.5 or twice those of their analogues. The introduction of these machines has to be the result of inventive or innovative projects. For all other new machines including modernized ones, the surcharge should not exceed 15 percent of the wholesale price or half of the estimated benefit (Rozenova, 1986, p.32).

The surcharge is ordinarily set for one year. For goods with complex technology, it is for two years, and for unique machines and equipment, for three years. If, during that period, the good is awarded a seal of quality, the term of the surcharge is extended for the standard terms of four, five, or six years, respectively. The seal of quality can be awarded for a second term, too. In this case, if there is improvement in the good's parameters, the surcharge and its standard term are approved again. Without improvement in a good's characteristics, the surcharge and its term are cut in half. This consideration means that a unique machine can receive a surcharge for quality for up to 15 years. One would hardly believe that, even with some minor improvements, a machine could be viewed as being in a high-quality category for such a long period. It may be logical to expect Soviet planners to eliminate awarding the seal of quality twice in a row, to reduce the general term of the surcharge for quality. (Assuming, of course, that they continue this odd practice.)

Along with raising the surcharge, the recent resolutions, and especially the 1985 one, have strengthened the role of price discounts for shabby goods. In a way similar to the application of the surcharge, *Goskomtsen* can now apply price discounts of up to 30 percent, to push for the discontinuance of obsolete machines and equipment. The existing rule states that, if a certification committee decides to discontinue a product, the normative profit incorporated in its price must be cut in half. The strange thing about such a price reduction is that the user will still pay the same price and, therefore, will not benefit; the whole sum of the price reduction will be withheld for the state budget. This approach prevents different technologies from competing in the market and contradicts the spirit of economic reform.

It should be noted that the system of price discounts has not worked in the Soviet economy so far. In spite of numerous resolutions and the attempts by planners to impose stiffer penalties for the lack of innovation, price discounts did not substitute for administrative punishment as a chief tool for stimulating quality improvements. For example, a study of the pricing policies of the Ministry of Electrotechnical Industry from 1972 to 1979 showed that, in half of the period, discounts were not practiced at all and, in the other half, were negligible (Shalimov, 1981A). This was also characteristic of the Ministries of the Heavy and Transport Machinery and of the Energy and Power Machinery, to name a few. The ruling of the 1979 resolution called for withholding half of a poor quality good's profit and, then, the remaining half if the good is not eventually substituted by a better one. Yet, in the early 1980s, price discounts were seldom imposed.

The surcharges and discounts are ignored when the plan is compiled, but they are taken into account when the meeting of plan targets is evaluated. In other words, if a product is entitled to a surcharge for quality, the firm's planned value of output will remain the same as if the surcharge did not exist. The surcharge will, however, be added to the actual output, thus improving the firm's success indicators. Similarly, price discounts are only counted toward the meeting of plan targets. As a result, the surcharges and discounts are supposed to ease the lives of producers who turn out good products and to hurt those that turn out inferior products. However, there are mechanisms in the Soviet economy that will work in the opposite direction. For example, a firm may lose money due to the manufacturing of an inadequate good that, nevertheless, could not be discontinued. In this case, which is common, the firm will be compensated for the loss either by the state budget or, under the new system of self-sufficiency and self-financing, by the ministry centralized fund created for such contingencies.

Chapter 4
Trends in Production, Prices, and Technological Change

4.1. Production, Prices, and Costs

The differences between Soviet and western methods of measuring growth and inflation were explained in Chapter 2. Since, within the same format, varying computational schemes are possible, the Soviet methodology has some peculiarities which are explored in the case studies presented in Chapters 6 through 8. Those case studies are for the branches of the Soviet MBMW sector. The trends in that sector's growth are examined in this chapter in order to provide a context for the case studies, while Chapter 5 is devoted to the MBMW sector and its branches.

To demonstrate the official perspective of the economic growth of the Soviet MBMW sector, Table 4.1 reports the sector's growth indices and average annual growth rates for the 1966-86 period. Official information will also be used in analyzing trends for other economic indicators. Since the pattern, not the growth rates themselves, is important to us, we may to an extent ignore here the issue of the reliability of official Soviet statistics which will be addressed in Chapter 9. The average annual growth rates in Table 4.1 follow from the relevant indices, and both are measured with respect to the starting period. Thus, the 1970 average annual rate of 11.8 percent refers to the 1966-70 five-year average, while the 1975 average annual rate of 11.7 percent refers to the 1966-75 ten-year average. Table 4.1 demonstrates the pattern of economic growth in the Soviet MBMW sector over the 21-year period, characterized by declining rates. This is distinctly seen as one goes from the left to the right

Table 4.1. Official Growth Indices and Average Annual Growth Rates for the Soviet MBMW Sector in the 1966-86 Period (Percent)

1965	1970		1975		1980		1985		1986	
Index	Index	Average Rate	Index	Average Rate	Index	Average Rate	Index	Average Rate	Index	Average Rate
100	175	11.8	303	11.7	448	10.5	606	9.4	649	9.3
	100	–	173	11.6	256	9.9	346	8.6	371	8.5
			100	–	148	8.2	200	7.2	215	7.2
					100	–	135	6.2	145	6.4

Source: *Narkhoz SSSR* (1980, p.126 and *za 70 let*, 1987, pp. 166-7).

and from the top to the bottom of Table 4.1. The average growth rates in the 1985 column can serve as an example: For the entire 20-year period (1966-85), the average growth rate is 9.4 percent, for the 15-year period, 1971-85, 8.6 percent, for the 10-year period, 1976-85, 7.2 percent, and, finally, for the 1981-85 period, 6.2 percent. Though declining (with the exception of 1986), the growth rates are still impressive.

The growth indices and average annual growth rates for selected branches of the MBMW sector are in Table 4.2. With the partial exception of the automotive industry, all produce investment rather than consumption goods. Resembling the pattern for the MBMW sector as a whole, the branches demonstrate decelerating growth, with the growth rates dropping by one percentage point for energy and power machinery to five percentage points for instrument making and the automotive industry. By ranking the growth rates in Table 4.2, one could guess which branches have greater opportunities to inflate their growth rates. As noted in Section 2.3, they could do this with the introduction of new products and with a gradual switch from less to more expensive outputs. For example, instrument making, with a rapid turnover and a great selection of manufactures, is in the most advantageous position. The material-intensive branches, such as energy and power machinery, have a slowly changing product mix and therefore the least opportunity for inflating growth. The growth rates in Table 4.2 reflect this.

The shares of different branches in the total MBMW output in 1972 and 1982 were computed from the input-output tables. They are shown in Table 4.3. The largest branch, with a 35.8 percent share in 1982, is the radio and electronics industry, a conglomerate of high technology industries chiefly engaged in military production. Among the smallest industries, along with logging, paper, and construction materials machinery and equipment, are the two serving the production of consumer goods – the food and light industry machinery branches.

Since Soviet labor productivity is measured as the output-to-employment ratio, measures of productivity growth rates must be affected by decelerating output. The correlation is, of course, only technical. Causality goes the opposite way, i.e., falling productivity growth must have led to decelerated output growth rates, given employment. Table 4.4 illustrates growth rates for labor productivity in the Soviet MBMW sector. The comparison of the declining growth rates in Tables 4.1 and 4.4 shows less deceleration for productivity than for output. Thus, whereas the 1986 average annual output growth rates in Table 4.1 range from 9.3 percent to 6.4 percent (a decline of 2.9 percentage points), similar productivity rates in Table 4.4 range from 6.9 percent to 5.5 percent (a decline of only 1.4 percentage points). Since labor productivity is measured as a ratio, its growth rates depend on the relationship between the changes in output and employment. If, for example, output and employment changed at the same rate, productivity would not change at all. But, since production rose, apparently employment growth rates were lower than those for the value of output. Thus there was room for an increase in productivity, as measured by Soviet statistics.

Table 4.2. Growth of Selected Soviet MBMW Branches in the 1971-86 Period (Percent, 1970=100 for Index Values)

Branch	1975		1980		1986	
	Index	Rate	Index	Rate	Index	Rate
Energy and Power M&E	138	6.7	172	5.6	243	5.7
Electrotechnical M&E	152	8.7	197	7.0	257	6.1
Machine Tools	161	10.0	238	9.1	340	7.9
Instruments	234	18.5	450	16.2	760	13.5
Automobiles	184	13.0	267	10.3	344	8.0
Tractors and Agricultural M&E	170	11.2	229	8.6	311	7.8
Total MBMW	173	11.6	256	9.9	371	8.8

Source: *Narkhoz SSSR* (*za 70 let*, 1987, p.166 and 1985, p.186).

The information about output and productivity growth rates presents an opportunity to estimate the growth rates for employment in the Soviet MBMW sector. It is shown in Section 2.2 that the relationship among the growth rates is

$$r^q = r^\ell + r^L + r^\ell r^L, \tag{4.1}$$

Table 4.3. Proportions of Branches in the Soviet MBMW Output
(Percent)

Branch	1972	1982
Energy and Power Machinery and Equipment	1.4	1.1
Mining and Metallurgical M&E	2.3	2.0
Hoist-Transport M&E	6.0	4.9
Electrotechnical M&E	8.4	7.4
Pumps and Chemical M&E	2.2	2.0
Logging and Paper M&E	0.3	0.3
Machine Tools	2.6	2.1
Instruments	5.1	3.5
Construction M&E	1.5	1.2
Construction Materials M&E	0.4	0.4
Automobiles	9.0	11.4
Tractors and Agricultural M&E	6.7	7.2
Light Industry M&E	0.6	0.5
Food Industry M&E	0.6	0.5
Radio and Electronics	31.7	35.8
Other Machines	1.7	1.3
Metalwares and Structures	5.5	5.0
Repair	14.0	13.4
Total MBMW	100.0	100.0

Source: Gallik, et al. (1983, pp. 68-70) and Kostinsky (1987).

where r^q, r^ℓ and r^L = growth rate for output, productivity, and employment, respectively. From formula (4.1) it follows that

$$r^L = \frac{r^q - r^\ell}{1 + r^\ell}.$$ (4.2)

Growth indices for employment in the Soviet MBMW sector, computed with the use of formula (4.2), and average annual growth rates corresponding to these indices are illustrated in Table 4.5. Thus, average annual growth rates for employment amounted to 3.9 percent in 1966-70, 2.8 percent in 1971-75, 1.9 percent in 1976-80, and, finally, 0.9 percent in 1981-86. These results are generally reliable since, unlike the results for output and productivity, they are not distorted by prices. This can be verified by analyzing the change in formula (4.2) when the current-year output is inflated. Using definitions of the three growth rates in formula (4.2),

$$r^q = \frac{Q_1}{Q_0} - 1,$$

$$r^\ell = \frac{Q_1}{L_1} \cdot \frac{L_0}{Q_0} - 1,$$

and

$$r^L = \frac{L_1}{L_0} - 1,$$

where Q_1 and L_1 = output and employment in current year 1 and Q_0 and L_0 = output and employment in base year 0. Multiplying Q_1 by the inflation index P, distorted growth rates are

$$r^{q'} = \frac{PQ_1}{Q_0} - 1$$

and

$$r^{\ell'} = \frac{PQ_1}{L_1} \cdot \frac{L_0}{Q_0} - 1.$$

Inserting these expressions in formula (4.2), the distorted growth rate for employment is

Table 4.4. Official Growth Indices and Average Annual Growth Rates for Labor Productivity in the Soviet MBMW Sector Percent

1965	1970		1975		1980		1985		1986	
Index	Index	Average Rate	Index	Average Rate	Index	Average Rate	Index	Average Rate	Index	Average Rate
100	145	7.5	219	8.2	296	7.5	383	6.9	407	6.9
	100	–	151	8.6	204	7.4	264	6.7	281	6.7
			100	–	135	6.2	174	5.7	186	5.8
					100	–	129	5.2	138	5.5

Source: *Narkhoz SSSR* (1982, pp. 125-7 and *za 70 let*, 1987, p.141).

Table 4.5. Growth Indices and Average Annual Growth Rates for Employment in the Soviet MBMW Sector (Percent)

1965	1970		1975		1980		1985		1986	
Index	Index	Average Rate	Index	Average Rate	Index	Average Rate	Index	Average Rate	Index	Average Rate
100	121	3.9	139	3.3	151	2.8	158	2.4	158	2.2
	100	–	115	2.8	126	2.3	131	1.8	131	1.7
			100	–	110	1.9	115	1.4	115	1.3
					100	–	105	1.0	106	0.9

Source: Tables 4.1 and 4.4.

$$r^{L'} = \frac{\dfrac{PQ_1}{Q_0} - \dfrac{PQ_1}{L_1} \cdot \dfrac{L_0}{Q_0}}{\dfrac{PQ_1}{L_1} \cdot \dfrac{L_0}{Q_0}} = \frac{L_1}{L_0} - 1 = r^L,$$

i.e., it equals the true growth rate r^L, and there is no effect of price inflation on the growth rate for employment computed with formula (4.2).

Official Soviet statistics demonstrate a consistent deflationary trend at the aggregate level whereas, at the same time, the Soviet literature has presented numerous examples of significant price hikes at a disaggregate level. Table 4.6 reports official price indices for the Soviet MBMW sector, with wholesale prices of enterprises used. As the table shows, MBMW prices declined by an average 28 percent over the 1966-85 period, with most of the decline taking place in the first ten years. It would be interesting to compare the direction of annual changes in prices and outputs, i.e., to look at the specifics of the information in Tables 4.1 and 4.6. For this purpose, Table 4.7 shows annual growth indices for outputs and prices of the Soviet MBMW sector in the 1964-85 period. To reflect annual growth, the indices are measured for every pair of consecutive years, so that, for instance, a value of 95 indicates a 5 percent decline from the previous year, and a value of 110 reflects a 10 percent rise from the previous year.

There are two distinctly different patterns in Table 4.7. Since prices do not rise, the price index either declines or remains 100. Since output does not decline, the output index is always greater than 100. However, the output growth rates can decelerate if, for example, an index of 107 follows a value of 110. As one can see from Table 4.7, the official price index declined in 15 years out of 22 under consideration. The deceleration of the output growth occurred in 10 years, of which seven years (1964, 1970, 1973, 1976, 1977, 1979, and 1982) were deflationary. Was it a mere coincidence, or did the decline in the price level affect the rates or "real" growth? This is not an easy question to answer, and we will be concerned with it in Chapters 6 through 9.

Table 4.6. Official Price Index for the Soviet MBMW Sector
(Percent)

1965	1966	1967	1968	1969	1970	1971	1972	1973	1974	1975
100	99	99	99	96	95	88	88	83	80	80

1976	1977	1978	1979	1980	1981	1982	1983	1984	1985
77	76	75	74	74	74	73	73	73	72

Source: *Narkhoz SSSR* (1970, p.175; 1975, p.231; 1977, p.142;
1978, p.138; 1979, p.164) and *Vestnik Statistiki* (9, 1982,
p.78 and 9, 1986, p.79).

For now, we can apply a simple nonparametric sign test which
will indicate whether the fact of the coincidence is statistically significant. This will be a one-sided test; we cannot look at the effect
of prices on growth acceleration because no rise in prices is reported
in Tables 4.6-4.7. A hypothesis stating that the decline in the price
index did not affect the growth rates for outputs will be tested. The
indifference of output growth to the price decline should be reflected
in an approximate equality of plus and minus signs for the first differences in output growth rates. The hypothesis will be tested for
the years in which the price declines took place. To give the hypothesis a formal interpretation, let p denote the probability of a negative
sign and q the probability of a positive sign. Then the hypothesis
is $p = 1/2$. Suppose a sample from this population is given, and we
wish to determine whether it differs significantly from the hypothesis. We then count the number of negative signs (call it N) and
compute the probability of obtaining, from the population for which
$p = 1/2$, a sample for which the number of negative signs differs as
much as N or more from the expected value.

Table 4.7. Official Annual Growth and Price Indices for the Soviet
MBMW Sector (Previous Year=100)

	1964	1965	1966	1967	1968	1969	1970	1971	1972
Output	110	110	112	112	112	112	111	111	113
Price	98	96	99	100	100	97	99	93	100

	1973	1974	1975	1976	1977	1978	1979	1980	1981
Output	111	113	111	110	107	109	108	107	106
Price	94	96	100	96	99	99	99	100	100

	1982	1983	1984	1985
Output	105	106	107	107
Price	99	100	99	99

Source: *Narkhoz SSSR* (1970, p.177; 1975, p233; 1979, p.165, and
1985, p.129), *Vestnik Statistiki* (9, 1986, p.79) and
Table 4.6.

In our example, we take into account the 15 years in which the
price index declined, i.e., n=15. Disregarding four cases in which the
growth index did not change at all, we find that in the remaining
sample of 11 cases seven are negative. By means of the binomial
distribution, we can find the probability that seven or more minus
signs are obtained, under the hypothesis of equal chance for plus and
minus signs. For the binomial distribution

$$m = np = 11(1/2) = 5.5, \qquad \sigma = \sqrt{npq} = \sqrt{11(1/2)(1/2)} = 1.66,$$

and, since a normal-curve approximation of the binomial distribution is used, a standardized ratio

$$z = \frac{7 - 5.5}{1.66} = .90,$$

with zero mean and unit variance, will be needed.

As indicated above, for the hypothesis of that a deceleration in the price index does not lead to a decline in the growth index, a one-tail test should be applied. In such a case, the area under the normal probability curve to the right of $x = 7$ will be needed. Choosing a 0.05 level of significance, we find that, for $z = .90$, $p = .1841$ which is greater than 0.05. Hence, at the 95 percent level of significance, the null hypothesis of no relationship between the change in the price and growth indices should be accepted. The sample we possess does not, therefore, suggest a statistically significant relationship between the deceleration in the growth rates and price declines for the Soviet MBMW sector.

Changing costs are frequently the driving force behind price changes. This must be especially true in the Soviet case where they set prices on the cost-plus-profit principle. We can therefore expect that the movement of prices will depend on the movement of costs. Table 4.8 shows the cost index for the Soviet MBMW sector in the 1966-86 period. As one can see from the comparison of this index and the price index in Table 4.6, there indeed is a resemblance in the two patterns. In the 20-year period, 1966-85, the official price index declined by 28 percent, while the cost index fell by 29 percent. Table 4.8 also indicates that most of the cost reduction happened in the 1966-75 period, i.e., in the first ten years, when the index fell by 20 percentage points; in the 1976-86 period, it only fell by 10 points. That translates into an average annual decline of 2.2 percent and 1.2 percent, respectively. One should realize that, in the context of the comparable-price principle, a cost decline only means a reduction in the costs of those goods that are already established in production. For a newly introduced good, the Soviet accounting scheme does not provide a relevant comparison with a good for which it substitutes. The new good's cost will start counting in the calculation of cost indices only when the producer receives a plan target for cost reduction, i.e., at the period's end. In other words, since the same principle is applied to the comparisons of both costs and prices, the close relationship in the movement of the two variables is not surprising.

Table 4.8. Cost Index for the Soviet MBMW Sector (Percent)

1965	1966	1967	1968	1969	1970	1971	1972	1973	1974	1975
100	97	95	93	91	90	87	85	84	82	80
1976	1977	1978	1979	1980	1981	1982	1983	1984	1985	1986
79	78	77	76	75	75	74	73	72	71	70

Source: *Narkhoz SSSR* (1970, p.173; 1975, p.229; 1980, p.152, and *za 70 let*, 1987, p.158).

Cost increases and declines have become the prime cause of price changes for the Soviet MBMW sector in the last two decades. As indicated in Section 1.3, the 1967 price reform brought a significant change in the cost structure for Soviet industry, including the MBMW sector. The 1967 price reform was followed by price corrections for MBMW products in 1969, 1970, and 1971. Each time, profit markups were driven into line with the movement of production costs, but it was possible to maintain an equilibrium only for a short time. Along with products barely making a profit because of rising costs of material inputs, there were many machines (and especially instruments) with "excessive" profit rates because of cost declines in the first several years of mass production. For this reason, a general revision of MBMW prices took place in 1973. During that time, 74 out of 85 *preiskuranty* for MBMW product groups approved by *Goskomtsen* were revised, and on average these prices were slashed by 12 percent (Lukinov, 1977, pp. 357-8).

Changes in MBMW prices also took place after 1973. Thus, in the 1976-77 period, there were price hikes for metal-intensive product groups, as a result of rising wholesale prices for rolled metals. At the same time, prices were discounted in the instrument making, electronics, and radio industries. Other developments in the Soviet economy, some of them external to the MBMW sector, also affected its prices. During that time, for example, wages were raised in the service sector of the economy, along with wage rates for the night shift. In another development, norms for mandatory depreciation payments on production capital rose sharply. It was also decided to reflect in prices the costs of geological survey and forest rehabilitation.

The MBMW sector of the Ukrainian economy can serve as an illustration of price changes. At the end of the 10th five-year plan (1976-80), one tenth of the sector's products were manufactured at a loss while a quarter of the output generated a profit exceeding the normative level by 1.5 to two times (Alferova and Kaleniuk, 1984, p.37). It was difficult for the authorities to keep prices up to date. In 1977 they revised *preiskuranty* for eight product groups and changed prices for both remunerative and unprofitable goods. In 1978 significant corrections were made for seven product groups, and in 1979 for ten. Since all of these changes affected the value indicators of the national economic plan, those indicators had to be corrected. This led to a chain process of plan alterations.

The perpetual price changes of the 1970s paved the way for the overall reform of prices in 1982. The reform was required by the following circumstances, both exogenous and endogenous to the MBMW sector: 1) price increase for raw materials, fuels, and energy that induced a chain reaction of price adjustments in manufacturing; 2) the discrepancy between the costs approved as the base of prices and the actual costs for many products; 3) unjustifiably high profit rates for products that were manufactured for a long time, some of which even became obsolete; 4) a broad range of profitability for MBMW products that had to be narrowed and brought in line with the targeted rates for different MBMW branches, and 5) the need to update prices in the *preiskurantly* last published in 1973. The first of these factors was exogenous and was the most important among those pushing MBMW prices upward. As a matter of fact, higher prices of raw materials and energy pushed MBMW costs up by an average of nearly 41 percent in the 1982 price reform, an increase that was in part offset by other factors (Ermak, 1982, p.11). In general, planners often use factors associated with improvements in production to justify decreasing operational costs and thus to offset exogenous shocks. But, in the 10th five-year period (1976-80), the pace of planned improvements in the technology and organization of production decelerated, and the role of exogenous factors consequently increased. As a result of interaction of the endogenous and exogenous factors, some MBMW branches received high profits, and others received low profits. Within each branch there were significant disparities among firms, and, even within the same firm, profit rates varied widely for different products. The situation was not unique for the 1982 price reform; as noted above, it was typical for revisions of the Soviet pricing system.

During the 1982 price reform, the idea of the net-value model of price described in Section 1.2 was implemented. For each good, the average branch-of-industry cost served as the base for price. In the averaging procedure, only specialized firms were considered. Those with obsolescent technologies and consequently greater costs were ignored, as were temporary expenses incurred for mastering new technological processes. The profit markup was divided among different products as a proportion of their costs net of material inputs, to reduce the effect of material expenditures on the level of profit and to discourage firms from using expensive raw materials. In addition to the change in the format for the computation, there also were quantitative changes in the targeted level of the profit markup. The markup was, on average, raised to allow the ministries and their firms to accumulate additional funds for self-financing their research, development and some investment costs.

New prices were introduced in 1982 for 94 product groups of the nomenclature of *Goskomtsen* and for many product groups of the nomenclature of ministries and republic authorities. Table 4.9 summarizes the average overall change of MBMW prices by three additive factors – cost of material inputs, other costs, and the profit markup – in 1982 compared to similar changes in 1967. The change

Table 4.9. MBMW Price Change by Factors in 1967 and 1982
          (Percent)

Factor	1967	1982
Cost of Raw Materials, Fuel, and Energy	9.5	10.5
Other Costs	-5.3	-2.9
Profit Markup	-4.5	-1.4
Overall Change	- .3	6.2

Source: Ermak (1982, p.10).

in costs of material inputs had similar effects on MBMW prices in 1967 and 1982. As Table 4.9 shows, the increase in these costs pushed MBMW prices up by 10.5 percent in 1982 as compared to 9.5 percent in 1967. As also seen from Table 4.9, the reserves for offsetting that increase were lower in 1982 than in 1967. Thus, while other costs, primarily wages, dropped in 1967 by 5.3 percent, in 1982 they fell by only 2.9 percent. The 1982 decline in the normative profit was also insignificant, 1.4 versus 4.5 percent in 1967. (The required decline in profit was determined as the difference between the total targeted profit incorporated in MBMW prices with the profit that could have been generated in the absence of the reform.) After totaling the effects of all three factors, an average overall increase of MBMW prices was 6.2 percent in 1982, while there was a symbolic price decline of 0.3 percent in 1967.

Table 4.10 specifies the increases in the costs of material inputs during the 1967 and 1982 price reforms. As one can see from Table 4.10, the costs of raw materials rose during the two reforms by almost the same proportion of 16.9 percent and 17 percent, respectively. The increase of the costs of fuel and energy was much higher, i.e., 59.3 percent in 1967 and 44.4 percent in 1982. The overall impact was greater in 1967 than in 1982 – 24.8 and 22.4 percent, respectively. But, as Table 4.9 shows, the net impact on the MBMW sector was the opposite, i.e., the role of the material component was greater in 1982 than in 1967. Although prices of all material inputs rose more significantly in 1967, those important to the MBMW sector, especially prices of metals, rose more in 1982. This explains a seeming contradiction between the information in Tables 4.9 and 4.10.

Table 4.10. Price Increase for Material Inputs during the 1967 and 1982 Price Reforms (Percent)

Cost	1967	1982
Raw Materials	16.9	17.0
Fuel and Energy	59.3	44.4
Total Material Inputs	24.8	22.4

Source: Ermak (1982, p.11).

The role of different costs in the MBMW sector is demonstrated in Table 4.11 where they are broken down into four items – materials and energy, depreciation, wages and social insurance deductions, and miscellaneous. As Table 4.11 shows, the materials and energy share of total MBMW costs grew consistently, and the proportion for wages declined. As a matter of fact, the share for wages fell by 10 percentage points over the 1956-86 period. This has made it more and more difficult for the authorities to pursue the policy of tightening production norms for workers as a means of offsetting the rising costs of material inputs.

For individual MBMW product groups, the range of cost and price changes was broad. In 1982 there were significant price increases for the material-intensive MBMW branches as a result of rising costs. Examples include heavy and transport machinery (an average price increase of 13.4 percent), agricultural machinery (13.2 percent), energy and power machinery (8.5 percent), and chemical machinery (8.3 percent). Among declines, the greatest was for instrument making (25.5 percent), the branch that has had one of the

Table 4.11. The Breakdown of MBMW Costs (Percent of Total)

Indicator	1955	1965	1976	1982	1986
Materials and Energy	59.0	60.6	64.5	64.9	66.3
Depreciation	4.1	4.8	5.7	7.0	8.0
Wages and Social Insurance Deductions	33.2	30.2	24.0	22.9	21.2
Miscellaneous	3.7	4.4	5.8	5.2	4.5

Sources: Gorfinkel' (1981, p.34) and *Narkhoz SSSR* (*za 70 let*, 1987, p.159 and 1982, p.139).

highest turnovers of products. Table 4.12 shows the MBMW price change in 1982 for three types of nomenclature for which prices are approved by *Goskomtsen*, ministries, and the republic authorities. In several cases, the standard MBMW branches are grouped together in Table 4.12 so that percentages indicated do not necessarily coincide with price changes for individual branches. As shown in Table 4.12, there were both similarities and differences in price changes for all three types of nomenclature. For the most important machines and equipment, whose prices are approved by *Goskomtsen*, price changes ranged from a 15 percent increase to a 25.5 percent decrease. The overall impact of these changes on MBMW prices depended on the proportions of different product groups in the sector's total value of output. If these proportions are taken into account, it then turns out that autotractive and agricultural machinery, with a roughly 47 percent share in the value of output of civilian MBMW, accounted for 61 percent of the sector's overall price increase in 1982.

It is possible to find examples in the Soviet economic literature illustrating the general pattern of the co-movement of costs and prices for the MBMW branches. Specific cases reveal much similarity in the rise of prices and costs, mentioned above, with costs usually as an exogenous factor for price increases. The first of the three examples considered below pertains to metal-cutting machines whose cost and price indices are given in Table 4.13.

As follows from Table 4.13, the average cost of metal-cutting machines rose by 57 percent, and the wholesale price rose by 64 percent in the 1967-74 period. The similarity in the movement of both indices is apparent; the correlation coefficient between the two equals 0.99. Moreover, it follows from Table 4.13 that, in the process of an increase in both indices, the price index always surpassed the cost index by two to nine percentage points. As a result, the average annual growth rate for costs was 5.8 percent, and for prices, 6.4 percent. The Soviet sources indicate that the example of metal-cutting machines is symptomatic, and that costs and prices also rose for trucks, tractors, combines, other agricultural machines and many other MBMW products (Lukinov, 1977, pp. 357-8). Similar indices for metal-cutting machines were reported for the 1968-72 period (Koshuta and Rozenova, 1977). In this case, the behavior of prices and costs of other specific machines was also investigated. For example, the loom's average price rose by 62 percent in compliance with an increase in production costs. In those cases, as well as in other Soviet studies, only permanent *preiskurant* prices were used; these exclude the newly introduced goods with generally higher temporary prices.

Table 4.14 illustrates an example of the cost and price indices for VAZ-2101 (*Zhiguli*), a Soviet car whose production began at the Volga automobile plant (VAZ) in 1970. As discussed in Chapter 5, VAZ is the largest car producer in the USSR, with 55 percent of Soviet annual car output reached by 1978 (Shugurov and Shirshov, 1980, p.85). Table 4.14 illustrates the effect of what could be considered as a typical phenomenon for the Soviet MBMW sector: as a new machine is introduced, its costs and prices are set at a relatively high level which can then be reduced sharply in the first several years of mass production. Very quickly, however, the reduction decelerates. As one can see from Table 4.14, the bulk of the cost reduction occurred in 1971 (30 points) and in 1972 (16 points). With the correlation coefficient of 0.99, the behavior of the price index was similar to that of the cost index. Though declining, the price index fell at a lower pace than the cost index. (Incidentally, the wholesale price decline for *Zhiguli* did not materialize in any reduction of the car's retail price and hence meant nothing to the Soviet consumer.)

Table 4.12. Percentage Price Change for MBMW Branches in 1982

Branch	Nomenclature		
	Goskomtsen	Ministries	Republics
Heavy, Transport, Energy, and Machinery for Coal Industry	15.0	12.4	7.4
Autotractive and Agricultural Machinery	7.1	–	3.8
Road-Construction and Machinery for Chemical, Light, and Food Industries	6.4	.8	4.8
Electrotechnical Industry	1.7	7.3	2.7
Machine-Tool Industry	- 2.8	- 6.0	4.8
Instrument Making	-25.5	-10.1	- .5
Capital Repair	16.9	1.7	6.3
Spare Parts	11.5	6.0	6.7

Source: Ermak (1982, p.8).

Table 4.13. Cost and Price Indices for Metal-Cutting Machines

Year	Cost Index	Price Index
1966	100	100
1967	118	120
1969	123	130
1970	132	140
1971	136	141
1972	142	151
1973	152	156
1974	157	164

Source: Lukinov (1977, p.357).

Table 4.14. Cost and Price Index for the Automobile VAZ-2101
(Percent)

Year	Cost Index	Price Index
1970	100	100
1971	70	73
1972	54	65
1973	49	58
1974	43	48

Source: Lukinov (1977, p.356).

The third example illustrated in Table 4.15 for a spike-tooth har-row is different in one respect. Instead of a pattern of costs declining consistently but at decelerating rates, here cost first systematically rose from 1966 to 1972 and then fell sharply in 1973. The pattern for the price index is similar, with the correlation coefficient between the price and cost of 0.98. In this case, as well as in the two previous cases, the price index always rises at a faster rate and declines at a slower rate than the cost index.

These examples demonstrate that the average wholesale prices of machines and equipment in the Soviet Union varied with the cost levels. There are two opposite tendencies in the movement of costs: they rise for machines established in production, because of rising costs of material inputs, and gradually decline for newly introduced machines, because of improvements in technology and organization. The upward tendency is generally the case when a rise in the costs of material inputs cannot be offset by a decline in the cost of labor. The example of *Zhiguli* illustrates that a decline in production cost usually occurs in the first several years after the introduction of a new good. If compared to existing goods, the new good's starting

Table 4.15. Cost and Price Indices for a Spike-Tooth Harrow

Year	Cost Index	Price Index
1966	100	100
1967	119	143
1969	127	150
1970	145	176
1971	177	212
1972	214	272
1973	135	184
1974	133	163

Source: Lukinov (1977, p.359).

cost and the price based on it are high. Eventually, as the technological process is mastered, it becomes possible to reduce the cost
and the price, to drive them into line with other products. Hence,
the introduction of a new good generally raises MBMW costs, but
that is not taken into account in planning. Only after some time will
a new good's first approved production cost establish the base with
which subsequently changing costs will be compared. As a rule, a
downward movement will prevail, and this explains the phenomenon
of the declining cost index for the Soviet MBMW sector. What
may also be characteristic of the Soviet MBMW sector is that price
increases there surpass but price reductions lag behind changes in
costs.

4.2. Technological Change and Modernization

Both Soviet leaders and western analysts accept as fact the low
pace of technological progress in the Soviet economy. Does it mean
that insufficient resources are available for Soviet technological change?
In a free-market economy, many firms may be involved in the same
type of research. Some will be redundant. High levels of industry

spending on research and development (R&D) do not always yield adequate output. Therefore, a positive correlation between input and output from the process of technological change may or may not be high, depending on the market structure in which the firm operates. According to Soviet political economy, the liquidation of the "anarchy of capitalist production" there led to better coordination and, as a result, less repetition in the R&D process. Consequently, the Soviet process of technological change should have been more efficient than in the West; the Soviets should need less inputs to achieve comparable output. But the results are the opposite. Soviet goods, especially machines, are heavier than their western counterparts, or less versatile, or less convenient for the user.[4] Some striking examples of production inefficiency are now openly admitted by Soviet economists and even the leadership (Shmelev, 1987, p.156 and Gorbachev, 1986, p.3). Moreover, systematic problems of waste and inefficiency must affect all sectors of the Soviet economy, including the process of technological change. Not surprisingly, then, significant spending on technological improvement since the mid-1960s failed to materialize in an adequate improvement of Soviet goods and services. Inadequate technological change aggravated inefficiency.

With an emphasis on technological modernization, the 12th five-year plan (1986-90) is declared the plan of efficiency, as in the past there were plans of quality or of productivity. The integral role of technological improvement in the national economic plan was significantly strengthened in the 1960s. One of the problems of controlling plans for the mechanization and automation of technological processes was the absence of a synthesizing indicator which could measure the overall change of the state of technology. It was then decided to stress the introduction of prototypes of new goods and their first production runs as central indicators of the plan for new technology and to link them closely to the production plan. Eventually, planning for high-quality category goods outweighed the other indicators of the plan for new technology in the late-1970s. More direct links were also established between this plan, on the one hand, and investment, labor, and cost-of-production plans, on the other.

The plan for technological change paid little attention to conservation of material inputs due to the ideas of the 1965 economic reform. The rationale was that, under incentive provisions, the firm would find it profitable to reduce the production uses of inputs on its own, without mandatory plan targets. But, since no incentives actually worked in that direction, rising production costs alarmed planners. Their appeal for a return to the direct planning of costs was heeded by the party authorities only when the supplies of metals and energy to the domestic market were further strained. As a result, the use of material inputs emerged as one of the most important indicators of the plan for new technology. To be sure, resolutions on conserving energy, metals and other materials had repeatedly been approved in the past, but only in the 1980s were they implemented in concrete targets specifying reductions of supplies to industrial ministries. Assignments for saving material inputs (*rezhim ekonomii*) have been strengthened in the 12th five-year plan. As a result, the ratio of material expenditure to national income is to decline by four to five percent (the decline reported for the 1981-85 period was 2.5 percent), the ratio of energy expenditure to national income by the same percentage, and the ratio of metal expenditure to national income by 13 to 15 percent (*Narkhoz SSSR*, 1985, p.57 and *Pravda*, Jan. 26, 1986, p.1). Construction is supposed to conserve 13 to 15 percent of rolled metals, 8 to 10 percent of cement, and 10 to 12 percent of timber materials. As is usual for national economic plans, these targets for saving material inputs are too taut to be realistic and, at the same time, too modest to incorporate the revolutionary changes in the efficiency of machines and equipment that were projected for the 12th five-year plan.

Along with conserving material inputs, the new, advanced technologies to be introduced in the 1986-90 period are supposed to improve work conditions by automating and mechanizing production. Automation has been a dream for all Soviet leaders since Stalin; they could not stand the idea of millions of workers employed in unproductive manual jobs. However, Gorbachev claims that little was actually done in the past to attain plan targets for automation. According to the new plan, automation is to double by 1990, with a special emphasis on the MBMW sector. The new plans are based on the introduction of flexible automation systems, rotor and conveyor lines, microprocessor devices, robots and computers. The Soviets have manufactured their computers since the 1960s, after the anathema was removed from cybernetics. Although significant progress was made, Soviet hardware and especially software remain of poor quality. The main problem, however, is that, counter to the intent and the whole idea of computerized data processing, the expanded use of computers led to a higher demand for data processing personnel. The use of computers is still a responsibility of a small group of programmers and analysts who are isolated from the rest of the employees in a research institute or an industrial firm. The authorities view the mass production of personal computers as a golden opportunity to involve a broader circle of white collar workers in computerized data processing. A western reader may be misled by the term "personal," but these computers will be produced by Soviet industry primarily for offices and schools, not for private, personal use. The production of computers is to surge 2.4 times in the 1986-90 period; of those, 1.1 million will be personal computers for which the technology of manufacturing is being established (Gorbachev, 1986, p.2). In comparison, between four and five million personal computers were manufactured annually in the U.S. in the 1983-85 period (*Statistical Abstract of the U.S.*, 1987, p.751).

For the economy to benefit from advanced technologies, automates and computers, the equipment must be delivered and used properly. That is why the Soviet authorities are concerned with the efficiency of their research and development (R&D) units and the misuse of sophisticated equipment. Although there is nothing new about these concerns, some organizational changes in R&D and some stiffer punishments for failures to promote technological change have been introduced. For example, the Central Committee has passed several resolutions including ones reprimanding the Ministry of Machine Tool and Tool Making Industry for manufacturing dated equipment and the Ministry of Radio Industry for manufacturing shabby consumer goods (*Ekonomicheskaia Gazeta* 7, 1986, p.3 and *Pravda*, June 3, 1986, p.1).

The Soviet system of research organizations includes R&D units at industrial firms, project and research institutes at the ministries and departments (including the Union-republic *Gosplan* system), institutes of the Academy of Sciences and research divisions at higher education institutions. According to Soviet sources, there were 1.5 million researchers in the country in 1986; this is reported to be one fourth of the world total (*Narkhoz SSSR za 70 let*, 1970, p.63).[5] In

1986 the state budget outlays for R&D were 29.5 billion rubles, or five percent of the national income used for consumption and accumulation (*Narkhoz SSSR za 70 let*, 1987, pp. 430 and 632). This may account for less than half of total R&D expenditures; the rest is covered by production costs. The figures characterize a large scale of inputs to the technological change process. Here, is, however, how Gorbachev (1986, p.2) sees the output:

> Our production structure remained rigid and fell short of the requirements of technological progress. The USSR produces much more of iron ore and steel than the U.S., with significantly lower output of machine-building products, prepares the same amount of wood but produces less wood products. Each incremental unit of national income, industrial and agricultural output requires from us more resources under these conditions.

Blaming Soviet designers for the failure to take the highest world standards into account, Gorbachev accuses them of having an inferiority syndrome and of peddling eyewash. Among the causes that Gorbachev notes are miscalculations in the investment policy, neglect of the needs of existing plants (especially in the MBMW sector), creation of artificial labor shortages, and waste. But those are effects rather than causes.

The new Soviet leadership realizes the need for reducing the overstaffing in their huge R&D system which, rightly or wrongly, has become legendary. Since what should be done may not have been clear, they have endorsed several experiments that were initiated earlier. One is aimed at the creation of research and production associations (*NPO – nauchno-proizvodstvennye ob'edineniia*) that began in the 1970s. Most of those *NPO*s were subordinate to the ministries. In spite of the intent, the links of many of the ministerial institutes to production firms remained loose. In 1985 it was decided to transfer most of the ministerial institutes to production associations, in order to raise incentives and to strengthen the researchers' responsibility for the application of their findings. In one of the attempts to remove the stumbling block in the way of *NPO*s – the separation of research and production – first *VNPO*s (*vsesoiuznye NPO*) have already been organized. The potential advantages of a *VNPO* are that, at such a gigantic level, it is possible to combine powerful research organizations, design and project institutes and production firms.[6] However, the industrial production associations, that replaced ministerial *glavki* and that in turn will probably be replaced by *VNPOs*, had that same authority over all organizations and firms subordinate to them. Still, they did not succeed. The appointment of more qualified management to *VNPOs* may make a difference, but the problem in combining research and production is that the Soviet leaders want to have their cake and eat it, too. If production targets are taut, all the units of any associations will work toward meeting those targets and will forget about experimentation with new goods and new technologies. If the plan targets are loose, so experimentation is stressed, they cannot expect great production and the acceleration (*uskorenie*) initially declared by Gorbachev.

Another new form of industrial organization praised by Gorbachev at the 27th party congress was the interbranch R&D complexes (*MNTK – mezhotraslevye nauchno-tekhnicheskie kompleksy*). Unlike *VNPOs*, *MNTKs* are not charged with both research and mass production; their responsibility will stop at the manufacturing of prototypes. The first brand new *MNTK* embraces 14 organizations of the Academy of Sciences and five ministries, the chemical, petrochemical, fertilizer, chemical machinery and instrument making industries (Zamaraev, 1988, p.21). The main organizational difficulties facing *MNTKs* are related to the decision making process and the distribution of investment and supplies. The Soviets have a negative experience of attempts at breaking ministerial barriers when, for example, the branch-of-industry and territorial aspects of planning had to be coordinated. Since the plan assumes a strict principle of responsibility for the use of each specific input (*adresnyi kharakter*), in most cases the ministries were recipients of funds, and the branch-of-industry clearly dominated over the territorial aspect. Only supraministerial power possessed by bureaucratic bodies such as the new Agroindustrial Committee and the Bureau on Machine Building will enable them to solve problems that involve several ministries. Since the new *MNTKs* cannot be given a supraministerial status, a related deputy minister will control each ministry's organizations involved in the *MNTK*, and a deputy director of the *MNTK* will be appointed to coordinate it with each of the ministries. This is a traditional Soviet approach, except that the people responsible for the coordination will have higher than usual ranks. One can be skeptical whether such a change will make any difference for the *MNTK* performance, especially with more of them organized and with declining preferential treatment in terms of supplies.

The wage structure in the Soviet R&D system has also been reformed. At the experimental stage, 70 research organizations of 33 ministries and employing 60,000 people were involved (Kozhevnikov, 1986, p.65). Directors of those organizations set guaranteed minimum wages at the level of 70 to 80 percent of existing base salaries for all employees. Depending on performance, every worker can "earn" an additional portion of his wage which, together with a payment from the incentive fund, may even exceed his former salary, up to a certain cap. Although subject to abuse, this new system will give some greater leverage to an administration that only has an ability to reward conscientious workers and cannot penalize those who shirk or are incompetent.

Soviet investment priorities are also being revised. The role of investment plans in inducing technological change in the Soviet economy has persistently grown since the 1960s. New targets linking the two plans were imposed, and industrial firms were required to submit their plans for investment in technological renovation and modernization. The following figures characterize Soviet investment growth since 1960 by five-year periods: 1961-65, 45.1 percent; 1966-70, 42.6 percent; 1971-75, 41.3 percent; 1976-80, 27.5 percent; 1981-85, 17.5 percent (*Narkhoz SSSR za 70 let*, 1987, p.324).[7] Of the several different versions, a 23.6 percent growth seems to be the last one approved for the 1986-90 period (Gorbachev, 1986, p.2).

There were many possible reasons for the low rate of investment growth foreseen in the 11th five-year plan. The sharp decline of projected growth puzzled western analysts when the guidelines for the 11th five-year plan were first published in 1981. The rationale, however, was an attempt to switch from "extensive" growth, based on the use of additional resources in the production process, to "intensive" growth, based on an increase in marginal productivity. With an emphasis on the use of more machines and equipment, the proportion of construction and installation work had to be decreased by several percentage points in the plan. There was also a projected shift to completion of projects started earlier, a slower process than new construction. These changes had to result in an unusually low volume of investment for the 11th five-year plan. As usual in Soviet planning, significant changes were reflected in the annual plans. While the five-year plan outlines how the economy *should* perform, the annual plan shows how the economy *can* perform. By making five-year plans more realistic and more concrete, the authorities have reduced that discrepancy, but it is still a big one. In the case of 1981-85 investment, the initiation of new construction projects at a pace higher than initially planned, and a corresponding reduction of funds available to renovation, led to the rare incident of surpassing the plan. (As a rule, the results fall short of the five-year investment plan projections.)

This time Gorbachev wants everything to go differently. He believes that slowing down investment growth was a bad idea. Instead, investment should grow faster, so the economy can modernize its huge capital stock. The highest growth is foreseen for investment in renovation, which is to increase 1.7 times in the 1986-90 period, and its share of total investment would rise from 38.5 percent in 1985 to 50.5 percent in 1990 (Ryzhov, 1986B, pp. 12-3). Accelerating the renovation process would cause a change in the composition of production capital stock: capital stock in machines and equipment will rise, while stock in buildings and structures will decline. This is to be accomplished by raising the retirement rates for capital stock, accelerating its turnover, and thus modernizing the technological base of all sectors of the economy.

There is much discussion in economic literature, including the Soviet literature, on the obsolescence of Soviet production capital and its declining rates of retirement. Table 4.16 shows the average ratios of the cost of retired capital to the cost of total industrial production capital for the 1971-85 period. For comparison, normative (planned) ratios for retirement, which rose in 1975, are also provided. The normative ratio shown is a weighted average for different industries whose individual normative ratios vary from 3.2 percent for energy machinery to 5.6 percent for instrument making (Senchagov and Ostapenko, 1981, p.37). As one can see from Table 4.16, actual retirement ratios were much lower than the normative ones; they even moved in the opposite directions. For machines and equipment the retirement ratios were more stable at about 2.5 percent in the 1971-85 period (*Narkhoz SSSR*, 1970, p.169; 1980, p.147, and 1985, p.124). While there are many reasons for the low actual retirement ratios, the shortage of new equipment is usually indicated as the most important one. In addition, in some instances production firms are simply not interested in replacing their old equipment by new machines that may have no advantages, may be more costly and may be more difficult to install and use.

The new retirement rates are compulsory and are much higher.

Table 4.16. Retirement Ratios for Soviet Industrial Production
Capital (Percent)

Indicator	1971-75	1976-80	1981-85
Total Retirement Ratio	11	8	8
Annual Retirement Ratio	2.2	1.6	1.6
Annual Normative Ratio	3.7	4.8	4.8

Sources: *Narkhoz SSSR* (1985, p.123) and Senchagov and
Ostapenko (1981, p.36).

The average retirement ratio for machines and equipment will increase to five to six percent (Ryzkov, 1986A, p.26). What growth
rates does that command for the MBMW sector? To figure it out,
one should take into account both the change in the retirement rates
and in the composition of production capital. First, as indicated
above, in 1985 the equipment retirement ratio was 2.5 percent of
the cost of production capital stock. That stock consists of buildings, installations, equipment and other, smaller items; equipment
was 39.9 percent of capital stock by the end of 1985 (*Narkhoz SSSR*,
1985, p.119). Hence, the retirement ratio with respect to the stock
of equipment was 6.27 percent (2.5÷0.399), and the average age of
equipment was 16 years (100÷6.27) in 1985. Second, the composition of capital is supposed to change gradually in favor of equipment,
whose share of 39.9 percent of capital stock rose at the average
annual rate of 0.82 percent in the 1981-85 period. Assuming this
average growth rate for the 1986-90 period, the proportion of machines and equipment may reach 42 percent by 1990. The average
5.5 percent retirement ratio for capital thus becomes 13.1 percent
(5.5÷0.42) of the cost of machines and equipment. Consequently,
this ratio implies an average projected age of machines of 7.6 years
(100÷13.1).

Reducing the age of the equipment stock would require heroic
expansion of the MBMW sector. At the existing production growth
rates for the MBMW sector, the average age of machines was 16

years in 1985. To achieve a 7.6 year age by 1990 would require MBMW production growth rates to be 2.1 times (16÷7.6) higher. Therefore, if the projected average age of machines and equipment stabilizes at between 7 to 8 years, the MBMW sector production must grow 2 to 2.3 times as rapidly as in the 11th five-year period. A Soviet writer arrives at similar results by finding that a twofold acceleration in MBMW growth will be needed to maintain a lower, 4 percent retirement ratio (Malygin, 1985, p.34).

Then what can be expected from the 43 percent growth rate planned for the sector in the 1986-90 period if the sector grew by 35 percent in the 11th five-year period? (Ryzhkov, 1986B, p.13 and *Narkhoz SSSR*, 1985, p.129). It is logical to expect that, unless new sources of production or import are found, the average age of machinery can be lowered from 16 to about 13 years; the retirement ratio consequently would rise only by about one percentage point from the existing 2.5 percent rate. This does not even take into account the fact that the pace of new construction will probably be higher than initially planned and that additional equipment will be siphoned off from the renovation process. Also, any improvements in machine quality, along with more generous incentive provisions, will hike machine prices and thus reduce real growth rates. Some Soviet authors have also expressed their concerns about the inconsistency between the plan targets for the renovation of capital stock in the economy and the projected growth for the MBMW sector.[8]

High turnover of capital by itself is not a panacea. For example, in the 1977-78 period when the retirement ratio for industrial capital was 2.4 percent, that ratio was 10.1 percent for agriculture and 7.6 percent for construction (Palterovich, 1980, p.103). But this is not a sign of superiority for those areas. Instead, it reflects misuse, poor maintenance and the lack of proper storage. In the process of capital replacement, the age of machines should not be decisive. What replaces the old machines? Soviet authors indicate that, if the efficiency of a new machine is not greater than 1.5 to two times that of the older one, the replacement is not economically justified (Palterovich, 1980, p.109). This puts the problem in the proper perspective of machine quality, rather than turnover alone. Meanwhile, in anticipation of the consequences of the capital turnover campaign, it is easy to imagine the amounts of useful equipment scrapped by Soviet managers. (In the U.S., the markets for used and renovated machines and equipment prevent the scrapping of useful capital stock, since market prices for such capital exceed the scrap values.)

Table 4.17. Efficiency of Different Investment Strategies

Type of Investment Strategy	Number of Projects	Share of Total Cost, Percent	Investment-to-Output Ratio	Number of Years per Million Rubles of Investment	Average Duration of a Project, Years
Renovation	42	34	.92	1.34	18.3
Expansion	31	49	.90	.49	15.7
New Construction	12	17	1.03	.30	8.9

Source: Fal'tsman (1981, p.77).

Many analysts, both in the West and in the Soviet Union, believe that renovation of Soviet industrial capital is more efficient than new construction. Thus, according to the *Gosplan's* Summary Department of Capital Investment, renovation pays off three times faster, requires a 27 percent shorter project duration and has a 1.5 times higher output-to-capital ratio than new construction (Stepun, 1981, p.35). Since renovation is not welcome everywhere, one may, without challenging these figures, suspect that the data must be somewhat hypothetical. Table 4.17 provides several alternative characteristics of efficiency for new construction, renovation and production expansion. (The latter is a process in which new shops are added to existing plants.) The information was obtained by surveying 85 construction projects for the machine tool industry. As Table 4.17 demonstrates, the investment-to-output ratio was lower for renovation than for new construction. However, the number of years required for the completion of a project per million rubles of investment and the average duration of a project were significantly higher for renovation than for new construction. Many other sources also point to problems with the renovation process, such as high labor costs and low profits of renovation projects (Rumer, 1982, p.60).

Yet the chief problem, in our view, is not the efficiency of the investment process by itself, but rather its effects on the improvement of product quality. From this standpoint, newly introduced plants are usually superior to those that are only partially renewed. Further, as indicated by Soviet sources, the correlation between fixed capital turnover and resulting improvement in product quality has not been significant thus far (Fal'tsman, 1981, p.177). Hence, the "optimization" of investment policies, even if all of the obstacles cited above are removed so that Gorbachev's plans for renovation can work, may not be sufficient for solving problems of Soviet product quality.

4.3. Plans for Quality Improvement and the Reality

Soviet authorities have for a long time stressed the necessity of approaching economic planning from the targeted final results, rather than from gross value indicators. Whether the change in emphasis can improve the final results is another story, but the fact of the matter is that some relevant adjustments have been made in the planning methodology. Looking at the final results of the industrial modernization drive, improvements in product quality seem to the logical prime target. What can and will Gorbachev do to attack the notorious problem of poor product quality? To the western reader, the problem of product quality may seem less important than other economic problems. He knows that, if a poor quality product is not sold, the producer will be forced to improve the product or, if it is sold, the producer will be forced to give the consumer a (*ceteris paribus*) better price. Yet this generally plausible assumption does not apply when products of different quality are not equally available, the condition in the Soviet case. Moreover, the quality problem becomes a quantity problem when defective goods are manufactured. The scale of the problem was illustrated by Gorbachev himself with an example of millions of meters of fabrics, pairs of shoes and other consumer goods returned to the producer or otherwise transferred to a low quality category in 1985 (Gorbachev, 1986A, p.5). He does not elaborate on the amount of damage but asserts that, as a result of the wasted material inputs and the wasted labor of hundreds of thousands of people, it was enormous.

Issues like investment priorities or introducing computers can be treated, at least in part, separately. The quality problem, on the other hand, is a systematic disease that makes the authorities feel uncomfortable about recommending treatment. They have used administrative controls and punishments, direct planning, standardization, price mechanisms, product certification, material incentives and moral persuasion. The policies for product quality improvements implemented in the 12th five-year plan are based on numerous resolutions approved prior to Gorbachev's rise to leadership. Even the new resolutions passed by the Central Committee mostly restated earlier decisions. Among the new provisions, there is one stating that after 1986 the cost of a producer's repair of defective products must come directly from the firm's material incentive fund (*fond material'nogo pooshchreniia*) (July 1985 Resolution, pp. 11-4). For each one percent of the share of defective products in the total value of output, the fund is to be reduced by 5 percent up, to a maximum of 20 percent of the material incentive fund. This provision is interesting because, so far, sanctions had been used against the firm but not against its workers.

One should yet realize that plant management does not create its own production plan. The decision rests with *Gosplan* or the ministry. Then why do they allow poor quality? One possible explanation is that, when a product grows obsolescent but is still in demand, it may not be discontinued without finding a substitute. If, however, an R&D facility could not be assigned to develop a new product, if the outcome of such a project is not adequate or if the deadline is not met, *Gosplan* will have no options but to permit the continued production of old goods. This type of a situation is illustrated by a director of an oil refinery from Baku who, in a Schiller style article, laments the "treachery" of shortages (Kuliev, 1986, p.11). His refinery turns out inferior motor oil. Since motor oil is in short supply, industrial users buy it and do not dare to complain. The refinery is incapable of upgrading the oil's quality, but when its director appeals for help to the ministry and its research institute, they do not listen. Why does he complain when his customers do not? The example, however, illustrates only one side of the story; if the ministry or its research institute told their stories, they could point to their own problems.

The authorities realize that it is impossible to introduce an integral characteristic of product quality. Since it is more difficult for the plan to take care of goods qualities than quantities, they use several procedures to besiege the fortress from different sides. One of the most important procedures is based on planning the proportion of goods in the high-quality category, while the awarding of the category to new machines and equipment involves comparisons to their analogues, i.e., existing similar models and/or standards.

Certification of goods according to quality categories has been considered one of the chief tools for planning quality improvements in the Soviet economy. According to the statute, its task is to stimulate the production of goods that meet the demands of the population, increase production efficiency, promote exports by improving the competitiveness of Soviet products and accelerate the modernization of technology and the discontinuation of obsolescent products. Following the provision of the Central Committee and Council of Ministers, experimental certification took place for the most important products manufactured by a certain limited number of firms in the late 1960s. The purpose was to award a special seal of quality (*znak kachestva*) and a surcharge on the price, to encourage the introduction of high-quality products. A firm applying for the seal of quality had to go through a painful process of coordinating and collecting approvals (visas) from the potential users of the product, research institutes, the ministries, the Exposition of the National Economy (*VDNKh*), and others.

To accelerate the introduction of new products and to ease the application procedures for the seal of quality, in 1972 certification became mandatory for all goods. Three categories of quality – the high, the first, and the second – were specified. A special instruction for the certification of MBMW products was issued in 1974. It spelled out the distinctions among the three categories. Products in the first category had to satisfy the requirements of certain standards in order to meet the demands of users. Products in the high category also had to be at or above the level of best domestic or imported products and to provide sufficient economic benefit to the user. The second category products were defined more vaguely as products whose "technical and economic characteristics did not meet modern requirements and became obsolescent."

The present state of certification is regulated by a special instruction approved in 1984 (Instruction, 1984). The instruction reduced the categories of quality to the first two only – the high and the first. The second category was not to be applied any more, and all products that either cannot be certified or are rejected certification should be discontinued. One may question the effects of the change in the number of categories, but the decision arose from the authorities' attempt to scrutinize the whole certification process. If one accepts such madness as the certification of all of the goods manufactured in the economy, the process should not be a farce. But it does seem to be a farce when widespread clamoring for better quality is belied by the rosy picture of few goods certified in the second category.

The issue of manufacturing the second-category products is not as simple as it may appear. Who should be punished for turning out shabby goods in the Soviet economy? The decision in this case, as explained above, so far rested with *Gosplan* or the ministry. Should they be punished? That seems to be going on in the Soviet economy now, with the ministries blamed for all the failures. The ministry is both responsible for meeting production plan targets and the improvement of goods quality. Under these conditions, the quantity target clearly dominates. This will still be the case as long as physical output is planned either in the form of production plan targets or state orders introduced recently.

The 1984 resolution also brought about another change in the certification process. In the past, a two-tier certification system – state and ministerial – existed. The state carried out the certification of high-category products, and the ministries took care of the first and second categories. The literature cited many examples, and planners were concerned about lax standards applied by ministerial certification committees. As a result, many products were certified for the first category while they did not belong there. The reason is that it is easy for a ministry to obtain an agreement from potential users on the certification of inferior goods as being of the first category. Since 1984 all of the certification has been taken over by state certification committees. In the past, when the committees processed the applications for the high category only, they dealt with 40 to 50 thousand cases a year (Isaev, 1983). Now, with the task of certification of all products in the Soviet economy, their load will be several times greater. State certification committees must be formed of representatives of three or more ministries, including those of the producer and the user. *Gosstandart's* representation on the committee is required. Depending on the nature of the good, other committees or ministries may maintain their presence as well; these may include the State Committee on Science and Technology (*GNTK*), the Ministry of Trade, and the Ministry of Foreign Trade.

Some products will be exempt from certification. Among noticeable exemptions are all food products (some of which, e.g., confectionery, had been certified), drugs and medical supplies, perfumes and cosmetics, jewelry, craft and art production, books and military hardware and supplies. Evidently, the Ministry of Defense does not need the state certification process because of its own network of quality control. But all the other items listed are consumer goods, and the Soviet consumer has no influence on such production. One would therefore expect that, under a system of compulsory quality certification, food and drug products would be the first to draw scrupulous attention from the state certification committees. But there is an embarrassing aspect to the certification of these products. Even if the second-category products would miraculously disappear, it is easy to forecast a reaction of a patient taking medicine or buying food certified in the first but not the high category. All foods and drugs must either be certified in the high category, which is unrealistic, or not certified at all, which is an easier thing to do, to avoid consumer reactions.

It may be difficult to discover the true values of quality characteristics. This is especially true in the case of technical characteristics required for the certification of new machines. Consider, for example, a machine's productivity when three different levels are possible – theoretical, technical, and actual. Theoretical productivity is measured on the basis of the machine's technical characteristics without accounting for time required for service and maintenance. For trucks, for instance, theoretical productivity reflects maximum hourly productivity as the product of freight-carrying capacity and maximum speed. Technical productivity significantly differs from that ideal since it takes into account all the labor time needed to produce a good. For example, a survey showed that technical productivity of Soviet excavators accounted for only 29 percent of theoretical (Gerasimova, 1976, p.47). Soviet standards, however, report theoretical productivity while even technical productivity is still a laboratory parameter that overstates the machine's actual productivity achieved by a user.

The modernization of the Soviet system of standards is viewed by the authorities as a necessary condition for product quality improvement. The Soviets have created thousands of standards – models on paper, the bulk of them for the MBMW sector. Along with the state standards (*GOSTy*), there are ministerial technical specifications. Should a standard be concerned with ideal or just acceptable properties of a new good? According to *GOST* 1, a standard for standards approved in the late 1960s, "optimal characteristics of quality should be established by the standards for manufactured products. They must include consumer and operational characteristics, reliability, durability, technological convenience, and aesthetic properties" (*Ekonomicheskaia Gazeta 9, 1971*). Optimality implies that the good's characteristics are the best under existing constraints, but what about the constraints? Moreover, the requirement of optimality turns into wishful thinking when it comes to defining technical characteristics in specific projects. Therefore, on a operational level, it was for a long time believed that standards should indicate the level of parameters acceptable for consumption and production use. Put differently, designers and technologists considered a standard as a threshold for the adequacy of a product's characteristics. If those characteristics met or exceeded the standard, the product had to be accepted; otherwise, the products had to be rejected. Consequently, no distinction was made among a variety of products of different quality as long as they met the minimum standard requirements. This treatment of standards has become less acceptable since the growing role of a normative approach to planning in the late 1970s.

In a broad context, the normative approach to planning means the use of a targeted set of indicators, such as norms of expenditure for material inputs, capital stock, labor, wages, incentive funds and profit. The normative approach has also been extended to technical characteristics of machines and equipment by requiring that a targeted level of characteristics be created for comparison purposes. Evidently, old standards that were oriented to minimum acceptable technical parameters could not serve those purposes, and new ones would be needed.

The 1983 and 1985 resolutions of the Central Committee and Council of Ministers on the acceleration of technological change in the Soviet economy demanded that managers and planners provide for outputs of goods at the level of the best world standards. According to the resolutions, new prospective standards (*perspektivnye standarty*) must play the leading role in mobilizing industrial firms for such a drastic improvement in product quality. But how can the Soviets create prospective standards reflecting the last word in design and technology? The organizational part of the problem has been solved. As usual in such cases, the industrial ministries are responsible for carrying out the projects for new standards. They appoint subordinate organizations, such as technological and project institutes, design bureaus and production associations, to prepare drafts for the projects. It turns out that those who design and produce machines and equipment are also responsible for standards. These are, of course, the best candidates for making qualified decisions. On the other hand, since their knowledge will be reflected in both products that they design and the standards for those products, it is difficult to imagine how the demands of the standards could become superior to the products. The idea of superiority is exactly the goal of the campaign: to have standards whose requirements may not be met by new goods at the beginning. According to the designers of the new system, at first an acceptable level of a good's characteristics could be established at the level of 70 to 80 percent of the value forecast by a prospective standard. Eventually, however, as good's quality improves, its characteristics would approach the ceiling of the standard's requirements; this would be a signal that the standard is to be raised again. So the scheme would work, in theory.

It is the responsibility of the State Committee on Standards (*Gosstandart*) to examine every single project for a new standard. It may either approve the standard or require a revision. If compared to *Goskomtsen* that examines products' projected costs, profits and prices, the position of *Gosstandart* is even more difficult. While costs and profits are formed for all product groups on a universal principle, *Gosstandart* has to go into details of all of the individual technical characteristics for thousands goods in different branches of industry. In such a situation, although *Gosstandart* has a qualified cadre, it must rely heavily on the expertise of designers and technologists from ministerial project institutes. Despite the caveats, planners expect to achieve at least some positive results from tougher requirements and the mass revision of the standards. A resolution of the Central Committee and the Council of Ministers calls for the creation of a national informational system on the best domestic and world standards (*Ekonomicheskaia Gazeta* 28, 1986, p.4). If and when created, it would be of much help to the designers.

However, even if it were possible to create fantastic prospective standards, adherence to them would present a much greater problem. Since tough standards slow down the meeting of plan targets, Gorbachev's predecessors "looked at the violations through their fingers." To combat the widespread abuse of the standards, he made a logical decision within the existing system, i.e., to apply the experience of military controllers (*voenpredy*) to civilian production. In 1987 a state quality control system (*gospriemka*) supervised by *Gosstandart* was introduced at many industrial firms. In addition to the controllers being independent of firm's management, their wages are also to be independent of the firm's meeting the plan targets, except of those for goods quality. Although a limited experiment with state quality control was going on since 1985, and the idea is generally a good one, it is not clear whether the controllers could go beyond enforcing the existing standards. It is, however, clear that the introduction of state quality control as well as the expansion of state product certification are geared toward further centralization of decision making in the Soviet economy. These moves will inevitably lead to a confrontation with the provisions of Gorbachev's economic reform aimed at enhancing producers' independence.

PART II

Studies of Growth
and Inflation

Chapter 5
The Soviet MBMW Sector and Its Branches

5.1. Machine Building as the Leading Sector of the Soviet Economy

According to Soviet classification, the MBMW sector combines industries that specialize in the production of machines, equipment, apparatus, instruments, and mechanisms for production use, consumption and services. The recent classification identifies the following branches of the MBMW sector: heavy and transport machinery, electrotechnical industry, chemical and petroleum machinery, machine-tool and tool-making industry, automotive and bearing industry, energy and power machinery, tractor and agricultural machinery, machinery for livestock breeding, construction, road, and municipal machinery, light and food-industry machinery and appliances, sanitary products and equipment, communications equipment, medical equipment, aircraft industry, shipbuilding industry, electronic industry, radio engineering and defense industry.

The MBMW sector's share of the Soviet gross material product (*valovoi obshchestvennyi produkt*) was 16.9 percent in 1986, the greatest among all the sectors (*Narkhoz*, 1987, pp. 122 and 132). The relationship of the leading MBMW indicators to the industry totals is shown for 1985 in Table 5.1. As one can see from the table, the MBMW sector commands over 27 percent of the Soviet industry gross value of output. Traditionally, the sector has specialized in producer durables, but its production of consumer goods has been growing since the late 1950s. In the last two decades, new incentives were created to encourage MBMW firms, especially those in the defense business, to produce consumer products (*shirpotreb*) from substandard and wasted materials. In 1985, the proportion of

Table 5.1. The Leading MBMW Indicators and Their Role in
Soviet Industry in 1985

Indicator	Value	Percent of Industry Total
Active Enterprises, Units	9,346	20.4
Gross Value of Output, Billions of Rubles	220	27.4
Fixed Production Capital, Billions of Rubles	189	24.7
Annual Investment, Billions of Rubles	15.9	24.3

Source: Kraiukhin (1987, p.14).

consumer goods was 11 percent of total MBMW output (Kraiukhin, 1987, p.14).

The Soviet MBMW sector is highly concentrated, in terms of both employment and production capital. Thus, Soviet machine-building enterprises are generally much larger (averaging 1,700 workers in 1985) when compared to other industrial enterprises (averaging 850 workers – Kraiukhin, 1987, p.14). The process of concentration was especially encouraged in the 1970s, when it took a form of a campaign. The advantages of economies of scale were stressed in the Soviet literature and numerous instructions for the ministries. The ministries were obliged to prepare proposals for long-term economic development of their branches (*general'nye skhemy razvitiia*). One of the elements of those proposals was a plan for large-scale mergers of their enterprises. In the 1980s, they have begun downplaying the efficiency of uniting several small plants under one management, admitting that big does not necessarily mean good.

The input-output links of the MBMW sector with all productive sectors of the Soviet economy are shown in Table 5.2. The percentages show that, beyond the MBMW sector itself, its chief suppliers are metallurgical and chemical industries. The chief consumers of machines and equipment are the MBMW sector, construction and agriculture. The service sector is not represented in Table 5.2 because it is not a part of the Soviet productive sphere. When it comes to the purchases of material inputs by the MBMW sector, services do not matter, but, when it comes to the distribution of the MBMW output, they consume a significant part of it.

Table 5.2. The Input-Output Links of the Soviet MBMW Sector (Percent of Total)

Sector and Branch	MBMW Purchases	MBMW Sales
Industry	91.7	66.8
Metallurgy	27.3	3.8
Chemical	8.7	3.4
Fuel	2.3	1.8
Electric Power	3.3	0.8
MBMW	42.8	46.5
Timber, Woodworking, and Paper	2.6	2.5
Construction Material and Glass	1.1	2.2
Light	3.2	1.2
Food	0.3	4.6
Other Sectors of the Economy	8.3	33.2
Construction	NA	18.8
Agriculture	NA	10.7
Transport and Communications	NA	2.4
Trade, Procurement, and Other Sectors	NA	1.3

Source: Kraiukhin (1987, p.43).

The components of MBMW cost are compared with those for the whole Soviet industry for 1985 in Table 5.3. The breakdown of MBMW cost has remained relatively stable since 1970. The share of wages dropped by almost four percentage points, to about 22 percent in 1985. But, as Table 5.3 shows, the wage share of cost was still greater for the MBMW sector than for Soviet industry, with the difference of almost eight percentage points. Within the MBMW sector, the wage component varies significantly, from seven percent of cost for cable products to 41 percent for instrument making (Kraiukhin, 1987, p.356).

Table 5.3. The Breakdown of Costs of the Soviet MBMW Sector
and Industry in 1985 (Percent of Total)

Component of Cost	MBMW	Industry
Raw Materials and Parts	62.8	67.7
Fuels and Energy	3.3	6.8
Depreciation	7.8	8.5
Wages and Social Insurance Withholdings	21.7	14.1
Other Costs	4.5	2.9

Source: Kraiukhin (1987, p.356).

The sources of financing the production of new machines and equipment in 1985 were: centralized investment (39 percent of total expenditures), the fund for production development (22 percent), the fund for science and technology (19 percent) and loans and other sources (20 percent) (Kraiukhin, 1987, p.89). The role of the fund for production development is supposed to grow rapidly since the approval of the new law on industrial enterprise (*Ekonomicheskaia Gazeta* 28, 1987). It has now absorbed the decentralized fund for science and technology and, in part, centralized investment. In addition, the newly created centralized fund of the ministry is to rise in prominence. The supply of goods by its enterprises will still remain the main responsibility of the ministry. It is also responsible for the conduct of the technological policy in the branch of industry and for the introduction of technological change.

Since Gorbachev's rise to power, the MBMW sector has received the most favorable treatment. According to Table 5.4, its average growth rates are supposed to be much higher in the 12th five-year plan (1986-90) than in the 11th five-year plan (1981-85). Investment growth rates are almost to quadruple, and the share of products manufactured for less than three years is almost to double. Ambitious targets are set for the terms of design and mastering production of new machines; they are forecast to decline three to four times. The productivity and durability of all newly produced machines will be

1.5 to twice those of their older analogues. The sector's own equipment is to be modernized first. Accelerated growth is planned for the output of machine tools, computers, instruments, electronics and electrotechnical products. The branches producing these products will surpass the average growth rates for the MBMW sector by 1.3 to 1.6 times.

Table 5.4. The MBMW Average Growth Rates for the 11th and 12th Five-Year Plans (Percent)

Indicator	Actual, 1981-85	Planned, 1986-90
Gross Value of Output	6.1	7.0-7.7
Investment	3.2	12.5
Labor Productivity	5.4	7.0-7.4
Proportion of Goods Manufactured for Less than Three Years	26.7	52.0

Source: Kraiukhin (1987, p.21).

What is the evidence? Since the information on the performance of the Soviet economy in the first two years of the 12th five-year period is available, it is possible to look at the first achievements of the MBMW sector. The production of important machines and equipment is in Table 5.5. Unfortunately, most of the product groups' output measures are inevitably in money terms. The indices of plan fulfillment in Table 5.5 deserve special attention. Not only are they extremely low by Soviet standards, but in 1987 they averaged seven to eight percentage points below the 1986 level. As annual plans become more ambitious, the supply of material inputs to the MBMW sector is further strained. Consequently, the plan fulfillment figures are thinner. This familiar outcome had been predicted by many Soviet economists in the process of discussing the published guidelines for the 12th five-year plan (1986-90).

Table 5.5. Soviet Production of Machines and Equipment in the 1985-87 Period

Product	1985		1986			198?		
	Output	Growth Index	Output	Growth Index Plan Fulfillment	Actual	Output	Growth Index Plan Fulfillment	Actual
Turbines, Millions of Kilowatts	21.6	101	20.9	95	104	22.5	82	108
Turbines Generators, Millions of Kilowatts	12.3	97	14.9	84	121	12.8	68	86
Electric Motors, Millions of Kilowatts	54.7	102	55.7	98	102	54.6	92	98
Machine Tools, Billions of Rubles	2.7	112	2.9	107	109	2.8	97	97
Forge and Press Machines, Millions of Rubles	660	100	687	94	105	645	83	94
Industrial Robots, Thousands	13.2	107	15.4	93	114	14.1	93	92
Instruments and Automation Devices, Billions of Rubles	4.5	105	4.8	102	105	5.0	98	104
Computers, Billions of Rubles	4.2	113	4.8	109	113	5.3	103	111
Oil Equipment, Millions of Rubles	229	109	248	97	108	241	87	98
Chemical Equipment, Millions of Rubles	936	110	968	96	103	941	85	97
Light and Food Industry Equipment, Billions of Rubles	1.7	105	1.8	98	104	1.8	89	97
Tractors, Millions of Horsepower	52.8	104	54.5	100.2	103	52.1	94	96
Agricultural Machines, Billions of Rubles	3.7	104	4.0	99	109	4.2	100.5	105
Excavators, Thousands	42.6	102	42.9	102	100.9	41.5	96	97

Sources: *Narkhoz SSSR za 70 let*, (1987 pp. 168-69 and 171-74), *Pravda*, Jan. 26, 1986, p.2; *Ekonomicheskaia Gazeta* 5, 1987, p.11 and 5, 1988, pp. 9-10.

Along with Gorbachev's modernization drive, the whole strategy of Soviet growth acceleration (*uskorenie*) counts on the availability of more and better machines. They are supposed to benefit all sectors of the Soviet economy in two ways. First, since new machines are more powerful, more versatile and more precise, goods produced with those machines will be of higher quality. Second, since the new machines are more efficient, they are expected to permit a switch to novel technologies which require less inputs, especially metals and energy. If so, more goods will be produced from a given amount of inputs. As Gorbachev promised (or was promised), 80 to 95 percent of Soviet manufacturers will be upgraded to the level of the world market standards by 1990, and all manufactures will meet the highest standards by 1991-93 (Gorbachev, 1986, p.2). The reality of the 12th five-year plan does not, however, appear to be so promising. According to the evidence provided by *Goskomtsen*, which prices new machines on the basis of improvements in their characteristics, three-fourths of all the goods introduced in 1986 did not differ significantly from the existing ones (Rozenova, 1987, p.17).

At a recent conference at the Central Committee, the problems of the further development of the Soviet MBMW sector were discussed. Unlike the past, the shortcomings are openly admitted now. Thus, the sector's growth is still "extensive," i.e., achieved with additional inputs, rather than by greater productivity (Leshchinskii, 1988, p.8). More than one third of all enterprises cannot meet plan targets for deliveries of MBMW goods. The production plan targets were met in 1987 for only 24 out of the 150 most important products. Light industry did not receive one quarter of all machines and equipment that were supposed to be delivered. In 1987 the producer introduced 2,700 new products; less than one tenth of them had the characteristics to exceed the level of world standards. Despite their attempts, the share of machines and equipment did not exceed 15 percent of the volume of Soviet exports and was stable at 40 percent of imports. To cure these problems, the necessity to accelerate retirement of production capital and to invest more in its modernization has been reemphasized, as noted in Section 4.2.

5.2. The Automotive Industry

The Soviet automotive industry (AI) is one of the leading branches of the MBMW sector and of Soviet manufacturing industries in gen-

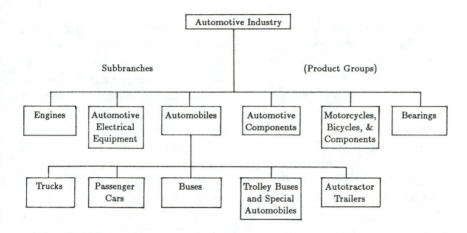

Figure 5.1. Organizational Structure of the Soviet Automotive Industry

eral. The role of the AI is determined by the fact that it makes products desperately needed by the Soviets – trucks, buses and cars – and, at the same time, helps to solve the consumer-goods problem by supplying passenger cars, motorcycles and bicycles. Figure 5.1 illustrates the organizational structure of the AI. There are 30 automotive plants in the Soviet economy. The biggest and best known of them are the following:

The Lenin *Komsomol* automobile plant (*AZLK*) in Moscow began operation as an assembly line in 1930 and first introduced its own make of car in 1940. Since 1947 the car has been named *Moskvich*. Depending on the model, *Moskvich* can be characterized as either a compact or a subcompact car. *Moskvich* may be the second most popular car in the USSR, but it is almost unknown outside of Eastern Europe.

The Belorussia automobile plant (*BelAZ*) near Minsk expanded its production in the 1960s. Since 1959 it has specialized in making powerful quarry dump trucks and coal trucks.

The Volga automobile plant (*VAZ*) in Togliatti was built by Fiat in 1970. The construction meant a revolutionary change in Soviet passenger car manufacturing. The output of passenger cars almost quadrupled in the first five years of operation of the new plant. The *Zhiguli* compact car manufactured by *VAZ* (with the export version *Lada*) is the most popular with the Soviet consumers. It has accounted for 55 percent of the total Soviet annual car output in recent years. This is the largest and most technologically advanced passenger car manufacturer in the Soviet Union. With the current reform of their export operations, the Soviets will probably attempt to increase the sale of *VAZ* models for hard currency.

The Gor'kiy automobile plant (*GAZ*) is the second largest in the country; production started in 1932. It is the only automaker that specializes in manufacturing both trucks and passenger cars. Traditionally the medium size trucks of the *GAZ* family are the best known in the USSR. They are also popular with the Soviet army. The *Volga* passenger car is medium sized and is the only "luxury" car available to the Soviet consumer. While it is more reliable and comfortable than other Soviet cars, it is produced in relatively small quantities and is very expensive.

The Zaporozh'ye automobile plant *(ZAZ) Kommunar* was founded in 1960, from a factory that manufactured agricultural combines. Later on, a branch was opened in Lutsk. The plant makes a subcompact car called *Zaporozhets*. It is the cheapest, the least reliable and the least popular Soviet car.

The Likhachev automobile plant (*ZIL*) in Moscow, the oldest automaker in the country, started production in 1924. The chief products are large trucks and truck engines. The plant also manufactures a small number of custom made limousines for top level Soviet officials.

The Izhevsk automobile plant (*IZh*) began production in 1966 as a branch of the Lenin *Komsomol* automobile plant. It continues manufacturing modifications of *Moskvich* which are now called *IZh*.

The Kama automobile plant (*KamAZ*) in Naberezhnye Chelny was built with heavy use of western technology. The construction began in the early 1970s and is still under way. The entire project is a complex of seven modern plants specializing in manufacturing heavy diesel trucks, dump trucks, saddle tractors and truck engines. *KamAZ* may be one of the most technologically advanced truck producers in the world.

The Minsk automobile plant (*MAZ*) began its production of trucks in 1947. The *MAZ* family includes heavy trucks, dump trucks, log transporters and specialized trucks for the oil industry and railways.

The L'vov bus plant (*LAZ*) began production in 1957, and it has eventually become the leading Soviet bus producer. It manufactures comfortable buses with both gasoline engines and diesels.

The Riga bus plant (*RAF*) started as a repair shop in 1954. Since 1957 it has specialized in the production of vans, limousines, and ambulances. The plant also carries out experiments with the production of electric cars.

One of the tendencies in the production of Soviet trucks is the growth in their capacity. The increase in the average load capacity, from 3.8 metric tons in 1965 to 5 metric tons in 1975 and to 5.5 metric tons in 1980, has been considered as an achievement of the trucking industry (Vlasov, 1978, p.40). This, however, may lead to a waste of both trucks and fuel when there is a need for smaller, not larger vehicles. Soviet sources note that the country's demand for small trucks is only 50 to 60 percent satisfied (Velikanov, 1984, p.33). As a result, powerful *GAZ* and *ZIL* trucks are used for shipment of small amounts of goods and therefore run partially empty.

The problems most important to the Soviet AI have been included in their new five-year plan (1986-90). The description below follows the guidelines for the five-year plan and provides a brief view of those problems (*Ekonomicheskaia Gazeta* 46, 1985, p.7). One of the industry's major tasks in this period is to increase production and improve the fuel efficiency of cars and trucks. Truck production is to include 40 to 45 percent of diesel trucks which will be 25 to 30 percent more fuel efficient than trucks with gasoline engines. The new buses are also to be diesels and are to be larger and more comfortable. As to the types of trucks, it is planned to raise the output of heavy quarry dump trucks with a carrying capacity of 110 to 180 metric tons, log transporters of higher capacity, small trucks and fork-lift trucks. Another, related task is to start or to increase the manufacturing of specialized trucks and trailers for construction, agricultural production and transportation of agricultural products.

Among the problems of the passenger car improvements, the five-year plan singles out the manufacturing of diesel and front-drive vehicles. The need to turn out more engines using liquefied natural gas is also stressed. In general, lower fuel consumption is expected to be achieved by the use of electronic devices and the improvement of the aerodynamic characteristics of both cars and trucks. Other ambitious targets are to reduce metal consumption in automobile production by 15 to 25 percent, to improve durability and to lower the maintenance cost for new vehicles. Analyzing the guidelines of the five-year plan for the Soviet AI, one gets an impression that the problem of vehicle efficiency is paid much more attention than the problem of producing more cars and trucks. This is generally a healthy approach to a Soviet industry. However, it is difficult to see to what extent the targets will have a "mobilizing" effect on the workers in the AI and to what extent they will be implemented in automotive technology.

5.3. The Electrotechnical Industry

The electrotechnical industry (EI) is one of the oldest branches of the Soviet MBMW sector; the industry was started long before the 1917 revolution. The importance of the EI to the Soviets is determined by the fact that it manufactures machines and devices for the production, transmission, transformation and use of electrical energy. At present, the EI includes some 20 subbranches, each of which can be viewed as a product group. These product groups are as follows: turbogenerators, hydrogenerators, large electrical machines, electric motors, crane electrical equipment, electric locomotives, tractive electrical equipment, power rectifiers, transformers, high and low tension apparatus, electrothermal equipment, electric welding equipment, storage batteries, illuminating fittings, X-ray equipment, electric insulation materials, cable products and electric bulbs.

The EI is material intensive, with the proportion of materials in total cost of 70 to 80 percent (Nikitin, 1984, p.25). It consumes rolled ferrous metals, copper, lead, silver and other metals. Around 70 percent of the metals used in the technological process is utilized, and 30 percent is wasted, a typical problem for the Soviet MBMW sector. As in some other Soviet industries, the EI needs many types of specialized equipment for its technological process which are not manufactured by the Soviet machine tool industry or other MBMW branches. For this reason, the EI turns out the machines, tools, and equipment it needs for winding, insulating, saturating, assembling and other specific functions.

Table 5.6 reflects the input-output links for the Soviet EI. Among the industries indicated are those that are either suppliers to or users of EI products. Industries with zero values are those whose share in a rounded form is less than one percent. According to Table 5.6, the two biggest suppliers are ferrous metallurgy and the EI itself, with a 25 percent share of total supplies of material inputs. The biggest consumer of EI products is the MBMW sector that takes 45 percent of output, with the EI excluded, and 69 percent, with the EI counted within the sector. The only industry outside of the MBMW sector with a big claim on EI products is construction, with a 20 percent share.

Table 5.6. The Input-Output Links of the Soviet Electrotechnical Industry (Percent of Total)

Sector and Branch	Electrotechnical Purchases	Electrotechnical Sales
Metallurgy	25	2
Chemical	10	1
Electric Power	2	1
MBMW		
(except Electrotechnical Industry)	6	45
Electrotechnical Industry	25	24
Timber, Woodworking, and Paper	4	0
Construction Materials	6	0
Transport and Communications	15	NA
Construction	NA	20

Source: Kurbatova and Sokolov (1978, pp. 45 and 58).

Taking into account the complex and specific nature of EI products, their output is concentrated at specialized firms of the Ministry of Electrotechnical Industry. The ministry has 20 scientific research institutes which conduct applied research in the field at the ministry's request. The ministry also has a significant fund for science and technology that covered more than 70 percent of its R&D expenditures in the early 1980s (Nikitin, 1984, p.26). According to the ministry's information, each year about 500 products are discontinued, and the same number of new ones are introduced. In a two-year period, 1979-80, the total value of the EI's surcharge for improved product quality rose fourfold. The proportion of products officially certified as of the high-quality category accounted for almost half of the total value of output in 1983, one of the largest proportions in the entire MBMW sector (Nikitin, 1984, p.27). This would be a good sign for the Soviet EI if there were not numerous complaints on the quality of its products. The information on output by product group in monetary terms, physical units, and parameters of quality for the Soviet EI is reconstructed in Chapter 7.

5.4. Energy and Power Machinery

Energy and power machinery (EPM) is one of the traditional branches of the Soviet MBMW sector. It manufactures power units and equipment for generating steam, gas and other energy sources. Four major product groups are combined in the branch: turbines (steam, gas and hydraulic), steam boilers, diesels and reactors for nuclear power plants. For different types of plants, there are different combinations of power units (Nelidov, 1979, pp. 15-8). A power unit used in steam power plants incorporates a steam generator, a steam turbine, an electric generator and other turbine boiler equipment. The equipment includes devices for chemical water treatment and supply and condensation pumps. For nuclear power plants, a power unit consists of a reactor, a heat exchanger, a turbine and a power generator. A gas turbine unit contains a combustion chamber, a gas turbine and a turbogenerator. A hydraulic power unit includes a hydraulic turbine and a hydrogenerator.

The following are the chief Soviet plants that manufacture turbines:[9]

The 22 Party Congress Leningrad metalworking plant produces all types of steam, gas and hydraulic turbines, with the spectrum of power from 50 to 1,200 thousand kilowatts. The most typical are large steam turbines K-800-240, K-300-240, K-200-130, K-100-90, and K-50-90 for condensation power plants. The plant mastered the production of the first Soviet superturbine of 1,200 thousand kilowatts (K-1200-240). Among hydraulic turbines the most typical are those of 1,200, 640 and 220 thousand kilowatts; among gas turbines, of 150 thousand kilowatts.

The Kirov Khar'kov turbine plant manufactures steam turbines K-500-65/3000, K-500-60/1500, K-500-240-2, K-300-240, K-2220-44 and K-100-360/3600. Among the most advanced products, there is the first superlarge steam turbine with power of one million kilowatts (K-1000-60/1500).

The Voroshilov Ural'sk turbomotor plant specializes in medium steam turbines T-200/300-240-2, PT-135/165-130/15, T-110/120-130-4, P-100/107-130-15, T-50/60-130-6 and R-40/130-31.

The Zdanov Izhorsk plant is a supplier of both medium steam turbines and, increasingly, equipment for nuclear power plants. The Neva machine-building plant manufactures small turbines, with power of 12 to 18 thousand kilowatts. The Polzunov Kaluga turbine plant turns out turbines from 1.5 to 50 thousand kilowatts. Similar small turbines are produced by the Kaunas turbine and Syzran' turbine-building plants.

The following are the main plants that specialize in the production of boilers:[10]

The Taganrog *Krasnyi Kotel'shchik* plant manufactures large steam boilers, with capacity of 3,950 metric tons of steam per hour, for power units of 1,200 megawatts. There are also boilers of 670, 500 and less metric tons of steam per hour.

The Ordzhonikidze Podol'sk machine-building plant specializes in the production of steam boilers used in power units of 800, 400, 300 and 200 megawatts.

The Barnaul boiler plant produces large boilers for condensation and heat and electric power plants (*TETs*), including drum water heaters for heat and electric power plants.

The Belgorod boiler plant produces medium boilers, 20 to 75 metric tons of steam per hour, and Biysk boiler plant is specialized in small boilers, 2 to 20 metric tons of steam per hour.

The following are the biggest specialized plants that produce diesels and diesel generators: the Gor'kiy *Dvigatel' Revoliutsii* plant, the *Russkiy Diesel'* plant and the *Ekonomizer* plant. They manufacture a variety of diesels for stationary and mobile power plants and for other diesel engines and ships.

The *Atommash* plant in Volgodonsk began operation in the late

1970s. It manufactures nuclear reactors and heavy equipment for nuclear power plants. Such equipment is also supplied by the 22 Party Congress Leningrad metalworking plant, the Zhdanov Izhorsk plant, the Ordzhonikidze Podol'sk machine-building plant, the Kirov Khar'kov turbine plant and many other machine-building firms. As a result of massive supplies of equipment and other investment, there has been a rapid buildup of Soviet nuclear energy production. The capacity of Soviet nuclear power plants more than doubled in the 1981-85 period, from 12.5 to 28 million kilowatts (Nekrasov and Troitskii, 1981, p.135 and Grigor'ev and Zorin, 1987, p.50). At the beginning of that period, there were nine nuclear power plants in the USSR – Leningrad, Chernobyl', Novovoronezh, Kursk, Kol'sk, Beloiarsk, Rovno, Armenian and Bilibinsk. By 1986 they were joined by seven new plants – Kalinin, Ignalinsk, Iuzhno-Ukrainsk, Zaporozh'ye, Smolensk, Balakovo and Shevchenko.

The Chernobyl' disaster has slowed the growth of Soviet nuclear energy production, but, at the same time, it should have boosted production and investment in the EPM. As a matter of fact, the EPM is to undergo further modernization in the 12th five-year plan (1986-90) (*Ekonomicheskaia Gazeta* 46, 1985, p.6). In particular, the issue of the industry's automation is stressed, and the level of automation will be raised on the basis of microprocessor devices. New and more advanced equipment, especially for nuclear power plants, will be turned out or will pass the design stage. Examples are power units of 800 thousand kilowatts with fast-neutron reactors, units of 1,500 thousand kilowatts with thermal- neutron reactors and units of 1,600 thousand kilowatts with fast-neutron reactors. New equipment will be manufactured for nuclear plants for heat supply. The needs of remote provincial regions for small power units will be met to a greater extent than in the past. Among new types of equipment, there will be steam turbine units of 800 thousand kilowatts for the Kansk-Achinsk fuel and energy complex. Attention is also to be paid to the production of large gas turbines, from 120 to 150 thousand kilowatts, and to hydraulic turbines for high headwater and water-storage plants. Actual fulfillment will, of course, fall short of these projections. As one can see from Table 5.5, plan targets for the output of turbines and turbine generators fell short of plan targets by 5 and 16 percentage points, respectively, in 1986 and by 18 and 32 percentage points in 1987.

Chapter 6
Estimating Growth of the Automotive Industry

6.1. The Reconstruction Process

The output of the Soviet automotive industry (AI), shown in Figure 5.1, includes trucks, passenger cars, buses and trolley buses, autotractors and trailers, motorcycles, bicycles, auto engines and components. Several sources of information can be used for reconstruction of the output of the Soviet AI; the results will accordingly differ. One of the sources is provided by the input-output tables created by the Center for International Research of the U.S. Bureau of the Census. Table 6.1 reflects the data on the value of the AI's output from the four input-output tables for 1959, 1966, 1972 and 1982. The data are given in both producers' and purchasers' prices, but the output of the AI in all further calculations, with the exception of Section 6.3, is measured in producers' prices. The difference between the two types of prices is primarily the turnover tax levied on passenger cars, motorcycles and bicycles sold to consumers. The two other available sources of the information are Soviet ones. The first is the official growth index published in the statistical yearbooks and shown in a spliced form in Table 6.2, with 1959 chosen as the base. The second source is a study by a Soviet author that indicates that the value of AI's output in 1972 and 1973 was 9,175 million rubles and 10,381 million rubles, respectively, in 1967 comparable prices (Bakis, 1975, p.111).

The role of prices in measuring the AI's growth deserves a special note. The 1972 and 1973 outputs mentioned above are measured in 1967 prices, and, though there have been several changes in the MBMW comparable prices, the Soviets have maintained an unal-

153

154

Table 6.1. Output of the Soviet Automotive Industry from the
Input-Output Tables (Millions of Rubles)

Year	Producers' Prices	Purchasers' Prices
1959	2,590	3,084
1966	4,367	5,365
1972	8,838	11,473
1982	20,789	22,294

Sources: Gallik, et al. (1975, pp. 57 and 75 and 1983, pp. 41 and
69) and Kostinsky (1976, pp. 17 and 73 and 1987).

tered continuity of their growth indices. This in particular means
that, as new years are added to the already existing series and a
switch to the new comparable prices occurs, no corrections are made
in the previous time series on indices. Two factors are responsible.
First, any distortions in the indices from the failure to account for a
price change may be insignificant. Second, the required alterations
in all the historic data on outputs may be too costly. Without going
into details of these circumstances, it is important that the analysis
of real and inflationary growth of a Soviet industry is based on the
officially reported information, not on the data adjusted for different purposes. Otherwise, if the data are not original, they will not
reflect one of the components, most likely the inflationary one. For
that reason, we will use the growth indices in the form presented by
the Soviets, i.e., those compiled in Table 6.2.

Table 6.3 reports the AI's output value calculated by applying
the growth indices from Table 6.2 to the data on outputs in 1972
and 1973 from the Soviet source (Bakis, 1975). To avoid inevitable
discrepancies that emerge because of rounding off the growth indices
from Table 6.2, the pre-1972 figures in Table 6.3 are computed on
the basis of the 1972 output, and the rest, on the basis of the 1973
output. Table 6.4 compares the outputs of the AI calculated from the

Soviet sources (Table 6.3) with those from the input-output tables
(Table 6.1). For this purpose the third column in Table 6.4 shows
the ratio of the data from input-output tables to the data based on
the Soviet sources. As one can see from the ratios, the two types
of outputs are relatively close with the exception of 1959, when the
input-output value exceeds the value from the Soviet sources by
almost 30 percent.

Table 6.2.   The Official Growth Index for the Soviet Automotive
Industry (1959=100)

Year	Growth Index	Year	Growth Index
1960	112	1973	518
1961	126	1974	580
1962	144	1975	631
1963	159	1976	679
1964	172	1977	737
1965	190	1978	813
1966	219	1979	875
1967	249	1980	916
1968	276	1981	962
1969	307	1982	989
1970	343	1983	1,017
1971	398	1984	1,063
1972	456	1985	1,118

Sources: *Narkhoz SSSR* (1964, p.182, 1970, p.205, 1974, p.238,
1980, p.164, and 1985, p.129).

At the following step of our analysis, we decompose the total AI
output by product group. In Soviet literature the appropriate percentage breakdowns are available for 1970 and 1976 (Vlasov, et al.,
1973, p.134 and 1978, p.103). These breakdowns will be the starting

point of the decomposition process. Unfortunately, the production of passenger cars and trucks is counted in Soviet statistics as one item, the automobiles group. Our plan is to divide this group, too, into two subgroups – passenger cars and trucks. After such a division is accomplished, we will use the resultant 1970 and 1976 proportions for estimating a similar breakdown for 1982. As a result, it will be possible to find the AI output by product group for 1970, 1976, and 1982. These outputs, in turn, will be used for estimating the real and inflationary components of the passenger car production growth in 1970, 1976 and 1982.

Table 6.3. The Output of the Automotive Industry Calculated from Soviet Sources (Millions of Rubles)

Year	Output	Year	Output
1959	2,012	1973	10,381
1960	2,254	1974	11,624
1961	2,535	1975	12,646
1962	2,897	1976	13,608
1963	3,199	1977	14,770
1964	3,461	1978	16,293
1965	3,823	1979	17,535
1966	4,406	1980	18,357
1967	5,010	1981	19,279
1968	5,553	1982	19,820
1969	6,177	1983	20,381
1970	6,901	1984	21,303
1971	8,008	1985	22,405
1972	9,175		

Sources: Table 6.2 and Bakis (1975, p.111).

The physical production of passenger cars and trucks is shown in Table 6.5. One of the purposes of this table is to demonstrate an unusually rapid expansion in Soviet passenger car production. While

Table 6.4. Comparison of the Automotive Industry's Outputs
Calculated from Soviet Sources and from Input-Output
Tables

Year	Input-Output X, Millions of Rubles	Soviet Sources Y, Millions of Rubles	The X/Y Ratio
1959	2,590	2,012	1.29
1966	4,367	4,406	.99
1972	8,838	9,175	.96
1982	20,789	19,820	1.05

Sources: Tables 6.1 and 6.3.

the output of trucks also steadily rose, a thirteen-year period, from 1965 to 1978, was necessary for it to double. Car production more than doubled in just two years, from 1970 to 1972. As a matter of fact, the greatest annual growth of output of passenger cars was in 1971 when the number of new cars rose by almost 54 percent, followed by gradually decelerating but impressive 1972, 1973, and 1974 growth rates of 38, 26, and 22 percent, respectively. This growth was caused by the construction of the *Volga* automobile plant that turned out its first vehicles in 1970 and reached its full production capacity by 1975.

The breakdowns of the AI outputs for 1970 and 1976 are reported in Table 6.6. The first item in Table 6.6, the proportion of automobiles in the total AI output, is of prime importance for the reconstruction process. This proportion rose from 50.7 to 52.5 percent in the 1970-76 period, while the proportions of other items dropped. Along with the greater attention paid to the production of trucks, the unprecedented growth of the passenger car output discussed above was the chief factor. Bearing in mind the goal of dividing the production of automobiles between passenger cars and

Table 6.5. Soviet Production of Passenger Cars and Trucks
(Thousands)

	Cars		Trucks	
Year	Production	Growth Rate, Percent	Production	Growth Rate, Percent
1960	139	11.2	362	3.7
1961	149	7.2	381	5.2
1962	166	11.4	382	0.3
1963	173	4.2	382	0
1964	185	6.9	385	0.8
1965	201	8.6	380	-1.3
1966	230	14.4	408	7.4
1967	252	2.6	437	7.1
1968	280	11.1	478	9.4
1969	294	5.0	504	5.4
1970	344	17.0	525	4.2
1971	529	53.8	565	7.6
1972	730	38.0	597	5.7
1973	917	25.6	629	5.4
1974	1,119	22.0	666	5.9
1975	1,201	7.3	696	4.5
1976	1,239	3.2	716	2.9
1977	1,280	3.3	734	2.5
1978	1,312	2.5	762	3.8
1979	1,314	0.2	780	2.4
1980	1,327	1.0	787	0.9
1981	1,324	-0.2	787	0
1982	1,307	-1.3	NA	
1983	1,315	0.6	NA	
1984	1,327	0.9	NA	
1985	1,332	0.4	NA	

Sources: *Narkhoz SSSR* (1968, p.261, 1974, p.249, 1980, p.171,
1983, p.188, and 1985, p.170) and *Kratkii avtomobil'nyi
spravochnik* (Moscow: Transport, 1985, p.6).

trucks, we apply the proportions from Table 6.6 to the 1970 and 1976 outputs from Table 6.3 to find production by product group. The results are shown in Table 6.7.

Table 6.6.   The Breakdown by Product Group of the Soviet
Automotive Industry (Percent)

Product Group	1970	1976
Automobiles	50.7	52.5
Buses	4.2	3.9
Engines	7.3	6.7
Special Automobiles	10.4	7.7
Autotractor Trailers	4.4	3.6
Automotive Electrical Equipment	6.2	5.6
Automotive Components	10.9	7.8
Motorcycles, Bicycles, and Components	5.9	3.7
Bearings	–	8.5
Total Automotive Industry	100.0	100.0

Sources: Vlasov (1973, p.134 and 1978, p.103).

To split the outputs of passenger cars and trucks, we will directly calculate the value of car output, so that the truck production will be the difference between the total output for automobiles and the calculated value. For this purpose, the information on car production by make and model and their prices is to be used. For every car model the Soviets publish the information on the time period when it was turned out. Collecting the makes and models for 1970 and 1976 yields the information on the types of cars produced in those two years shown in Table 6.8. We include only prime models in Table 6.8. In addition, there are some modifications of those models, especially by the *Volga* automobile plant. There are also several smaller plants that mostly produce the modifications of the cars listed in Table 6.8. Although some less important modifications are not explicitly listed, they will be counted in total production figures for 1970 and 1976.

Table 6.7. Output by Product Group of the Soviet Automotive Industry (Millions of Rubles)

Product Group	1970	1976
Automobiles	3,499	7,144
Buses	290	531
Engines	504	912
Special Automobiles	718	1,048
Autotractor Trailers	303	490
Automotive Electrical Equipment	428	762
Automotive Components	752	1,061
Motorcycles, Bicycles, and Components	407	503
Bearings	–	1,157
Total Automotive Industry	6,901	13,608

Sources: Tables 6.3 and 6.6.

According to the Soviet sources, the planned index of individual wholesale prices in the Soviet AI did not change in the 1970-75 period (Iakovets, 1974, p.95). Based on this assumption and taking into consideration that, in the process of the revision of the 1973 wholesale prices, the price lists (*tsenniki*) were published, we will use the prices from a *tsennik* as prices for the 1970 models, as reported in Table 6.9.

To estimate the value of the passenger car production for 1970, we then turn to the data on physical output by make and model. The official Soviet statistical sources do not publish this information. The only Soviet source available to us demonstrates the distribution of the *Zhiguli* make by model in the 1970-75 period; these data are in Table 6.10. We will also use the information available in this country that specifies Soviet production by make of car (Welihozkiy,

Table 6.8. Types of Soviet Cars Produced in 1970 and 1976

Plant	Model	
	1970	1976
Volga Automobile Plant (VAZ)	VAZ-2101 *Zhiguli*	VAZ-2101, 2102, 2103, 2106 *Zhiguli*
Lenin Komsomol Automobile Plant (AZLK)	*Moskvich*-408	*Moskvich*-2136, 2137, 2138, 2140
Izhevsk Automobile Plant (IZh)	*Moskvich*-412	IZh-2125
Zaporozh'ye Automobile Plant (ZAZ)	ZAZ-966, 966V, 969, 969V *Zaporozhets*	ZAZ-968A, 969A *Zaporozhets*
Gor'kiy Automobile Plant (GAZ)	GAZ-24, 24-01 *Volga*, GAZ-13 *Chaika*	GAZ-24, 24-01, 24-02 *Volga*, GAZ-13 *Chaika*

Source: *Kratkii automobil'nyi spravochnik* (1985, p.25-43).

Table 6.9. Wholesale Prices of Soviet Passenger Cars in 1970
(Rubles)

Model	Price
VAZ-2101 *Zhiguli*	2,930
Moskvich-408	1,380
Moskvich-412	1,700
ZAZ-966 (968) *Zaporozhets*	1,780
ZAZ-966V *Zaporozhets*	1,530
ZAZ-969 *Zaporozhets*	1,490
GAZ-24 *Volga*	2,730

Source: *Tsennik No. 42* (1972, pp. 71-9).

1979, p.815). The 1970 output from this source is shown in the
second column of Table 6.11; the models in Table 6.11 are listed
in accordance with their specification in Table 6.8. However, estimated from different sources, plant outputs in the second column
of the table do not sum to the official total physical output of 344
thousand cars, the number which follows from Table 6.5. To arrive
at this total, we adjusted the data in Table 6.11 for the discrepancy.
For that purpose, all the outputs with the exception of *Zhiguli*, for
which the official production is given in Table 6.10, were raised by
the same proportion. The adjusted outputs are shown in the third
column of Table 6.11. In essence, the adjustment takes care of the
overlooked modifications of the base models. The last column in Table 6.11 shows the percentage of each make of car in total physical
production.

Table 6.10. Production of VAZ *Zhiguli* by Model in the 1970–75
Period (Physical Units)

Year	VAZ-2101	VAZ-2102	VAZ-2103	VAZ-21011	Total
1970	21,530				21,530
1971	172,175	185			172,360
1972	311,273	11,533			322,806
1973	379,007	46,233	67,060		402,300
1974	371,620	53,540	195,043	18,006	638,209
1975	212,871	55,282	220,522	178,510	667,185

Source: Vlasov (1978, p.31).

Table 6.11. Soviet Production of Passenger Cars by Model in
1970 (Thousands)

Model	Estimated Output	Adjusted Output	Percent of Total
VAZ-2101 *Zhiguli*	22	22	6.4
Moskvich-408 and Modifications	104	122	35.5
Moskvich-412 and Modifications	32	38	11.0
ZAZ-966 and ZAZ-969 *Zaporozhets* and Modifications	87	102	29.7
GAZ-24 *Volga* and Modifications	51	60	17.4
Total	296	344	100.0

Sources: Table 6.8 and Welihozkiy (1978, p.815).

The value of Soviet production of passenger cars is estimated in
Table 6.12 by multiplying the wholesale prices from Table 6.9 and
adjusted physical outputs from Table 6.11. What we need for this
computation are individual outputs and prices by model. Yet what

Table 6.12. The Value of Soviet Production of Passenger Cars in
1970 (Millions of Rubles)

Model	Production	Percent of Total
VAZ-2101 *Zhiguli*	64	10.3
Moskvich-408	168	26.9
Moskvich-412	65	10.4
Zaporozhets	163	26.1
VAZ-24 *Volga*	164	26.3
Total	624	100.0

Sources: Tables 6.9 and 6.11.

we may possess, as in the case of *Zaporozhets*, is the combination
of individual prices and outputs by the make of car. In such a case
we find the average price of the make of car as a sample mean from
the model prices, i.e., we assume equal proportions for the models
produced by a given plant. (In light of the close distribution of
individual prices, this assumption may be plausible in most cases.)

Now, after estimating the value of the passenger car production
in 1970, we can estimate the truck production. From Table 6.7, the
total output of automobiles was equal to 3,499 million rubles in 1970
and, from Table 6.12, the output of passenger cars amounted to 624
million rubles. Finding the value of the truck production as the
difference between the two numbers yields 2,875 million rubles. We
detail Tables 6.6 and 6.7 for 1970 by splitting the entries for automobiles production in accordance with our findings. The reconstructed
outputs and breakdown for 1970 are reported in Table 6.13.

The second part of the reconstruction process is focused on the
1976 output. This part is similar to the 1970 part, but it has its own
specifics in terms of both outputs and prices. To begin with, Table
6.14 provides the data on physical outputs by make of car which,
this time, sum to the official total car production from Table 6.5.

As one can see from the comparison of Tables 6.11 and 6.14, the *Volga* automobile plant's share of physical production of Soviet cars rose from 6.4 to 55.2 percent in the 1970-76 period.

Table 6.13. The Reconstructed Outputs and Breakdown of the Soviet Automotive Industry in 1970 (Millions of Rubles)

Model	Value	Percent of Total
Passenger Cars	624	9.0
Trucks	2,875	41.7
Buses	290	4.2
Engines	504	7.3
Special Automobiles	718	10.4
Autotractor Trailers	303	4.4
Automotive Electrical Equipment	428	6.2
Automotive Components	752	10.9
Motorcycles, Bicycles, and Components	407	5.9
Total Automotive Industry	6,901	100.0

Sources: Tables 6.6, 6.7, and 6.12.

We use the information on total production of *Zhiguli* from Table 6.14 to detail it by model. Table 6.10 provides such a specification, but only until 1975. Applying the 1975 proportions from Table 6.10 to the 1976 output, we estimate the 1976 *Zhiguli* production by model. The actual distribution by model may, of course, be different. The difference is not likely to be significant, given the low 2.5 percent growth of output between 1975 and 1976. The results of estimation are indicated in Table 6.15.

Table 6.14. The Output of Passenger Cars in 1976 (Thousands)

Make	Output	Percent of Total
VAZ *Zhiguli*	684	55.2
Moskvich (AZLK)	176	14.2
Moskvich (IZh)	166	13.4
Zaporozhets	143	11.5
GAZ-24 *Volga*	70	5.7
Total	1,239	100.0

Source: Welihozkiy (1979, p.815).

No information is available on the 1976 wholesale prices for Soviet passenger cars. There are two standard problems with using the 1973 prices from Table 6.9 for that purpose: wholesale prices might have changed, and some of the 1976 models were not manufactured in 1973. Therefore, we use the information from Table 6.9 in combination with another source on the 1981 prices presented in Table 6.16. The comparison of the 1973 and 1981 wholesale prices of *VAZ-2101 Zhiguli* in Tables 6.9 and 6.16 shows that the price index was 0.75 in that eight-year period (2183÷2930). Since a reduction in Soviet car wholesale prices is the result of initially high and eventually declining production costs, we assume a constant rate of reduction. As a result, in the case of *VAZ-2101*, the wholesale price dropped 3.5 percent annually $(1 - .75^{1/8})$. Applying this rate of decline to the 1973 price of 2,930 rubles yields the 1976 price of 2,633 rubles. Since the 1973 prices for *VAZ-2102* and *VAZ-2103 Zhiguli* were not available, we use the 1981 prices for those models. (Despite the fact that these two models were manufactured since 1971 and 1972, respectively, *tsennik* for the 1973 price revision was prepared two to three years in advance and omits their prices.) If there was an actual difference between the 1976 and 1981 prices, the 1981 prices must have been lower by analogy with the *VAZ-2101*. Therefore, assuming the 1981 instead of 1976 prices would probably underestimate the inflationary component of growth.

Table 6.15.   The Production of *VAZ Zhiguli* by Model in 1976
(Thousands)

Model	Output	Percent of Total
VAZ-2101 and Modifications	401	58.6
VAZ-2102 and Modifications	56	8.2
VAZ-2103 and Modifications	227	33.2
Total	684	100.0

Sources: Tables 6.10 and 6.14.

Unlike the *VAZ* case, the wholesale prices of *Moskvich*-412 increased in the 1973-81 period. From Tables 6.9 and 6.16, the index value would be 1.48 (2511÷1700). This may be explained by the fact that the price of *Moskvich* reported in Table 6.16 is an average for many modifications. Average prices may rise as a result of the introduction of more expensive new models, despite the general tendency of prices for given models to decline. Taking this into account, we assume a constant rate of price increase, of 5 percent ($1.48^{1/8}$ - 1). Applying this rate to the 1973 price of 1,700 rubles results in the 1976 price of 1,968 rubles.

Since there is no information on the prices of *Zaporozhets* in Table 6.16, we will use the 1973 prices for the *ZAZ* models. In other words, we make an assumption that there were no price increases for that make of car between 1973 and 1976. For the *GAZ Volga* models, the comparison of the data in Tables 6.9 and 6.16 for the base model *GAZ*-24 *Volga* reveals that its price rose by less than 3 percent between 1973 and 1981. Because of such an insignificant change and because of the lack of the 1973 prices for the modifications *GAZ*-24-01 and *GAZ*-24-02 *Volga*, the 1981 prices are used here for the *GAZ* models. The 1976 wholesale prices resulting from our estimation and assumptions are in Table 6.17, where the prices of *Zaporozhets* are averaged. Multiplying the prices from Table 6.17 by the physical outputs from Tables 6.14 and 6.15 yields the estimates of the value of the 1976 production of passenger cars in Table 6.18. As one can see from the comparison of Tables 6.12 and 6.18, the *Volga* automobile plant's models, as a percentage of the total value of Soviet passenger car production, rose sixfold from 1970 to 1976. In money terms, the plant's share approaches two-thirds of total output while, in physical terms, it remains within a 55 percent range.

Table 6.16.   The 1981 Wholesale Prices of Soviet Passenger
Cars (Rubles)

Model	Price
VAZ-2101 *Zhiguli* and Modifications	2,183
VAZ-2102 *Zhiguli* and Modifications	2,138
VAZ-2103 *Zhiguli* and Modifications	2,716
Moskvich-412	2,511
GAZ-24 *Volga*	2,800
GAZ-24-01 *Volga*	2,661
GAZ-24-02 *Volga*	2,980

Source: Working Papers.

As in the procedure for 1970, we estimate truck production in 1976. From Table 6.7, the total value of 1976 automobile production was 7,144 million rubles, and, from Table 6.18, the value of passenger car production was 2,891 million rubles. Hence, the value of truck production, as a residual, was 4,253 million rubles. On this basis, the relevant total output and total percentage in Tables 6.6 and 6.7 can be decomposed. The reconstructed outputs by product group and the percentage breakdown of the AI in 1976 are reported in Table 6.19. The comparison of Tables 6.13 and 6.19 shows that, as a result of a rapid buildup of Soviet passenger car production in the 1970-75 period, its share in the total AI output made an impressive gain from 9 percent in 1970 to 21.2 percent in 1976.

Table 6.17. Estimated 1976 Wholesale Prices of Soviet Passenger
Cars (Rubles)

Make and Model	Price
VAZ -2101 *Zhiguli*	2,633
VAZ-2102 *Zhiguli*	2,138
VAZ-2103 *Zhiguli*	2,716
Moskvich	1,968
Zaporozhets	1,600
GAZ-24 *Volga*	2,800
GAZ-24-01 *Volga*	2,661
GAZ-24-02 *Volga*	2,980

Sources: Tables 6.9 and 6.16.

Table 6.18. The Value of Soviet Production of Passenger Cars in
1976 (Millions of Rubles)

Make of Car	Production	Percent of Total
VAZ *Zhiguli*	1,792	62.0
Moskvich	673	23.3
ZAZ *Zaporozhets*	229	7.9
GAZ *Volga*	197	6.8
Total	2,891	100.0

Sources: Tables 6.14, 6.15, and 6.17.

Table 6.19. The Reconstructed Outputs and Breakdown of the
Soviet Automotive Industry in 1976 (Millions of Rubles)

Model	Value	Percent of Total
Passenger Cars	2,891	21.2
Trucks	4,253	31.3
Buses	531	3.9
Engines	912	6.7
Special Automobiles	1,048	7.7
Autotractor Trailers	490	3.6
Automotive Electrical Equipment	762	5.6
Automotive Components	1,061	7.8
Motorcycles, Bicycles, and Components	503	3.7
Bearings	1,157	8.5
Total Automotive Industry	13,608	100.0

Sources: Tables 6.6, 6.7, and 6.18.

The third step of the estimation process is intended to estimate
the 1982 production. The problem is more complex than at the first
two steps since there is no breakdown of the AI for 1982 similar to
those for 1970 and 1976. Along with other indicators, we estimate
such a breakdown. We begin with the outputs by make of car. Our
starting point is the total physical production of passenger cars of 1.3
millions in 1982 (*Narkhoz SSSR*, 1982, p.171). According to another
Soviet source, in the 1981-85 period the *Volga* automobile plant was
not supposed to raise its annual production above the 1980 level of
720 thousand vehicles (Boldyreva, 1985, p.132). Other than that,
we do not have the distribution of 1982 production by make of car.
We therefore turn to the 1976 distribution and, comparing, notice
that the total production of all cars with the exception of *Zhiguli*

Table 6.20. The Output of Passenger Cars in 1982 (Thousands)

Make	Output	Percent of Total
VAZ *Zhiguli*	720	55.1
Moskvich (AZLK)	186	14.2
Moskvich (IZh)	176	13.5
Zaporozhets	151	11.5
GAZ-24 *Volga*	74	5.7
Total	1,307	100.0

Sources: Table 6.14, *Narkhoz SSSR* (1982, p.171), and
Boldyreva (1985, p.132).

was 555 and 587 thousand cars in 1976 and 1982, respectively. This nearly constant level of outputs may justify the assumption made above that the 1976 and 1982 percentage distributions by make of car other than *Zhiguli* were similar. The 1982 outputs estimated on the basis of this assumption are shown in Table 6.20.

The information on the major types of models produced in 1982 is provided in Table 6.21. Although, as one can see from comparing Tables 6.8 and 6.21, more *Zhiguli* models were manufactured in 1982 than in 1976, most of them were the continuation of the base *VAZ*-2101 or *VAZ*-2103 models. For this reason, we still consider here the base models *VAZ*-2101, *VAZ*-2102 and *VAZ*-2103 *Zhiguli*. Table 6.22 presents the distribution of the total *VAZ* production by base model; it is the same as the 1981 distribution, which was available.

To find the value of 1982 production, the 1981 wholesale prices from Table 6.16 are multiplied by physical outputs from Table 6.20. But, to estimate the output of *Zaporozhets*, we have to assume constant prices in the 1973-82 period and use the prices from Table 6.9. The resultant value of 1982 production is shown in Table 6.23. By relating the data in Tables 6.3 and 6.23, we find that passenger cars were 15.5 percent of the total value of the AI's output in 1982. The other product groups' proportions cannot, however, be estimated so directly. We must instead relate the 1976 proportions from Table 6.19 to the growth rates by product group. These growth rates are shown in the third column of Table 6.24. They were obtained for trucks, buses, autotractor trailers, and automotive components on the basis of growth figures from Soviet sources for 1976-80. In cases when the percentages for other groups were not available, they were estimated by analogy with other similar items. For motorcycles and bicycles, we assume that their value of production rose at the same rate as in the previous 1970-76 period. Using the 1976 proportions and the data on output growth, we calculated the 1982 proportions for product groups other than passenger cars. The estimation process is a simple mathematical problem.

Table 6.21. Major Types of Soviet Passenger Cars Produced in 1982

Plant	Model
Volga Automobile Plant (VAZ)	VAZ-2101, 2102, 2103, 2105, 2106, 2107 *Zhiguli* and Modifications
Lenin *Komsomol* Automobile Plant (AZLK)	*Moskvich*-2137, 2140 and Modifications
Izhevsk Automobile Plant (IZh)	IZh-2125
Zaporozh'ye Automobile Plant (ZAZ)	ZAZ-968M, ZAZ (LuAZ)-969M *Zaporozhets*
Gor'kiy Automobile Plant (GAZ)	GAZ-24, GAZ-24-01, 24-02 *Volga*, GAZ-14 *Chaika*

Source: *Kratkii avtomobil'nyi spravochnik* (1985, pp. 25-43).

Table 6.22.   The Production of *VAZ Zhiguli* by Model in 1982
(Thousands)

Model	Output	Percent of Total
VAZ-2101 and Modifications	386	53.6
VAZ-2102 and Modifications	50	7.0
VAZ-2103 and Modifications	284	39.4
Total	720	100.0

Source: Working Papers.

Table 6.23.   The Value of Soviet Production of Passenger Cars in
1982 (Millions of Rubles)

Make of Car	Production	Percent of Total
VAZ *Zhiguli*	1,721	55.9
Moskvich	909	29.5
ZAZ *Zaporozhets*	242	7.9
GAZ *Volga*	208	6.7
Total	3,080	100.0

Sources: Tables 6.9, 6.16, 6.20, and 6.22.

Suppose total output z consists of n components $x_1, ..., x_n$. Find the proportions $w_1^1 = x_1^1/z^1, ..., w_n^1 = x_n^1/z^1$ in the current year 1, given the proportions $w_1^0 = x_1^0/z^0, ..., w_n^0 = x_n^0/z^0$ in the base year 0 and the growth ratios $r_1 = (x_1^1 - x_1^0)/x_1^0, ..., r_n = (x_n^1 - x_n^0)/x_n^0$. Using this information, the base year components are $x_1^0 = w_1^0 z^0, ..., x_n^0 = w_n^0 z^0$, and the current year components, accordingly, are $x_1^1 = (1 + r_1)w_1^0 z^0, ..., x_n^1 = (1 + r_n)w_n^0 z^0$. Choosing one of the components, for example x_n^1, as a *numeraire*, we can obtain the ratios

$$d_1 = \frac{x_1^1}{x_n^1} = \frac{(1+r_1)w_1^\circ}{(1+r_n)w_n^\circ}$$

$$\vdots$$

$$d_{n-1} = \frac{x_{n-1}^1}{x_n^1} = \frac{(1+r_{n-1})w_{n-1}^\circ}{(1+r_n)w_n^\circ}$$

$$d_n = 1.$$

Table 6.24. Estimated Breakdown of the Soviet Automotive Industry for 1982

Product Group	1976 Breakdown	1982/1976 Growth	1982 Breakdown
Passenger Cars	21.2	6.5	15.5
Trucks	31.3	19.5	28.6
Buses	3.9	49.7	4.5
Engines	6.7	19.5	6.1
Special Automobiles	7.7	19.5	7.0
Autotractor Trailers	3.6	171.5	7.5
Automotive Electrical Equipment	5.6	62.7	7.0
Automotive Components	7.8	62.7	9.7
Motorcycles, Bicycles, and Components	3.7	23.6	3.5
Bearings	8.5	62.7	10.6

Sources: Tables 6.3, 6.19, and 6.23 and *Avtomobil'naia Promyshlennost'* (1, 1977, pp. 1-2 and 1, 1981, p.1).

It is easy to demonstrate that the unknown weights can be found as $w_1^1 = d_1 / \Sigma d_i, ..., w_n^1 = d_n / \Sigma d_i$.

In the computation of d ratios, the proportions w_i° are the breakdowns from the second column of Table 6.24, and the growth ratios

r_i are the decimal equivalents of the percentages in the third column of Table 6.24. These proportions then can be used to determine the values of output by product group in 1982. The estimates are in Table 6.25. Since passenger car production in Table 6.25 was estimated independently, not as a percentage of total production, and then related to truck production, the product group outputs in Table 6.25 do not sum exactly to the AI total.

This concludes the reconstruction process for the output of the AI in 1970, 1976, and 1982. This information can now be used to estimate the real and inflationary components of the growth of passenger car production. For that purpose, we also consider the issue of estimating passenger car quality. Change of quality is an important factor; an adjustment is needed when the output growth in value terms is to be split between its real and inflationary components.

Table 6.25. Reconstructed Outputs of the Soviet Automotive
Industry for 1982 (Millions of Rubles)

Model	Output
Passenger Cars	3,080
Trucks	5,668
Buses	892
Engines	1,209
Special Automobiles	1,387
Autotractor Trailers	1,486
Automotive Electrical Equipment	1,387
Automotive Components	1,922
Motorcycles, Bicycles, and Components	694
Bearings	2,101
Total Automotive Industry	19,820

Sources: Tables 6.3 and 6.24.

Table 6.26. The Value of Soviet Passenger Car Production
(Millions of Rubles)

Year	Production	Percent of Total Automotive Industry
1970	624	9.0
1976	2,891	21.2
1982	3,080	15.5

Sources: Tables 6.13, 6.19, 6.23, and 6.24.

6.2. Quality and Growth of Soviet Passenger Car Production

The results of our reconstruction process indicate that there was a dramatic increase in the value of Soviet passenger car production from 1970 to 1976. As Table 6.26 shows, that value rose more than 4.6 times from 1970 to 1976 and then almost ceased growing in the 1976-82 period. How much of that overall growth was real and how much inflationary? Physical output would be the best measure of real growth, as some Soviet economists have suggested, but if there are quality improvements, they would be overlooked. Our plan is first to adjust physical output for quality change and then to compare the adjusted growth in physical output with the growth of output in money terms. For that purpose, we use the index of average price adjusted for quality (2.18) which we will rewrite here:

$$\bar{I}_t^r = \frac{\sum p_{it} q_{it}}{\sum r_{it} q_{it}} \bigg/ \frac{\sum p_{io} q_{io}}{\sum r_{io} q_{io}}, \tag{6.1}$$

where $\bar{I}_t^r$ = index of product group's average price adjusted for quality in year t; p_{io}, q_{io}, and r_{io} = price, quantity, and indicator (index) of quality of the ith product in the base year 0, respectively; p_{i1}, q_{i1}, and r_{i1} = price, quantity, and indicator (index) of quality of the ith product in the current year t, respectively.

What formula (6.1) basically does is to compare the average price of a product group $(\sum p_i q_i / \sum q_i)$ per average unit of product quality

$(\Sigma r_i q_i / \Sigma q_i)$ for the two time periods. While the values of output computed above allow us to find the average prices, indicators of quality are yet to be defined in each specific case. For some product groups, a single important characteristic of quality could be selected; this is done in Chapters 7 and 8. However, passenger cars are not such a group. Therefore, we build an index based on several important characteristics of passenger car quality. In other words, the idea of this approach is that several characteristics of passenger cars important to quality should be integrated in a single measurable index of product quality.

In the West, different characteristics of passenger car quality such as comfort, durability, fuel economy, horsepower, maneuverability, maintenance cost, and style are valued, but some are not measurable. Different proxies have been used, especially in studies on hedonic price indices. Thus, in studying hedonic price indices for British passenger cars, the following characteristics were considered: fuel consumption, horsepower, length and passenger area (Cowling and Cubbin, 1972). There are no "objective" parameters of quality, and different researchers may choose varying sets of proxies for the same theoretical characteristics. The characteristics may even be interpreted differently depending on cultural traditions, the extent of urbanization, the state of the roads, the availability of alternative means of transportation, income disparities and other conditions.

Comfort is usually characterized by the indicators that depend on either interior volume or passenger area, such as leg room, elbow room and front head room. *Gas Mileage Guide* reports an interior volume index for each vehicle sold in the U.S. However, there is no similar information on Soviet passenger cars; the closest data measure either car length and width, or base and gauge, which correlate with car passenger area.

Durability is generally a variable that can be represented by several proxies. One, for example, is the number of engine crankshaft revolutions for each mile of travel in high gear. Assuming that total engine crankshaft life-revolutions for each car are fixed and that maintenance habits do not influence inter-model comparisons of survival rates, then the lower the engine revolutions per mile, the longer the engine's life. Unfortunately, the availability of reliable information for the measurement of durability is a problem that is especially crucial in the case of Soviet products. The Soviets' indicator of vehicle durability is the mileage before the first capital repair, but this is an unreliable measure even if the data were available.

Fuel economy means high mileage per gallon (MPG) of gasoline. Both *Consumer Reports* and *Gas Mileage Guide* provide MPG for the U.S. auto market, but the data are based on different testing procedures. The U.S. manufacturer's tests may exaggerate fuel economy. This is especially true in the Soviet case, where testing conditions are far from realistic. Thus, Soviet instructions specify that car fuel consumption is to be measured "at a dry straight section of a flat highway." (*Za Rulem*, 11, 1966, p.5). This prevents a direct comparison of fuel consumption data for the U.S. and the Soviet Union. The Soviet data probably correspond to the U.S. data on fuel consumption on highways, with no traffic and in ideal weather conditions.

Horsepower is measured as the maximum horsepower output of a standard engine equipped as it would be when installed in the vehicle. Other things being equal, the greater the horsepower of the car, the more powerful and more expensive it is. In the U.S., *Consumer Reports* publishes the information on "advertised net horsepower." Of all the parameters of vehicle quality, horsepower is one of the most reliable; even though in the Soviet Union it is measured under laboratory conditions.

Maneuverability is measured as the turning circle divided by the overall car length. To an extent, car length also characterizes car luxury, and in some instances it is actually used as a crude index for luxury.

It is impossible to establish an unambiguous set of indicators of car quality since it is the consumer who is to make the final determination. But some characteristics of passenger cars are relevant to quality and affect production costs. To put it differently, we see the issue of quality improvement as a factor raising the cost of production. (This is similar to a Soviet approach of looking at product quality from the producer's, rather than the consumer's standpoint.) For example, the greater the horsepower or the size of a car, the more costly is it to produce the car. On the basis of these considerations, the following characteristics of Soviet cars are studied here: capacity as a number of occupants, size, weight, engine volume, horsepower and fuel consumption. These characteristics are used in building a quality index for Soviet cars the production of which was reconstructed for 1970, 1976, and 1982.

Table 6.27 reports the characteristics of Soviet passenger cars manufactured in 1970. In this case as well as in others, the characteristics are taken from different Soviet sources. In many instances, different sources provide different magnitudes of the same technical parameters. This may be caused by the fact that the same model might have been produced over a long period of time, with gradually changing parameters. Therefore the timing of the publications is important. We tried to choose the sources in the proper historic perspective which, in the case of Table 6.27, means the data published closer to 1970. This approach would guarantee that any later changes in technical characteristics would not be reflected in the set of data pertinent to an earlier period. One of the changing characteristics, for example, is the fuel consumption, and its reliability is difficult to determine. The hope is that, if it is exaggerated, the extent of the exaggeration is the same for different time periods.

The first step in building the quality index is the averaging of the characteristics in Table 6.27 by make of car. In all cases when the composition of output by model was estimated, the quality characteristics of an "average" car are found as a weighted average, with physical outputs of cars serving as weights. When the composition of output by model is not given, as in the case of *Zaporozhets*, the average characteristics of a car make are computed as a sample mean. The results produced by averaging the data in Table 6.27 are depicted in Table 6.28. One of the problems of using the information in Table 6.28 for the computation of the quality index is that the weight of each of the six factors depicted there would depend on the unit of account and scale. Thus, should we switch from square meters to square centimeters in measuring the size, the weight of this variable in the index would accordingly rise. This is a rather standard problem. To eliminate the effect of scale, we introduce a normalization procedure.

Table 6.27. The Characteristics of Soviet Passenger Cars Produced in 1970

Model	Occupants	Size (Length times Width), Square Meters	Weight, Kilograms	Engine Volume, Cubic Centimeters	Horsepower	Fuel Consumption, MPG
VAZ-2101 *Zhiguli*	5	4.073·1.611=6.56	955	1,198	60	26
Moskvich-408	4	4.120·1.510=6.22	990	1,358	50	21
Moskvich-412	4-5	4.120·1.550=6.39	1,045	1,475	75	21
Moskvich-412IE	4-5	4.120·1.550=6.39	1,045	1,475	75	27
ZAZ-966 *Zaporozhets*	4	3.765·1.490=5.61	780	1,198	40	32
ZAZ-966V *Zaporozhets*	4	3.765·1.490=5.61	820	887	30	29
ZAZ-969 *Zaporozhets*	4	3.765·1.490=5.61	870	887	40	26
GAZ-24 *Volga*	5	4.760·1.820=8.66	1,420	2,445	100	25
GAZ-24-01 *Volga*	5	4.760·1.820=8.66	1,420	2,445	85	25

Sources: *Za Rulem* (11, 1964, pp. 12-3; 11, 1966, pp. 5-6; 5, 1969, p.16; 4, 1972, p.8; 11, 1972, pp. 6-7; 7, 1977, p.19) and *Tsennik No. 42* (1972, pp. 71-9).

To normalize the data in Table 6.28, the characteristics of one of the makes of car will be used as a unit of scale and divided into the similar characteristics of all the cars. Although, in principle, any of the rows in the table could be picked for that purpose, we chose *Zaporozhets* as a car whose characteristics are generally inferior. In such a case, the greater the difference between a normalized characteristic and 1, the better the corresponding car's quality. As a result, the entries of the following row vector from Table 6.28 serve as the standard units of scale: (4; 5,61; 823; 991; 37; 29), and the variables in each of the columns in Table 6.28 are divided by the corresponding element of the vector. The results are shown in Table 6.29.

The row totals in the last column of Table 6.29 are intended to indicate an overall measure of car make's quality r_i in the quality index $\sum r_i q_i$ in formula (6.1). The fact that the weights are equal in the summation reflects an underlying assumption that all of the characteristics are equally important and equally treated. This may not be the case from the consumer's viewpoint, but we analyze the problem from the viewpoint of the cost of "producing" quality improvements. At different stages of the production process some improvements may, of course, be more costly, and improvements in some characteristics (like occupants, size, and weight) are clearly correlated. However, no alternative assumption that would provide practically acceptable estimates of the weights seems more plausible.

Using the row totals from Table 6.29, the 1970 quality index can be computed for Soviet passenger cars. In the procedure, the adjusted physical outputs from Table 6.11 are used as weights:

$$R_{70} = \sum r_{i70} q_{i70} = 7.31(22) + 7.14(160) + 6(102) + 10.36(60)$$

$$= 2537 \text{ thousand.} \tag{6.2}$$

The average quality index for 1970, consequently, equals

$$\bar{R}_{70} = \frac{R_{70}}{\sum q_{i70}} = \frac{2537}{344} = 7.38. \tag{6.3}$$

This information will be used for intertemporal comparison, after we build the two other quality indices. The data on characteristics of Soviet passenger cars made in 1976 are in Table 6.30. We average

Table 6.28. Average Characteristics of Soviet Passenger Cars in 1970

Model	Occupants	Size, Square Meters	Weight, Kilograms	Engine Volume, Cubic Centimeters	Horsepower	Fuel Consumption, MPG
VAZ Zhiguli	5	6.56	955	1,198	60	26
Moskvich	4.5	6.26	1,003	1,386	56	22
ZAZ Zaporozhets	4	5.61	823	991	37	29
GAZ Volga	5	8.66	1,420	2,445	93	25

Sources: Tables 6.11 and 6.27.

Table 6.29. Normalized Average Characteristics of Soviet Passenger Cars in 1970

Make of Car	Occupants	Size	Weight	Engine Volume	Horsepower	Fuel Consumption	Row Total
VAZ Zhiguli	1.25	1.17	1.16	1.21	1.62	.90	7.31
Moskvich	1.13	1.12	1.22	1.40	1.51	.76	7.14
ZAZ Zaporozhets	1	1	1	1	1	1	6
GAZ Volga	1.25	1.54	1.73	2.47	2.51	.86	10.36

Source: Table 6.28.

Table 6.30. The Characteristics of Soviet Passenger Cars Produced in 1976

Model	Occupants	Size (Length times Width), Square Meters	Weight, Kilograms	Engine Volume, Cubic Centimeters	Horsepower	Fuel Consumption, MPG
VAZ-2101 Zhiguli	5	4.073·1.611=6.56	955	1,198	62	24
VAZ-2102 Zhiguli	5	4.059·1.611=6.54	1,010	1,198	64	24
VAZ-2103 Zhiguli	5	4.116·1.611=6.63	1,030	1,452	77	22
VAZ-2106 Zhiguli	5	4.116·1.611=6.63	1,030	1,568	80	26
VAZ-21011 Zhiguli	5	4.043·1.611=6.51	955	1,294	70	24
Moskvich-2136	4	4.210·1.550=6.53	1,120	1,358	50	21
Moskvich-2137	4	4.210·1.550=6.53	1,120	1,475	75	21
Moskvich-2138	4	4.250·1.550=6.59	1,080	1,358	50	21
Moskvich-2140	4	4.250·1.550=6.59	1,080	1,478	75	21
IZh-2125	4	4.196·1.550=6.50	1,085	1,475	75	21
ZAZ-968A Zaporozhets	4	3.730·1.570=5.86	840	1,198	45	29
ZAZ-969A Zaporozhets	4	3.765·1.490=5.61	870	887	40	29
GAZ-24 Volga	5	4.760·1.820=8.66	1,420	2,445	95	18
GAZ-24-01 Volga	5	4.760·1.820=8.66	1,420	2,445	85	18
GAZ-24-02 Volga	7	4.735·1.820=8.62	1,550	2,445	95	17

Sources: *Za Rulem* (5, 1969, p.16; 1,1972, pp. 34-5; 11, 1972, pp. 6-7; 7, 1977, p.19), Shugurov and Shirshov (1980, p.80), Velikanov (1894, p.59), Vershigora, et al. (1984, p.4), Demikhovskii, et al., (1985, pp. 6-10), and Fuchadzhi and Struik (1984, pp. 5-6).

them as we did for the 1970 data, above. The physical outputs from Tables 6.14 and 6.15 are used as weights. The resultant average characteristics are in Table 6.31.

The normalization procedure for the data in Table 6.31 differs in one respect from that described above at the first step. Instead of picking the normalization row from the table, we use for 1976 the same normalization vector as for 1970. The rationale is that we want to depict the variability of quality not only by make of car, but also by time period. Since this can only be accomplished when the base for normalization does not change over time, the normalization vector should be the one from Table 6.28: (4; 5.61; 823; 991; 37; 29). The results of the normalization are reported in Table 6.32.

In the computation of the quality index for 1976, the physical outputs from Table 6.14 are used as weights:

$$R_{76} = \sum r_{i76} q_{i76} = 7.70(684) + 7.42(342) + 6.27(143) + 10.33(70)$$

$$= 9424 \text{ thousand.} \tag{6.4}$$

The average quality index for 1970 is

$$\bar{R}_{76} = \frac{R_{76}}{\sum q_{i76}} = \frac{9424}{1239} = 7.61. \tag{6.5}$$

At the last step of building the quality index for Soviet passenger cars, we estimate it for 1982. The characteristics of Soviet passenger cars made in 1982 are in Table 6.33 and, after averaging by model, in Table 6.34. Dividing the data from Table 6.34 by the normalization vector (4; 5,61; 823; 991; 37; 29), i.e., by the 1970 characteristics of *Zaporozhets* used in both the 1970 and 1976 computations, above, yields the normalized characteristics shown in Table 6.35. Using the physical outputs from Table 6.20 as weights, the 1982 quality index is as follows:

$$R_{82} = \sum r_{i82} q_{i82}$$

$$= 7.82(720) + 8.13(362) + 6.51(151) + 10.37(74)$$

$$= 10324 \text{ thousand.} \tag{6.6}$$

Table 6.31. Average Characteristics of Soviet Passenger Cars in 1976

Make of Car	Occupants	Size, Square Meters	Weight Kilograms	Engine Volume, Cubic Centimeters	Horsepower	Fuel Consumption, MPG
VAZ Zhiguli	5	6.88	984	1,310	69	24
Moskvich	4	6.55	1,097	1,429	65	21
ZAZ Zaporozhets	4	5.74	855	1,043	43	29
GAZ Volga	5.7	8.65	1,463	2,445	92	18

Sources: Tables 6.14, 6.15, and 6.30.

Table 6.32. Normalized Average Characteristics of Soviet Passenger Cars in 1976

Make of Car	Occupants	Size	Weight	Engine Volume	Horsepower	Fuel Consumption	Row Total
VAZ Zhiguli	1.25	1.23	1.20	1.33	1.86	.83	7.70
Moskvich	1	1.17	1.33	1.44	1.76	.72	7.42
ZAZ Zaporozhets	1	1.02	1.04	1.05	1.16	1	6.27
GAZ Volga	1.43	1.54	1.78	2.47	2.49	.62	10.33

Sources: Tables 6.28 and 6.31.

Table 6.33. The Characteristics of Soviet Passenger Cars Produced in 1982

Model	Occupants	Size (Length) times Width), Square Meters	Weight, Kilograms	Engine Volume, Cubic Centimeters	Horsepower	Fuel Consumption, MPG,
VAZ-2101 Zhiguli	5	4.073·1.611=6.56	955	1,198	64	29
VAZ-2102 Zhiguli	5	4.059·1.611=6.59	1,010	1,300	64	28
VAZ-2103 Zhiguli	5	4.116·1.611=6.63	1,030	1,450	77	28
VAZ-2105 Zhiguli	5	4.128·1.611=6.65	995	1,300	69	32
VAZ-2106 Zhiguli	5	4.116·1.611=6.63	1,045	1,570	80	28
VAZ-2107 Zhiguli	5	4.128·1.611=6.65	1,030	1,450	77	32
VAZ-21051 Zhiguli	5	4.128·1.611=6.65	890	1,198	63	33
VAZ-21011 Zhiguli	5	4.043·1.611=6.51	955	1,300	69	29
VAZ-21021 Zhiguli	5	4.059·1.611=6.54	1,010	1,300	64	26
VAZ-21023 Zhiguli	5	4.059·1.611=6.54	1,010	1,450	64	25
VAZ-21033 Zhiguli	5	4.116·1.611=6.63	1,030	1,300	77	29
VAZ-21061 Zhiguli	5	4.116·1.611=6.63	1,045	1,300	80	29
VAZ-21063 Zhiguli	5	4.116·1.611=6.63	1,045	1,450	80	29
Moskvich-2137	5	4.210·1.550=6.53	1,095	1,480	75	30
Moskvich-2140	4-5	4.250·1.550=6.59	1,045	1,480	75	32
Moskvich-21406	4	4.250·1.550=6.59	1,080	1,480	68	32
IZh-21251	4-5	4.196·1.550=6.50	1,100	1,480	75	28
ZAZ-968M Zaporozhets	4	3.765·1.490=5.61	840	1,198	41	35
ZAZ (LuAZ)-968M Zaporozhets	4	3.390·1.610=5.46	960	1,198	40	29
GAZ-24 Volga	5	4.760·1.820=8.66	1,420	2,445	95	21
GAZ-24-01 Volga	5	4.760·1.820=8.66	1,420	2,445	85	21
GAZ-24-02 Volga	7	4.735·1.820=8.62	1,550	2,445	95	20
GAZ-3102 Volga	5	4.960·1.820=9.03	1,350	2,445	109	28

Sources: *Kratkii automobil'nyi spravochnik* (1985, pp. 25-43); Shugurov and Shirshov (1983, pp. 84-5 and 108-9), Velikanov (1984, p.59), Vershigora et al. (1984, p.4), Demikhovskii (1985, pp. 6-10), and Fuchadzhi and Striuk (1984, pp. 5-6).

Table 6.34. Average Characteristics of Soviet Passenger Cars in 1982

Make of Car	Occupants	Size, Square Meters	Weight, Kilograms	Engine Volume, Cubic Centimeters	Horsepower	Fuel Consumption, MPG
VAZ Zhiguli	5	6.58	983	1,307	70	29
Moskvich	4.5	6.53	1,086	1,480	74	30
ZAZ Zaporozhets	4	5.54	900	1,198	41	32
GAZ Volga	5	8.74	1,435	2,445	96	22

Sources: Tables 6.20, 6.22, and 6.33.

Table 6.35. Normalized Average Characteristics of Soviet Passenger Cars in 1982

Make of Car	Occupants	Size	Weight	Engine Volume	Horsepower	Fuel Consumption	Row Total
VAZ Zhiguli	1.25	1.17	1.19	1.32	1.89	1	7.82
Moskvich	1.13	1.16	1.32	1.49	2	1.03	8.13
ZAZ Zaporozhets	1	1	1.09	1.21	1.11	1.10	6.51
GAZ Volga	1.25	1.56	1.74	2.47	2.59	.76	10.37

Sources: Tables 6.28 and 6.34.

The average quality index is:

$$\bar{R}_{82} = \frac{R_{82}}{\sum q_{i82}} = \frac{10324}{1307} = 7.90. \tag{6.7}$$

The quality indices of passenger cars for 1970, 1976, and 1982 can now be combined with the output data reconstructed in Section 6.1 to estimate the real and inflationary components of the growth of Soviet car production. We first estimate the inflationary growth rates for the 1970–76 and 1976–82 periods. The index of the average price adjusted for quality (6.1) is used for that purpose. In this index, with the numerator as the value of output and the denominator as the quality index estimated above, we obtain a measure of output per unit of quality. At the next step, we decompose the official growth rates into the real and inflationary components.

From Tables 6.12 and 6.18, the 1970 and 1976 values of passenger car production are 624 and 2,891 million rubles, respectively. As found in the computation (6.2) and (6.4), in those two years the quality indices are equal to 2,537 thousand and 9,424 thousand, respectively. Inserting this information in formula (6.1), the average price index adjusted for quality equals

$$\bar{I}^r_{76/70} = \frac{2891000}{9424} \bigg/ \frac{624000}{2537} = 1.25.$$

The result means that there was a 25 percent increase in the average price of a Soviet passenger car in the 1970-76 period that was not matched by quality improvements.

This result could also be obtained by comparing the growth of the average price with the rise of the average quality index. This version of the index illustrates the idea of the approach. Using the 1970 and 1976 values of output and the data on physical production from Table 6.5, the average wholesale price

$$\bar{p}_{70} = \frac{624000}{344} = 1814 \text{ rubles,}$$

and

$$\bar{p}_{76} = \frac{2891000}{1239} = 2333 \text{ rubles.}$$

Hence, the average wholesale price of a passenger car rose in that period by 29 percent (2333÷1814). At the same time, the computation (6.3) and (6.5) shows that the average quality index rose in that period from 7.38 to 7.61, or by only 3 percent. The overall index of a price growth therefore was 1.25 (i.e., $1.29 \div 1.03$). A price increase of 25 percent over a six-year period reflects an average annual rate of 3.8 percent ($1.25^{1/6}-1$). We may conclude that the average inflation rate for Soviet passenger car production in the 1970-76 period was 3.8 percent.

How can inflation in the Soviet production of passenger cars be interpreted? Two factors are generally responsible. The introduction of new models is the first. As shown above, the 1970-76 period witnessed a rapid expansion in car output. As a result of improvements in the new models, higher prices were allowed. When a Soviet manufacturer introduces a new product, he has to demonstrate that cost increases are accompanied by a better product quality. It is well known that quality improvements lagging behind cost increases have contributed to inflation in Soviet producer goods markets. The producer is frequently able to demonstrate to the pricing authorities that a good's quality change is adequate when, indeed, it is not. But we believe that, in the case of passenger cars, the role of this factor should have not been significant. The reason is that we are talking about a product which is highly "visible" in the sense that pricing authorities carefully control each step in the technological process and in the price setting procedures of the producer. The situation is similar to that in the U.S. where a passenger car is the good whose costs and quality improvements are most familiar to the Bureau of Labor Statistics.

The second factor is related to the manufacturer's alterations of the product mix by reducing the output of less expensive items and increasing the output of more expensive ones. This factor was probably the chief contributor to inflation in passenger car production. A gradual shift from less to more expensive models may also be reflected in the quality index. Even though the wholesale prices set for new passenger cars may generally be justified, those prices are based on the highest cost of the first year's production. In several subsequent years the production cost would fall drastically, but the discounts in wholesale price usually lag behind. The discrepancies in the rates of cost reductions among the models, in combination with different lags in price reductions, leave the producer room for maneuvering. (If prices reflected consumer preferences, such a producer's behavior would be quite rational from the society's standpoint.)

Turning now to the 1976-82 period, the 1976 and 1982 values of output amounted to 2,891 million and 3,080 million rubles, respectively (Tables 6.18 and 6.23). These data, along with the quality indices of 9,424 thousand and 10,324 thousand units, respectively, found in the computation (6.4) and (6.6), are used to calculate the average price index adjusted for quality:

$$\bar{I}^r_{82/76} = \frac{3080000}{10234} \bigg/ \frac{2891000}{9424} = .97.$$

The index means that there was a 3 percent deflationary change in Soviet passenger car production in the 1976-82 period. This result corresponds to the Soviet policy of slowing down the expansion in car production and concentrating on their quality improvements in the late 1970s and the 1980s.

We economists can easily explain everything *a posteriori*. But the fact that it is easy to explain a disinflationary change from 1976 to 1982 does not, of course, mean that it could have been expected. On the contrary, in light of the general policies in the MBMW sector, it is surprising. The comparison of the rise of the wholesale average price and the average quality index illustrates the actual developments. On the basis of outputs in physical and value terms from Tables 6.25 and 6.23, the 1982 average price is

$$\bar{p}_{82} = \frac{3080000}{1307} = 2367 \text{ rubles.}$$

Divided by the 1976 average wholesale price of 2,333 rubles found above, it translates into only a 1 percent rise of the average price (2357÷2333). But, as found in the computation (6.5) and (6.7), the average quality index rose from 7.61 to 7.90 in that period, i.e., by 4 percent (7.90÷7.61). Consequently, the price index for that period equals .97 (i.e., 1.01÷1.04).

In the entire 1970-82 period there was an inflationary growth of 21 percent which follows from the chain index

$$\bar{I}_{82/70} = 1.25(.97) = 1.21,$$

which could alternatively be obtained from the information we used for each of the two periods, 1970–76 and 1976–82. This result reflects an annual 1.6 percent inflation rate over the twelve-year period we analyzed $(1.21^{1/12}-1)$. Such a rate can be considered quite moderate, in light of the rapid growth of passenger car production in the 1970s. With all the information estimated in this study, we are in a position now to isolate the real and inflationary components of that growth.

By analogy with (2.10), the following relationship always holds

$$r^v = r^q + r^p + r^q r^p, \tag{6.8}$$

where r^v, r^q, and r^p = nominal, real, and inflationary growth rate, respectively. In formula (6.8), the only unknown is the real growth rate; the other two rates follow from the data we estimated. Since, from this formula, the real growth rate equals

$$r^q = \frac{r^v - r^p}{1 + r^p}, \tag{6.9}$$

it can be isolated from the data we estimated. The information inserted in and resultant from using formula (6.9) is summarized in Table 6.36. The output values in Table 6.36 are the estimates from Tables 6.12, 6.18, and 6.23. The growth index and the nominal growth rates are, in turn, derived from those output values. The inflation rates are the estimates obtained above. The real growth rates are found with the use of formula (6.9): For the 1970–76 period,

$$r^q = \frac{.291 - .038}{1 + .038} = .244, \text{ i.e., } 24.4 \text{ percent,}$$

and, for the 1970–82 period,

$$r^q = \frac{.142 - .016}{1 + .016} = .124, \text{ i.e., } 12.4 \text{ percent.}$$

This estimation shows how, with the account of the inflationary component, the nominal growth rates of Soviet passenger car production are discounted. They actually drop from 29.1 to 24.4 percent, i.e., by 4.7 percentage points, for the 1970–76 period and from 14.2 to 12.4 percent, i.e., by 1.8 percentage points, for the entire 1970–82 period. Although these discounts, especially one from 1970 to 1976, should be viewed as significant, the overall performance of

Table 6.36. Estimated Real Growth and Inflation Rates for Soviet Passenger
Car Production in 1970-82

Year	Value of Output, Millions of Rubles	Nominal Growth Index	Nominal Rate, Percent		Inflation Rate, Percent		Real Rate, Percent	
			76/70	82/70	76/70	82/70	76/70	82/70
1970	624	100						
1976	2,891	463	29.1		3.8		24.4	
1982	3,080	494		14.2		1.6		12.4

Sources: Tables 6.12, 6.18, and 6.23 and the estimates from this
section.

Table 6.37. Retail Prices of Soviet Passenger Cars Produced in
1970 (Rubles)

Model	Retail Price
VAZ-2101 *Zhiguli*	5,500
Moskvich-408	4,511
Moskvich-412	4,936
ZAZ-966 *Zaporozhets*	3,500
GAZ-21 *Volga*	5,602

Source: Radio Liberty Research (CRD 661/67, CRD 355/70, and
PC 357/76).

Soviet passenger car production should be evaluated as impressive in the analyzed period.

6.3. Real and Inflationary Growth of Passenger Car Production at the Retail Level

Was inflation much higher at the retail level than at the wholesale level of Soviet passenger car production? The western press, and the Soviet press lately, quote numerous examples of unjustifiably high retail prices of Soviet autos sold in the domestic market. If the actual retail prices are two to five times the wholesale prices, they are doubtless inflated. Yet this may not necessarily be inflation in the statistical sense, i.e., inflation measured by a price index, if the ratio of retail to wholesale prices does not grow over time. To put it differently, retail prices may be as unjustifiably high as they are, but if they are equally high over the entire period, this will not show up in our analysis of inflation. With this comment in mind, we start the process of estimation.

At the first step, we have to reestimate the value of output of Soviet passenger cars in retail prices. For that purpose, we collected retail price data from different sources. As before, we use outputs in 1970, 1976, and 1982. Table 6.37 contains the data on retail prices of the models that were produced in 1970. Multiplying these prices by the adjusted physical outputs from Table 6.11, the 1970 values of output in retail prices are as shown in Table 6.38. On the basis of this information and physical output from Table 6.11, the average retail price in 1970 was

$$\bar{p}^r_{70} = \frac{1552000}{344} = 4512 \text{ rubles.}$$

(More accurately, the average retail price should have been computed from the data on domestic sales, with exports excluded. But, since outputs in value and physical terms would both be reduced by about the same proportion, an assumption is that the magnitude of the average price would not be affected significantly.) The 1970 average retail price of 4,512 rubles thus was 2.5 times the average wholesale price of 1,814 rubles found earlier.

Table 6.38. The Value of Soviet Passenger Car Production in
Retail Prices in 1970 (Millions of Rubles)

Make	Output	Percent of Total
VAZ *Zhiguli*	121	7.8
Moskvich	738	47.6
ZAZ *Zaporozhets*	357	23.0
GAZ *Volga*	336	21.6
Total	1,552	100.0

Sources: Tables 6.11 and 6.37.

The 1976 retail prices of Soviet passenger cars are as presented in
Table 6.39. The data will be used for switching from these prices to
average prices by make of car. In the case when car's physical output
is known from Tables 6.14 or 6.15, the average price can be found
as a weighted average. When the composition of output by model
is not available, the average price is computed as a sample mean.
Since we were not able to find the retail price for *VAZ-2102 Zhiguli*,
we assumed that it was related to the retail price for *VAZ-2101
Zhiguli* by the same proportion as their wholesale prices in Table
6.16. That seems plausible. The *VAZ-2102 Zhiguli* rounded retail
price was consequently estimated to be 5,390 rubles $\left(\frac{2138}{2183} \cdot 5500\right)$. The
estimated 1976 outputs in retail prices are in Table 6.40. Taking
physical output from Table 6.14, the 1976 average retail price is

$$\bar{p}_{76}^r = \frac{7703000}{1239} = 6217 \text{ rubles.}$$

Comparing this price with the average wholesale price of 2,333 rubles
yields a 2.7 ratio of the average retail to wholesale price for 1976.

Table 6.39. Retail Prices of Soviet Passenger Cars in 1976
(Rubles)

Model	Retail Price
VAZ-2101 *Zhiguli*	5,500
VAZ-21011 *Zhiguli*	6,030
VAZ-2103 *Zhiguli*	7,500
VAZ-2106 *Zhiguli*	8,300
Moskvich-2140	6,346
Moskvich-412 (AZLK)	6,376
Moskvich-412 (IZh)	6,100
ZAZ-968 *Zaporozhets*	3,500
ZAZ-968A *Zaporozhets*	3,750
GAZ-24 *Volga*	9,223

Source: Radio Liberty Research (PC 357/76, Bulletin No. 21,
Oct. 26, 1979, and CIR 40332).

The retail prices of Soviet passenger cars manufactured in 1982
are in Table 6.41. We average these prices in a procedure similar
to that for Table 6.39, and then we multiply the average prices by
physical outputs from Tables 6.20 and 6.22. The results, the 1982
outputs in retail prices, are shown in Table 6.42. On the basis of the
information from Tables 6.20 and 6.42, the average retail price for a
Soviet passenger car in 1982 is

$$\bar{p}_{82}^r = \frac{9910000}{1307} = 7582 \text{ rubles.}$$

Since, as calculated in Section 6.2, the 1982 average wholesale price
is equal to 2,357 rubles, the ratio of the retail to the wholesale price
is therefore 3.2 for that year.

Table 6.40. The Value of Soviet Passenger Car Production in
Retail Prices in 1976 (Millions of Rubles)

Make	Output	Percent of Total
VAZ *Zhiguli*	4,407	57.2
Moskvich	2,132	27.7
ZAZ *Zaporozhets*	518	6.7
GAZ *Volga*	646	8.4
Total	7,703	100.0

Sources: Tables 6.14, 6.15, 6.16, and 6.39.

These data permit us to estimate the inflationary growth in Soviet passenger car production in the 1970-76 and the 1976-82 periods. The easiest way to do so would be to apply the index of average price adjusted for quality (6.1) in the form that compares the growth of average prices with average quality indices estimated in Section 6.2. As a result,

$$\bar{I}^r_{76/70} = \frac{6217}{4512} \bigg/ \frac{7.61}{7.38} = 1.34$$

and

$$\bar{I}^r_{82/76} = \frac{7582}{6217} \bigg/ \frac{7.90}{7.61} = 1.17.$$

Hence, inflationary growth at the retail level is equal to 34 percent in the 1970-76 period and 17 percent in the 1976-82 period. On an annual basis, the results translate into 5 and 2.7 percent, respectively ($1.34^{1/6}-1$ and $1.17^{1/6}-1$). For the entire 1970-82 period, the inflationary growth consequently amounts to 57 percent which follows from the chain index

$$\bar{I}^r_{82/70} = 1.34(1.17) = 1.57.$$

This index reflects a 3.8 percent annual rate of inflation ($1.57^{1/12}-1$).

Table 6.41.   Retail Prices of Soviet Passenger Cars in 1982
(Rubles)

Model	Retail Price
VAZ-2101 *Zhiguli*	6,786
VAZ-21011 *Zhiguli*	7,300
VAZ-2103 *Zhiguli*	8,600
VAZ-2106 *Zhiguli*	9,100
VAZ-2121 *Niva*	10,300
Moskvich-412IE	7,394
Moskvich-2140	7,491
ZAZ-968M	5,375
ZAZ-968MZ	5,600
ZAZ-968M-005	5,160
ZAZ-968A	5,300
ZAZ-968AE	5,300
LuAZ-969M	5,100
GAZ-24 *Volga*	10,200*

Sources: *Trud* (July 11 and 23, 1982 and Jan. 10, 1985, p.4),
Radio Liberty Research (RL 380/82), and Working
Papers.

*Estimate

Summarizing, while at the wholesale level the inflation rates are
equal to 3.8 and 1.6 percent for the 1970-76 and the 1970-82 periods,
they were respectively 5 and 3.8 percent at the retail level. Using
these inflation rates and the values of output found above, we can
estimate the real growth component at the retail level. The results
of computation are illustrated in Table 6.43. The real growth rates,
shown in the last column of Table 6.43, are obtained with the use of
formula (6.9): For the 1970-76 period,

$$r^q = \frac{.306 - .050}{1 + .050} = .244, \text{ i.e., } 24.4 \text{ percent,}$$

Table 6.42. The Value of Soviet Passenger Car Production in
Retail Prices in 1982 (Millions of Rubles)

Make	Output	Percent of Total
VAZ *Zhiguli*	5,659	57.1
Moskvich	2,695	27.2
ZAZ *Zaporozhets*	801	8.1
GAZ *Volga*	755	7.6
Total	9,910	100.0

Sources: Tables 6.20, 6.22, and 6.23.

Table 6.43. Estimated Real Growth and Inflation Rates for Soviet
Passenger Car Production at the Retail Level in 1970-1982

Year	Value of Output, Millions of Rubles	Nominal Growth Index	Nominal Rate, Percent		Inflation Rate, Percent		Real Rate, Percent	
			76/70	82/70	76/70	82/70	76/70	82/70
1970	1,552	100						
1976	7,703	496	30.6		5		24.4	
1982	9,910	639		16.7		3.8		12.4

Sources: Tables 6.38, 6.40, and 6.42 and the estimates from this section.

and, for the 1976-82 period,

$$r^q = \frac{.167 - .038}{1 + .038} = .124, \text{ i.e., } 12.4 \text{ percent.}$$

As follows from Table 6.43, the 1970-76 period was one of a rapid expansion in the values of passenger car production in retail prices, at the nominal rate of 30.6 percent. Although the average nominal rate fell drastically in the next, 1976-82 period, on average it is still high at 16.7 percent for the entire 1970-82 period (compared to 14.2 percent at the wholesale level, Table 6.36). After adjusting for inflationary growth of 5 percent from 1970 to 1976 and 3.8 percent from 1970 to 1982, the real growth rates still remain impressive at 24.4 and 12.4 percent, respectively. (As could have been expected, the latter coincide with the growth rates at the wholesale level from Table 6.36.)

6.4. Quality and Growth of Soviet Truck Production

The methodology suggested for passenger cars is used here for estimating a quality index for Soviet trucks. There are, of course, both similarities and differences in the importance attached to technical characteristics of quality for trucks and passenger cars. In both cases it is more costly to produce a bigger, or heavier, or more powerful vehicle. Therefore, on the same basis as for passenger cars, the following characteristics of truck quality are taken into account: size, weight, engine volume and horsepower. Further, in both cases fuel consumption is one of the most important characteristics of efficiency, and it is also included in the quality index for trucks. On the other hand, cars and trucks have different uses, and this should be reflected in the treatment of their capacity. While the maximum number of passengers is used as a proxy of capacity for cars, it is natural to characterize the capacity of a truck as its maximum load. The quality index for Soviet trucks therefore incorporates the following six characteristics: maximum load, size, weight, engine volume, horsepower and fuel efficiency.

The official Soviet information on truck technical characteristics is used in this analysis, even though it is more reliable in some instances than in others. Characteristics such as size, weight, engine volume, and horsepower are verifiable by their mere nature. Maximum load and fuel efficiency are not so reliably reported. The reasons for that are well known. The technical characteristics of Soviet trucks and passenger cars are determined by testing when the first samples are produced. Since the tests are carried out under ideal road and operating conditions, they result in inflated capacity and efficiency reports. One can find much evidence in the Soviet press on the discrepancy between nominal and actual truck capacity, not to mention the problem of the underutilization of capacity. It is interesting that the issue of fuel efficiency is not raised very frequently. To speculate on the reason, the waste of gasoline from low efficiency may be less significant than losses from theft and resale by truckers.

Despite the inaccuracy of some characteristics, the methodology of estimation has not changed over time. This means that any distortion of those characteristics' true magnitudes is likely to be about the same for all periods, and that the bias is constant. If so, then the indices for 1972, 1976 and 1982 will not be affected significantly. There is a difference in the procedure for trucks as compared to passenger cars. While quality comparisons are carried out by make of car, there is no similar information for trucks. For this reason, a hypothetical "average" truck is found by averaging the characteristics of all of the trucks for each of the three years under consideration. The normalization procedure is accordingly performed over the characteristics of the "average" truck, not by make of vehicle, as in the case of passenger cars.

Table 6.44 reports the characteristics of Soviet trucks produced in 1972. As indicated above, the purpose of the table is to find the characteristics of the "average" truck produced in 1972. As one can see from Table 6.44, the characteristics of this average truck are as follows: 10.28 metric tons maximum load, 8.7 square meters in size, 7.56 metric tons in weight, 8,987 cubic centimeters of engine volume, 174 horsepower and 7 miles per gallon for fuel consumption. To eliminate the effect of scale, the normalization of the average characteristics is also performed in Table 6.44. Since 1972 is the base year, the simplest way to normalize the characteristics is to equate each of them to 1, as done in the table. Of course, the average characteristics are not needed for this normalization, but they are used for the normalization of the characteristics in 1976 and 1982.

Table 6.44. The Characteristics of Soviet Trucks Produced in 1972

Model	Maximum Load, Metric Tons	Size (Base times Gauge), Square Meters	Weight, Metric Tons	Engine Volume, Cubic Centimeters	Horsepower	Fuel Consumption MPG,
		Flat-Bed Trucks and Vans				
GAZ-51A	2.5	3.3×1.65=5.45	2.5	3,485	70	10
GAZ-66-01	2.0	3.3×1.8=5.94	3.47	4,254	115	8
GAZ-66-02	2.0	3.3×1.8=5.94	3.64	4,254	115	8
GAZ-53A	4.0	3.7×1.69=6.25	3.25	4,254	115	9
GAZ-52-03	2.5	3.7×1.65=6.11	2.82	3,485	75	10
TA-942	2.7	3.75×1.65=6.11	4.97	3,485	82	11
ZIL-157K	2.5	7.485×1.755=13.14	5.8	5,555	100	6
ZIL-130	5.0	3.8×1.79=6.80	4.3	5,966	150	7
ZIL-131	3.5	4.6×1.82=8.37	6.46	5,966	150	5
KrAZ-257	12.0	6.45×1.95=12.58	11.3	14,860	240	6
KrAZ-255B	7.5	6.0×2.16=12.96	11.95	14,860	240	6
Ural-375D	4.5	4.925×2.0=9.85	8.35	6,959	180	4
Ural-377	7.5	4.95×2.0=9.85	7.28	6,959	180	5
MAZ-500	7.5	3.85×1.95=7.51	6.5	11,150	180	9
MAZ-516	14.0	5.305×1.97=10.45	8.8	11,150	180	8
UAZ-451DM	1.0	2.3×1.442=3.32	1.51	2,445	72	15
UAZ-452D	0.8	2.3×1.442=3.32	1.67	2,445	72	13
		Tow Trucks				
GAZ-51P	4.0	3.3×1.65=5.45	2.6	3,485	70	9
ZIL-157kV	7.5	7.485×1.755=13.14	5.7	5,555	110	5
ZIL-130V1	7.5	3.3×1.8=5.94	3.86	5,966	150	6
ZIL-131V	5.5	4.6×1.82=8.37	6.23	5,966	150	5
Ural-375S-K1	10.0	4.925×2.0=9.85	7.4	6,959	180	4
Ural-377S	13.5	4.925×2.0=9.85	6.83	6,959	180	4
KAZ-608	11.5	2.9×1.8=5.22	4.0	5,966	150	6
MAZ-504	13.5	3.2×1.95=6.24	6.85	11,150	180	6
MAZ-509,509A	16.0	3.95×1.95=7.70	8.8	11,150	180	8
KrAZ-258	25.0	5.48×1.95=10.59	10.1	14,860	240	8
KrAZ-255V	25.0	6.0×2.16=12.96	10.6	14,860	240	5
KrAZ-255L	23.0	6.0×2.16=12.96	12.39	14,860	240	5
MoAZ-546P	20.0	5.4×2.23=12.04	10.08	14,860	215	5
BelAZ-531	30.0	7.5×2.53=18.98	17.0	22,300	360	2

(Continued)

Table 6.44. (cont.)

Model	Maximum Load, Metric Tons	Size (Base times Gauge), Square Meters	Weight, Metric Tons	Engine Volume, Cubic Centimeters	Horsepower	Fuel Consumption, MPG
		Dump Trucks				
GAZ-SAZ-53B	3.5	3.7 ×1.69=6.25	3.75	4,254	115	7
SAZ-3502	3.2	3.7 ×1.69=6.25	4.03	4,254	115	8
ZIL-MMZ-555	4.5	3.3 ×1.8=5.94	4.58	5,966	150	6
MAZ-503	7.0	3.2 ×1.95=6.24	6.75	11,150	180	8
KrAZ-256B	12.0	5.48 ×1.95=10.69	11.42	14,860	240	5
BelAZ-540	27.0	3.55 ×2.8=9.94	21.0	22,300	360	2
BelAZ-548A	40.0	4.2 ×2.8=11.76	28.87	22,300	500	2
		Average Characteristics				
Average Truck	10.28	8.70	7.56	8,987	174	7
		Normalized Characteristics				
Average Truck	1	1	1	1	1	1
		Sum of Normalized Characteristics				6

Sources: *Tsennik No. 110* (1970, pp. 8-20), *Tsennik No. 42* (1972, pp. 10-40), Shugurov and Shirshov (1983, pp. 86-9 and 110-3), and *Kratkii avtomobil'nyi spravochnik* (1985, pp. 53-87).

The characteristics of Soviet trucks produced in 1976 and 1982 are in Tables 6.45 and 6.46, respectively. If the same truck was produced in two or in all three years, its characteristics, whenever possible, were picked from different publications in order to note their change over time. As it turned out, however, most changes in the average characteristics occurred due to the introduction of new models, rather than due to the modification of old ones. Each table ends with a row of normalized average characteristics that are obtained by dividing the 1972 average characteristics from Table 6.44 (10.28; 8.70; 7.56; 8,987; 174; 7) into the 1976 and 1982 average characteristics.

The sums of normalized characteristics obtained in Tables 6.44, 6.45, and 6.46 play the role of average quality indices as did those estimated for passenger cars in Section 6.2. Using these indices, the real and inflationary components of the growth of Soviet truck production can be estimated. In this estimation, we use the index of average price adjusted for quality in its reduced form, i.e., the one which compares the growth of the average price

$$\bar{p} = \frac{\sum p_i q_i}{\sum q_i} \qquad (6.10)$$

with the growth of the average quality index

$$\bar{R} = \frac{\sum r_i q_i}{\sum q_i} \qquad (6.11)$$

where $\bar{p}$ and $\bar{R}$ = average price and average quality index per vehicle in a given time period, q_i and r_i = price and index of quality of the ith vehicle in the same period.

The sum of normalized average characteristics computed in each of the Tables 6.44, 6.45, and 6.46 is used as a consequent value of $\bar{R}$. The average wholesale prices of trucks are found in Table 6.47 by dividing physical outputs into the values of production. The latter are the estimates from Tables 6.13, 6.19, and 6.25. The physical outputs through 1981 are from the Soviet sources (Table 6.15), and the 1982 output is an estimate. The Soviets published the data on physical production of trucks only until 1981. Looking at the pattern of growth demonstrated by the data, one may infer the reason for terminating such reports. Output rose through 1980, when 787,000 trucks were made. For 1981, the production of 786,600 trucks is

Table 6.45. The Characteristics of Soviet Trucks Produced in 1976

Model	Maximum Load, Metric Tons	Size (Base times Gauge), Square Meters	Weight, Metric Tons	Engine Volume, Cubic Centimeters	Horsepower	Fuel Consumption, MPG
		Flat-Bed Trucks and Vans				
GAZ-66-01	2.0	3.3×1.8=5.94	3.47	4,254	115	10
GAZ-66-02	2.0	3.3×1.8=5.94	3.64	4,254	115	10
GAZ-53A	4.0	3.7×1.69=6.25	3.25	4,254	115	9
GAZ-52-03	2.5	3.7×1.65=6.11	2.82	3,485	75	10
GAZ-52-04	2.5	3.3×1.69=5.58	2.71	3,485	75	11
GAZ-52-05	2.5	3.3×1.69=5.58	2.52	3,485	75	11
GESA-3706	3.25	3.7×1.69=6.25	4.0	4,254	115	8
GESA-3721	3.0	3.7×1.69=6.25	4.27	4,254	115	8
T-140	7.0	3.4×2.1=7.14	5.9	4,254	115	8
ZIL-157K	2.5	7.485×1.755=13.14	5.8	5,555	100	6
ZIL-131	3.5	4.6×1.82=8.37	6.46	5,966	150	5
ZIL-133G1	8.0	5.11×1.85=9.45	6.88	5,966	150	6
KrAZ-257	12.0	6.45×1.95=12.58	11.3	14,860	240	6
KrAZ-255B	7.5	6.0×2.16=12.96	11.95	14,860	240	6
Ural-375D	4.5	4.925×2.0=9.85	8.35	6,959	180	4
Ural-377	7.5	4.925×2.0=9.85	7.28	6,959	180	5
Ural-375	7.5	4.925×2.02=9.95	7.73	6,959	180	5
Ural-375H	5.0	4.925×2.02=9.95	7.7	6,959	180	5
TA-943D	2.0	3.3×1.69=5.58	3.05	3,485	75	11
TA-943H	2.0	3.3×1.69=5.58	3.01	3,485	75	11
MAZ-500A	8.0	3.95×1.97=7.78	6.6	11,150	180	7
MAZ-7310	20.0	7.7×2.375=18.29	23.9	38,800	525	2
KamAZ-5320	10.0	5.01×2.026=10.15	8.2	10,850	210	9
UAZ-451DM	1.0	2.3×1.442=3.32	1.51	2,445	72	16
UAZ-452D	0.8	2.3×1.442=3.32	1.67	2,445	72	16
ErAZ-762A	1.0	2.7×1.42=3.83	1.45	2,445	72	20
ErAZ-762V	1.15	2.7×1.42=3.83	1.45	2,445	72	20
IZh-2715	0.4	2.4×1.237=2.97	1.1	1,478	75	26
IZh-27151	0.35	2.4×1.237=2.97	1.05	1,478	75	26
Moskvich-2734	0.4	2.4×1.27=3.05	1.09	1,478	75	26
		Tow Trucks				
ZIL-157KV	7.5	7.485×1.755=13.14	5.7	5,555	110	5
ZIL-131V	5.5	4.6×1.82=8.37	6.23	5,966	150	5
ZIL-130V1	7.5	3.3×1.8=5.94	3.86	5,966	150	6
Ural-375S-K1	10.0	4.925×2.0=9.85	7.4	6,959	180	4
Ural-377S	13.5	4.925×2.0=9.85	6.83	6,959	180	4

Continued

Table 6.45. cont.

Model	Maximum Load, Metric Tons	Size (Base times Gauge), Square Meters	Weight, Metric Tons	Engine Volume, Cubic Centimeters	Horsepower	Fuel Consumption, MPG
Ural-375SH	12.5	4.925×2.02=9.95	7.26	6,959	180	4
Ural-377SH	13.5	4.925×2.02=9.95	6.93	6,959	180	4
KAZ-608	11.5	2.9×1.8=5.22	4.0	5,966	150	6
KAZ-608V	11.5	2.9×1.8=5.22	4.0	5,966	150	6
MAZ-509	16.0	3.95×1.95=7.70	8.8	11,150	180	8
MAZ-504A	13.5	3.4×1.97=6.70	6.4	11,150	180	8
MAZ-504G	13.0	3.4×1.97=6.70	6.3	11,150	180	8
MAZ-515B	25.0	4.9×1.97=9.65	8.7	14,860	300	6
KrAZ-255V	25.0	6.0×2.16=12.96	10.6	14,860	240	5
KrAZ-255L	23.0	6.0×2.16=12.96	12.39	14,860	240	5
KrAZ-258	25.0	5.48×1.95=10.69	10.1	14,860	240	5
KamAZ-5410	14.0	4.16×2.01=8.36	6.8	10,850	210	7
MoAZ-546P	20.0	5.4×2.23=12.04	10.0	14,860	215	5
MoAZ-36401-9585	20.0	4.45×2.32=10.32	18.0	14,860	190	6
BelAZ-531	30.0	7.5×2.53=18.98	17.0	22,300	360	2
Dump Trucks						
GAZ-SAZ-53B	3.5	3.7×1.69=6.25	3.75	4,254	115	8
SAZ-3502	3.2	3.7×1.69=6.25	4.03	4,254	115	8
SAZ-3503	2.4	3.3×1.69=5.58	2.75	3,485	75	12
SAZ-3504	2.25	3.3×1.69=5.58	2.9	3,485	75	12
ZIL-MMZ-555	4.5	3.3×1.8=5.94	4.58	5,966	150	7
ZIL-MMZ-5551A	4.5	3.3×1.8=5.94	4.61	5,966	150	8
ZIL-MMZ-4502	5.25	3.3×1.8=5.94	4.8	5,398	110	8
MAZ-503A	8.0	3.4×1.97=6.70	7.1	11,150	180	8
MAZ-7310	20.0	7.7 ×2.375=18.29	23.9	38,800	525	2
MAZ-5335	8.0	3.925 ×1.97=7.73	6.72	11,150	180	10
KrAZ-256B	12.0	5.48×1.95=10.69	11.4	14,860	240	5
BelAZ-540A	27.0	3.55×2.8=9.94	21.0	22,300	360	2
BelAZ-548A	40.0	4.2×2.8=11.76	28.8	22,300	500	2
BelAZ-7420	120.0	15.4×3.99=61.45	101.0	58,800	1,300	2
BelAZ-549	80.0	4.45×4.1=18.25	68.4	43,700	1,050	2
Average Characteristics						
Average Truck	12.11	9.15	9.41	9,713	198	8
Normalized Characteristics						
Average Truck	1.18	1.05	1.24	1.08	1.14	1.14
Sum of Normalized Characteristics						6.83

Sources: Shugurov and Shirshov (1983, pp. 110-3), *Kratkii avtomobil'nyi spravochnik* (1985, pp. 53-87).

Table 6.46. The Characteristics of Soviet Trucks Produced in 1982

Model	Maximum Load, Metric Tons	Size (Base times Gauge), Square Meters	Weight, Metric Tons	Engine Volume, Cubic Centimeters	Horsepower	Fuel Consumption, MPG
		Flat-Bed Trucks and Vans				
GAZ-66-01	2.0	3.3×1.8=5.94	3.47	4,254	115	10
GAZ-66-02	2.0	3.3×1.8=5.94	3.64	4,254	115	10
GAZ-53A	4.0	3.7 ×1.69=6.25	3.25	4,254	115	9
GAZ-52-04	2.5	3.3 ×1.69=5.58	2.71	3,485	75	11
GAZ-52-05	2.5	3.3 ×1.69=5.58	2.52	3,485	75	11
GAZ-52-07	2.5	3.3 ×1.69=5.58	2.69	3,485	70	11
GAZ-53-07	4.0	3.7 ×1.69=6.25	3.44	4,254	115	8
GESA-3706	3.25	3.7 ×1.69=6.25	4.0	4,254	115	8
GESA-3721	3.0	3.7 ×1.69=6.25	4.27	4,254	115	8
T-140	7.0	3.4 ×2.1=7.14	5.9	4,254	115	8
PAZ-3742	2.5	3.6 ×1.69=6.08	2.52	4,254	115	8
ZIL-131	3.5	4.6 ×1.82=8.37	6.46	5,966	150	5
ZIL-133G1	8.0	5.11 ×1.85=9.45	6.88	5,966	150	6
ZIL-130-76	6.0	3.8 ×1.8=6.84	4.3	5,966	150	8
ZIL-130G-76	6.0	4.5 ×1.8=8.10	4.58	5,966	150	6
ZIL-130GV-76	6.0	5.6 ×1.8=10.08	4.99	5,966	150	6
ZIL-138	6.0	3.8 ×1.8=6.84	4.42	5,966	150	6
ZIL-157KD	3.0	4.785 ×1.755=8.40	5.8	5,398	110	6
ZIL-133GIa	10.0	6.02 ×1.85=11.14	7.79	10,850	210	9
ZIL-133G2	10.0	6.02 ×1.85=11.14	6.88	10,850	210	5
KrAZ-257B1	12.0	6.45 ×1.95=12.58	10.29	14,860	240	6
KrAZ-260	9.0	6.4 ×2.16=13.82	12.78	14,860	300	7
KrAZ-255B1	7.5	6.4 ×2.16=13.82	12.78	14,860	240	7
Ural-375D	4.5	4.925 ×2.0=9.85	8.35	6,959	180	4
Ural-377	7.5	4.925 ×2.0=9.85	7.28	6,959	180	5
Ural-375	7.5	4.925 ×2.02=9.95	7.23	6,959	180	5
Ural-375H	5.0	4.925 ×2.02=9.95	7.7	6,959	180	5
Ural-4320	5.0	4.925 ×2.02=9.95	8.62	10,850	210	9
TA-943D	2.0	3.3 ×1.69=5.58	3.05	3,485	75	11
TA-943H	2.0	3.3 ×1.69=5.58	3.01	3,485	75	11
MAZ-7310	20.0	7.7 ×2.375=18.29	23.9	38,800	525	2
MAZ-5335	8.0	3.925 ×1.97=7.73	6.72	11,150	180	10
MAZ-53352	8.4	3.925 ×1.97=7.73	7.45	11,150	180	8

Continued

Table 6.46. cont.

Model	Maximum Load, Metric Tons	Size (Base times Gauge), Square Meters	Weight, Metric Tons	Engine Volume, Cubic Centimeters	Horsepower	Fuel Consumption, MPG
KamAZ-5320	8.0	4.51 ×2.026=9.14	7.08	10,850	210	9
KamAZ-53212	10.0	5.01 ×2.026=10.15	8.2	10,850	210	9
UAZ-451DM	1.0	2.3 ×1.442=3.32	1.51	2,445	72	16
UAZ-452D	0.8	2.3 ×1.442=3.32	1.67	2,445	72	16
IZh-2715	0.4	2.4 ×1.237=2.97	1.1	1,478	75	26
IZh-27151	0.35	2.4 ×1.237=2.97	1.05	1,478	75	26
Moskvich-2734	0.4	2.4 ×1.27=3.05	1.09	1,478	75	26
Tow Trucks						
GAZ-52-06	4.0	3.3 ×1.69=5.58	2.44	3,485	75	7
ZIL-131V	5.5	4.6 ×1.82=8.37	6.23	5,966	150	5
ZIL-130V1-76	7.5	3.3 ×1.8=5.94	1.86	5,966	150	6
ZIL-133GIa	18.5	5.1 ×1.85=9.44	7.1	10,850	210	9
ZIL-157KDV	7.5	4.785 ×1.755=8.40	5.7	5,398	110	5
Ural-375S-K1	10.0	4.925 ×2.0=9.85	7.4	6,959	180	4
Ural-377S	13.5	4.925 ×2.0=9.85	6.83	6,959	180	4
Ural-375SH	12.5	4.925 ×2.02=9.95	7.26	6,959	180	4
Ural-377SH	13.5	4.925 ×2.02=9.95	6.93	6,959	180	4
Ural-4420	12.5	4.925 ×2.0=9.85	7.0	10,850	210	9
KAZ-608V	11.5	2.9 ×1.8=5.22	4.0	5,966	150	6
MAZ-504G	13.0	3.4 ×1.97=6.70	6.3	11,150	180	8
MAZ-5429	13.45	3.4 ×1.97=6.70	6.54	11,150	180	7
MAZ-6422	26.0	3.6 ×2.05=7.38	9.05	14,860	320	5
MAZ-5432	16.0	3.4 ×1.97=6.70	7.05	14,860	280	6
KrAZ-255B1	16.0	6.4 ×2.16=13.82	10.43	14,860	240	5
KrAZ-258B1	21.0	6.4 ×2.16=13.82	9.2	14,860	240	5
KamAZ-5410	14.0	4.16 ×2.01=8.36	6.8	10,850	210	7
KamAZ-54112	20.0	4.16 ×2.01=8.36	7.1	10,850	210	7
MoAZ-546P	20.0	5.4 ×2.23=12.04	10.0	14,860	215	5
MoAZ-36401-9585	20.0	4.45 ×2.32=10.32	18.0	14,860	190	6
BelAZ-531	30.0	7.5 ×2.53=18.98	17.0	22,300	360	2

Continued

Table 6.46. cont.

Model	Maximum Load, Metric Tons	Size (Base times Gauge), Square Meters	Weight, Metric Tons	Engine Volume, Cubic Centimeters	Horsepower	Fuel Consumption, MPG
			Dump Trucks			
GAZ-SAZ-53B	3.5	3.7 ×1.69=6.25	3.75	4,254	115	8
SAZ-3502	3.2	3.7 ×1.69=6.25	4.03	4,254	115	8
SAZ-3503	2.4	3.3 ×1.69=5.58	2.75	3,485	75	12
SAZ-3504	2.25	3.3 ×1.69=5.58	2.9	3,485	75	12
ZIL-MMZ-555GA	4.5	3.3 ×1.8=5.94	4.61	5,966	150	8
ZIL-MMZ-554M	5.25	3.8 ×1.8=6.84	5.04	5,966	150	8
ZIL-MMZ-4502	5.25	3.3 ×1.8=5.94	4.8	5,398	110	8
ZIL-MMZ-45021	5.25	3.8 ×1.8=6.84	4.8	5,398	110	8
MAZ-5549	8.0	3.4 ×1.97=6.70	7.23	11,150	180	8
KrAZ-256B1	12.0	4.08 ×1.95=7.69	10.85	14,860	240	7
KamAZ-5511	10.0	4.16 ×2.01=8.36	8.77	10,850	210	9
KamAZ-55102	7.0	4.51 ×2.026=9.14	8.48	10,850	210	10
MoAZ-522A	20.0	3.55 ×2.5=8.88	8.9	14,860	300	7
MoAZ-6507	20.0	3.55 ×2.5=8.88	8.9	14,860	300	7
BelAZ-540A	27.0	3.55 ×2.8=9.94	21.0	22,300	360	2
BelAZ-548A	40.0	4.2 ×2.8=11.76	28.8	22,300	500	2
BelAZ-7510	27.0	3.55 ×2.8=9.94	21.4	22,300	350	2
BelAZ-7525	40.0	4.2 ×2.8=11.76	29.3	22,300	500	2
BelAZ-7420	120.0	15.4 ×3.99=61.45	101.0	58,800	1,300	2
BelAZ-549	80.0	4.45 ×4.1=18.25	68.4	43,700	1,050	2
BelAZ-7519	110.0	15.4 ×3.99=61.45	101.0	59,300	1,300	2
			Average Characteristics			
Average Truck	13.13	9.71	10.34	10,497	219	8
			Normalized Characteristics			
Average Truck	1.28	1.12	1.37	1.17	1.26	1.14
Sum of Normalized Characteristics						7.34

Sources: Shugurov and Shirshov (1983, pp. 83-89 and 110-3), *Kratkii avtomobil'nyi spravochnik* (1985, pp. 53-87), and Azamatov, et al. (1984, p.8).

reported. Since the pattern of decline had apparently persisted, the figures disappeared from publications. We assume that the annual production did not fall far below the 786 thousand level, which appears to be a reasonable rounded estimate for 1982.

Table 6.47. The Production and Average Prices of Soviet Trucks

Year	Physical Production, Thousands	Value of Output, Millions of Rubles	Average Price, Rubles
1970	525	2,875	5,476
1976	716	4,253	5,940
1982	786	5,668	7,211

Sources: Tables 6.5, 6.13, 6.19, and 6.25.

As indicated above, the reduced formula of the index of average price adjusted for quality

$$\bar{I}_t^r = \frac{\bar{P}_t}{\bar{P}_o} / \frac{\bar{R}_t}{\bar{R}_o},$$ (6.12)

based on average parameters defined by (6.10)-(6.11), is used for the estimation of inflationary growth in the 1970-76 and 1976-82 periods. Inserting the average prices from Table 6.47 and average quality indices from Tables 6.44 and 6.45 in formula (6.12), the 1976 index of average price adjusted for quality is

$$\bar{I}_{76/70} = \frac{5940}{5497} / \frac{6.83}{6} = .95.$$

This means that there was a 5 percent deflationary change in Soviet truck production in the 1970-76 period. Looking at this computation as a two-step procedure, the average price of a truck rose by over 8 percent (5940÷5496), while the average quality index rose by 14 percent (6.83÷6). Since the average index of quality rose by more than the average price in that period, the overall change was deflationary.

Using the average quality indices from Tables 6.45 and 6.46 and the average prices from Table 6.47, the 1982 index of average price adjusted for quality was

$$\bar{I}^r_{82/76} = \frac{7211}{5940} / \frac{7.34}{6.83} = 1.13,$$

i.e., there was an inflationary growth of 13 percent in Soviet truck production in the 1976-82 period. In that period, a 7 percent (7.34÷6.83) rise in the average quality index fell short of the 21 percent (7211÷5940) rise in the average price of trucks.

Why was there a shift from deflationary change in the 1970-76 period to inflationary growth in the 1976-82 period? The chief contributing factor, according to our data, is a change in the growth of fuel efficiency. As one can see from the comparison of Tables 6.45 and 6.46, it rose by an average 14 percent in the 1970-76 period and stopped rising later, in the 1976-82 period. One of the reasons for that was the expansion of output and the introduction of several new models of powerful and fuel-intensive dump trucks at the Belorussia automobile plant.

On an annual basis, the 1970-76 growth is characterized by an average annual deflationary change of about 1 percent ($.95^{1/6}$-1), and the 1976-82 period by an average rate of inflationary growth of 2 percent ($1.13^{1/6}$-1). It can be deduced from these results that the entire 1970-82 period experienced a low level of inflationary growth, at the average rate of under 1 percent. At a more accurate level, this result follows from the 1970-82 average price index adjusted for quality:

$$\bar{I}^r_{82/70} = 95(1.13) = 1.07.$$

These estimates can now be used to isolate the real and inflationary components of the growth of Soviet truck production. The computation is summarized in Table 6.48. It is based on the estimated output values from Table 6.47 and the estimated price deflation and inflation rates obtained above. The real growth rates are calculated with the use of formula (6.9). For the 1970-76 period, the real growth rate equals

$$r^q = \frac{.068 - (-.008)}{1 + (-.008)} = .077, \text{ i.e., } 7.7 \text{ percent,}$$

for the 1976-82 period,

$$r^q = \frac{.049 - .021}{1 + .021} = .027, \text{ i.e., } 2.7 \text{ percent,}$$

and, for the entire 1970-82 period,

$$r^q = \frac{.058 - .006}{1 + .006} = .052, \text{ i.e., } 5.2 \text{ percent.}$$

6.5. Real and Inflationary Growth of the Automotive Industry

Having obtained the growth estimates for passenger cars and trucks, we are in a position to estimate the real and inflationary growth of the AI as a whole. The value of passenger car and truck production was equal to about half of the total AI output in the 1970-82 period. This is a representative sample of production. In addition, one should take into account the other items of the AI breakdown – autotractor trailers, special automobiles, engines, automotive electrical equipment and components – that are closely associated with cars and trucks. It would be realistic to expect that their prices move together with car and truck prices. The combined output of all these product groups, along with cars and trucks, constitutes some 90 percent of the AI production. On the basis of these considerations, we assume that the change in car and truck prices approximates the AI as a whole.

At the final step, we therefore estimate the AI price index for the 1970-76 and the 1976-82 periods. To do this we simply estimate a weighted average price index, with car and truck outputs at the end of each period, i.e., in 1976 and 1982, as weights. On the basis of the information from Table 6.49, the AI price index is:

For the 1970-76 period,

$$\bar{I}^r_{76/70} = \frac{125(2891) + 95(4253)}{7144} = 107.1,$$

and, for the 1976-82 period,

$$\bar{I}^r_{82/76} = \frac{97(3080) + 113(5668)}{8748} = 107.4.$$

Table 6.48. Estimated Real Growth and Inflation Rates for Soviet Truck
Production in the 1970-82 Period

Year	Value of Output, Millions of Rubles	Nominal Growth Index	Nominal Rate, Percent		Inflation Rate, Percent		Real Rate, Percent	
			76/70	82/70	76/70	82/70	76/70	82/70
1970	2,875	100						
1976	4,253	148	6.8		-0.8		7.7	
1982	5,668	197		5.8		0.6		5.2

Sources: Tables 6.47 and the estimates from this section.

Table 6.49. The Information for the Computation of the Price
Index for the Soviet Automotive Industry

Indicator	1976	1982
Value of Output, Millions of Rubles		
Cars	2,891	3,080
Trucks	4,253	5,668
Total	7,144	8,748
Price Index (1976=100 for 1970-76 and 1976=100 for 1976-82)		
Cars	125	97
Trucks	95	113

Sources: Tables 6.36 and 6.48 and estimates from Sections 6.2
and 6.4.

These virtually equal indices reflect the average growth rates of 1.1 and 1.2 percent, respectively $(1.071^{1/6}-1$ and $1.074^{1/6}-1)$. For the entire 1970-82 period, the price index found as a chain index equals

$$\bar{I}^r_{82/70} = 107.1(1.074) = 115,$$

with an expected average growth rate of 1.2 percent $(1.15^{1/12}-1)$.

The real growth rates can now be estimated with the use of formula (6.9):

For the 1970-76 period,

$$r^q = \frac{.126 - .011}{1 + .011} = .114, \text{ i.e., 11.4 percent,}$$

and, for the 1970-82 period,

$$r^q = \frac{.079 - .012}{1 + .012} = .066, \text{ i.e., 6.6 percent.}$$

The nominal growth rates used in this computation are from Table 6.50. The resultant real growth rates for the AI, i.e., 11.4 percent for the 1970-76 period and 6.6 percent for the whole 1970-82 period, are also in Table 6.50. These results mean that the inflationary component of the economic growth was modest for the AI in the 1970-82 period. As a matter of fact, the average nominal growth rate of 7.9 percent should be discounted to 6.6 percent, i.e., by only 1.3 percentage points.

We summarize the findings of this chapter. For the automotive industry, we have built a rather complex index of quality since it is impossible to single out a characteristic of cars or trucks that would dominate over or represent the others. For this reason, the quality index for passenger cars includes such characteristics as: the number of occupants, size, weight, engine volume, horsepower and fuel efficiency. A similar index for trucks also includes the indicator of maximum load, instead of the number of occupants for cars.

For passenger car production, inflationary growth was studied at both the wholesale and retail levels. An important conclusion is that inflation at the retail level of Soviet passenger car production was significantly higher than at the wholesale level. As a matter of fact, the overall inflation rate at the retail level was more than twice that at the wholesale level (3.8 versus 1.6 percent). Other than the difference in magnitudes, however, there is similarity in the behavior of the inflationary component. At both levels inflation plays a much greater role in the first of the two six-year periods and tends to subside in the second. The differences in the inflation rates between the 1970-76 and the entire 1970-82 periods also remain close at both levels.

Another conclusion is that the parallel analysis of the output growth in both wholesale and retail prices sheds some light on the important question of the driving force behind price increases in the Soviet economy. Our analysis demonstrates that the Soviet authorities were more successful in controlling price inflation at the wholesale level of Soviet car production than at the retail. (More accurately, when it comes to the retail level, one should rather speak of the willingness or desire to control the price increases.) At the same time, we are confronted with a widespread belief that plant management introduces cosmetic alterations in product quality and, under that umbrella, inflates prices. One should note that the chief conduit for management's inflating wholesale prices is in cost increases that are claimed to be necessary for reported improvements in product quality. If that were the case, the wholesale prices would be the first to reflect it. By controlling production cost, plant management has evidently had some impact on the level of wholesale prices, and retail prices as well, in cases when there is little difference between the two. But that is hardly true for Soviet passenger autos whose retail prices are several times wholesale, so that any given cost increase would be a higher percentage of the wholesale price than of a retail price. A simple example will illustrate. Suppose that a good's production cost is 80 rubles, profit 20 rubles, and turnover tax 300 rubles. The wholesale price is then 100 rubles, and the retail price 400 rubles. Further, suppose that the cost rises to 90 rubles, in which case the new wholesale price equals 110 rubles (a 10 percent increase) and the retail price 410 rubles (a 2.5 percent increase).

What follows from our analysis and this simple arithmetic is that the prices of Soviet passenger cars have grown at the discretion of

Table 6.50. Estimated Real Growth and Inflation Rates for the Soviet Automotive Production in 1970-82

Year	Value of Output, Millions of Rubles	Nominal Growth Index	Nominal Rate, Percent		Inflation Rate, Percent		Real Rate, Percent	
			76/70	82/70	76/70	82/70	76/70	82/70
1970	3,499	100						
1976	7,144	204	12.6		1.1		11.4	
1982	8,748	250		7.9		1.2		6.6

Sources: Tables 6.36, 6.48, 6.49 and the estimates from this section.

central authorities rather than plant managers. This was shown by the rise in the ratio of retail to wholesale car prices from 2.5 in 1970 to 2.7 in 1976 to 3.2 in 1982. It is accounted for by changes in the turnover tax, the wedge between wholesale and retail prices. This explains the fact of greater retail than wholesale price inflation over the 1970-1982 period. At the wholesale level, the inflation rates for Soviet passenger car production were 3.8 percent for the 1970-76 period and 1.6 percent for the entire 1970-82 period. Passenger car retail prices rose at a rate of 5 percent between 1970 and 1976 and 3.8 percent in the entire twelve-year period.

What about Soviet truck production? Here we find the lowest inflationary rates among the MBMW branches we studied. The overall inflation rate from 1970 to 1982 was only 0.6 percent, and the 1970-76 period even experienced a deflationary growth. (That also happened to passenger car production but in the 1976-82 period.) The analysis shows that one of the reasons for that was a reported rise in the fuel efficiency of trucks in the first of the two periods. In the second period, quality improvements became less visible, and a resultant inflation rate rose to 2 percent. (Adjusting fuel efficiency to reflect load capacity could affect this conclusion.) As a combination of passenger car and truck production, the automotive industry is characterized by a modest annual inflation rate.

Although the inflation rates we found discount the official growth indices of Soviet passenger car and truck production, they nevertheless do not undermine the fact of impressive growth, especially for cars (12.4 percent per annum). Usually rapid growth in the past, in combination with the importance attached to an industry, would in the Soviet case mean the continuation of high growth in the future. This may be true for trucks, but Soviet passenger car production is an interesting exception from this rule. The great buildup of the industry, when physical output of Soviet autos rose almost fourfold from 1969 to 1974, was largely the result of building one very large plant. This drained other MBMW branches of significant investment and, therefore, has been followed by a long period of slack. The revival of the industry may be expected in the 1990s, probably with the use of western loans and technology.

Chapter 7

Estimating Growth of the Electrotechnical Industry

7.1. The Reconstruction Process

The chief purpose of the statistical reconstruction process is to find the output of the electrotechnical industry (EI) by product group in money terms, in physical units, and in accepted units of quality. We begin with the aggregate input-output information. Table 7.1 contains the output data from the four input-output tables (1959, 1966, 1972, and 1982) for the EI. They are divided into two groups – the electrotechnical machinery and equipment and the cable products groups. The column totals in Table 7.1 represent the gross values of the output of the EI that are used in reconstructing the information by product group.[11]

To divide a total among its components, we might use the percentage breakdowns of the EI if a consistent set of those could be obtained. We found Soviet sources illustrating the EI's output breakdowns for the following years: Astaf'ev, et al. (1967, p.11), 1966; Astaf'ev, et al. (1975, p.35), 1940, 1950, 1960, 1965, and 1972; Astaf'ev, et al. (1977, p.14), 1975; and Karlik (1977, p.35), 1965, 1970, and 1977. Unfortunately, the information provided in these sources pictures different structures of the EI for the same years. To some extent, the discrepancy can be attributed to the possible use of different comparable prices which are not specified by the authors. Thus, it is quite possible that the 1955 or 1967 comparable prices were used, depending on which were valid at the time of publication. The discrepancy might also be the result of different ways of aggregating product growth. It is clear from the context that Karlik uses

217

Table 7.1. Output of the Electrotechnical Industry in Producers'
Prices (Millions of Rubles)

Branch	1959	1966	1972	1982
Electrotechnical Machinery and Equipment	1,724.6	4,929.9	6,996.1	11,297.8
Cable Products	748.9	1,286.4	1,934.0	3,131.5
Total	2,473.5	6,217.4	8,930.1	14,429.3

Sources: Gallik, et al. (1975, p.71 and 1983, p.68) and Kostinsky
(1976, p.69 and 1987).

the proportions for pure product groups, while Astaf'ev et al. goes
by a broader measure specifying the organizational division of the
EI. For example, there is a difference even for such a monoproduct
group as transformers, since Astaf'ev et al. uses the proportions for
the entire process of building transformers which, along with transformers *per se*, also includes transformer substations and reactors,
while Karlik uses proportions for a more narrowly defined product.
Therefore, when we used the proportions from different sources, we
also tried to take into consideration some control factors, in order
to maintain consistency. For example, it is often possible to verify
the proportions by using total constraints on output or the growth
rates estimated in the same comparable prices.

Of the possible breakdowns, the one provided by Karlik is more
detailed than the others and, as indicated above, is built around pure
product groups. The use of pure product groups for the computation
of outputs in money terms is advantageous from our standpoint,
since we compare this output with output in physical units. The
breakdowns are provided for 1965, 1970 and 1977. We complement

Table 7.2. The Proportions of Electrical Machines in the
Electrotechnical Output in 1965 (Percent)

Product Group	Percent
Turbine Generators	1.4
Large Electrical Machines	3.9
Small Electrical Machines	1.7
Electric Motors, 100 Kilowatts and over	.9
Electric Motors, under 100 Kilowatts	5.0
Total	12.9

Source: Karlik (1977, p.55).

this information with the breakdowns for 1960. To reconstruct these, other available sources are used.

We make an assumption that, if the 1960 breakdowns were given by Karlik, their ratios to the 1965 breakdowns would be the same as the 1960/1965 ratios for Astaf'ev et al. (1967, p.11) data. If so, then the following proportion can be applied

$$\frac{w_{60,K}}{w_{65,K}} = \frac{w_{60,A}}{w_{65,A}}, \tag{7.1}$$

where $w_{60,K}$ and $w_{65,K}$ = the weight of a given product group in the total EI output for Karlik's specification in 1960 and 1965, respectively; $w_{60,A}$ and $w_{65,A}$ = the same weights for Astaf'ev's specification. However, the Astaf'ev et al. source combines several important product groups into a combined group of electrical machines which we should decompose. Astaf'ev et al. indicates that the proportion of electrical machines in the EI output in 1960 and 1965 was 18 and 17.4 percent, respectively, but no detailed breakdown of those percentages is given. Such a percentage breakdown is reported by Karlik for 1965 as shown in Table 7.2.

It follows from Table 7.2 that the total share of electrical machines in the EI output was 12.9 percent in 1967. This total share, along with the percentages for this group for 1960 and 1965 given by Astaf'ev et al., above, can be used to correct the share of electrical machines, to make it consistent with the Astaf'ev classification. Applying formula (7.1) yields:

$$w_{60,K} = \frac{w_{65,K} \cdot w_{60,A}}{w_{65,A}} = \frac{12.9 \cdot 18}{17.4} = 13.3 \text{ percent.}$$

The resultant 13.3 percent for the electrical machines' share in the total EI output for 1960 should be divided among the five groups listed in Table 7.2. To do so, the constant product group-to-total proportion is assumed, i.e.,

$$\frac{w_{g,60}}{w_{60}} = \frac{w_{g,65}}{w_{65}},$$

where $w_{g,60}$ and $w_{g,65}$ = the weight of a given product group in the total EI output in 1960 and 1965, respectively; w_{60} and w_{65} = the same weight for the total group of electrical machines. Using the percentages for product groups from Table 7.2 as $w_{g,65}$, with w_{60} = 13.3 percent and w_{65} = 12.9 percent, the reconstructed weights $w_{g,60}$ are reported in Table 7.3.

To reconstruct the weights of other product groups for 1960, formula (7.1) will be applied. The resultant weights and the basis on which they can be computed – the 1960 and 1965 percentages given by Karlik and Astaf'ev et al. – are in Table 7.4. For example, the proportion of transformers according to formula (7.1) equals

$$w_{60,K} = \frac{3.6 \cdot 3.6}{3.8} = 3.4,$$

as shown in Table 7.4.

Table 7.5 is the final step of reconstructing the breakdowns of the EI by product group. It combines the reconstructed percentages for 1960 from Tables 7.3 and 7.4 with the 1965, 1970, and 1975 data provided by Karlik. Each column total represents the combined share of the listed product groups in the total of EI's gross output. For example, in 1975 this combined share was 79.1 percent. Although the listed product groups exhaust almost all of the EI's branches, the EI also manufactures many other goods that are peripheral to its specialization.

Table 7.3. Reconstructed Proportions of Electrical Machines in the
Electrotechnical Output in 1960 (Percent)

Product Group	Percent
Turbine Generators	1.5
Large Electrical Machines	4.0
Small Electrical Machines	1.7
Electric Motors, 100 Kilowatts and over	.9
Electric Motors, under 100 Kilowatts	7.2
Total	13.3

Source: Table 7.2

Given the percentages, the outputs for the product groups listed
in Table 7.5 are computed. To do so, the total EI output could be
multiplied by the percentages given in Table 7.5 for 1960, 1965, 1970
and 1975. However, in Table 7.1 the information on the EI output
is provided for 1959, 1966, 1972 and 1982, i.e., does not correspond
to the years for which the breakdowns are reconstructed in Table
7.5. To find the outputs for 1960, 1965 and 1970, the official growth
indices are applied to the data from Table 7.1. Given the set of the
growth indices, the results of the reconstruction would differ depending on the choice of the output from Table 7.1. The discrepancies
are likely to be minimized if, to estimate an unknown output, the
closest possible output from Table 7.1 is picked. Specifically, it pays
to use the 1959 output and the 1959/1960 growth to estimate the
1960 output, the 1966 output and the 1966/1965 growth to estimate
the 1965 output, and the 1972 output and the 1972/1970 growth to
estimate the 1970 output. The rounded official growth indices used
in this procedure are in Table 7.6. The results of the application of
the indices from Table 7.6 to the 1959, 1966 and 1972 outputs are in

Table 7.4. Reconstructed Proportions of Product Groups, other than Electrical Machines, in the Electrotechnical Industry in 1960 (Percent)

Product Group	Percent	Basis for Computation		
		1965 Proportion, Karlik	1960 Proportion, Astaf'ev	1965 Proportion, Astaf'ev
Transformers	3.4	3.6	3.6	3.8
High-Voltage Equipment	2.8	3.3	3.3	3.9
Low-Voltage Equipment	8.2	8.7	8.8	9.3
Electric Locomotives	2.5	2.4	2.7	2.6
Electric Welding Equipment	2.1	2.2	2.1	2.2
Electrothermal Equipment	.8	1.1	.9	1.2
Lighting Engineering Fittings	1.9	.4	3.0	3.8
Cable Products	29.3	26.3	32.6	29.3
Electric Light Bulbs	2.2	2.6	2.9	3.4

Sources: Astaf'ev, et al. (1975, p.35) and Karlik (1977, p.35).

Table 7.7. The 1975 value in Table 7.7 is taken as computed by the
Center for International Research of the U.S. Bureau of the Census.

Table 7.5.   Reconstructed Breakdowns by Product Group of the
Electrotechnical Industry (Percent)

Product Group	1960	1965	1970	1975
Turbine Generators	1.5	1.4	.9	.9
Large Electrical Machines	4.0	3.9	3.6	2.6
Small Electrical Machines	1.7	1.7	2.3	2.0
Electric Motors,				
100 Kilowatts and over	.9	.9	1.0	.7
Electric Motors,				
under 100 Kilowatts	5.2	5.0	5.2	5.5
Transformers	3.4	3.6	4.6	6.1
High-Voltage Equipment	2.8	3.3	4.0	4.2
Low-Voltage Equipment	8.2	8.7	12.6	14.1
Electric Locomotives	2.5	2.4	1.6	1.5
Electric Welding Equipment	2.1	2.2	2.7	2.5
Electrothermal Equipment	.8	1.1	1.6	2.0
Lighting Engineering Fittings	1.9	2.4	6.0	5.7
Cable Products	29.3	26.3	28.5	26.7
Electric Light Bulbs	2.2	2.6	4.4	4.6
Total	66.5	65.5	79.0	79.1

Applying percentages from Table 7.5 to the EI outputs in Table
7.6 yields outputs for the product groups identified in Table 7.7. The
results are in Table 7.8. As one can see from Table 7.8, the growth
indices for electrotechnical products vary significantly in the 1960-75
period. The lowest index is recorded for "big" items such as turbine
generators and electric locomotives (236) and the greatest index for
"small" items with high turnover of varying products such as electric

Table 7.6.   Official Growth Indices of the Electrotechnical Industry
Used in the Reconstruction Process

Year	Index		
1959	100		
1960	121		
1965		100	
1966		109	
1970			100
1972			117

Source: *Narkhoz SSSR* (1964, p.182, 1970, p.206, and 1972, p.256).

engineering fittings (1,181). Table 7.8 concludes the first step of the
reconstruction process.

At the second step, production in physical units and quality parameters is determined. In Soviet economic planning, the main quality parameter of machines and equipment is singled out whenever
possible. Usually it is the parameter of productivity or capacity. For
the EI, the more powerful the machine, *ceteris paribus,* the higher
its price. In the case of the automotive industry there was no single
characteristic of quality that would dominate others, but for the EI
it is possible to use the machine's capacity or power for this purpose.

For some electrotechnical machines and equipment, the number
of units is used as a physical indicator. Products such as wires
are measured in metric tons. Quality parameters, such as kilowatt,
kilowatt-hour or kilovolt-ampere, characterize the capacity or the
productivity of equipment. For some machines, e.g., electric motors,
both physical units and quality parameters are reported. For others, total production is given either in physical units or in quality
parameters. There are also machines and equipment for which no
such information is available.

Table 7.7. Reconstructed Output of the Electrotechnical Industry
in Producers' Prices (Millions of Rubles)

Year	1960	1965	1970	1975
Value	2,993	5,689	7,633	11,790

Sources: Table 7.1; *Narkhoz SSSR* (1972, p.222) and Tretiakova
(Working Paper, 1979, p.21).

Table 7.9 summarizes the available information on output of electrotechnical products in physical units and in quality parameters.
In addition to the information provided by official Soviet statistics,
Astaf'ev, et al. (1975, p.20) indicates the data for several product groups – electric furnaces, electric welding equipment, porcelain
ware, and electric wire – that are not published in Soviet statistical
yearbooks. But this information is only available for 1960 and 1975,
and there are no estimates for 1965 and 1970. The Astaf'ev source
includes the indicators of physical output for cable products. The
importance of this information is shown by the fact that, according
to Table 7.5, the cable product group is the largest for the entire EI,
accounting for 26 to 29 percent of its output. With this in mind, it
is useful to consider the information for 1960 and 1975 when a direct
comparison is made for these two years.

7.2. Real and Inflationary Growth of the Electrotechnical Industry

Since we are given different types of physical indicators for electrotechnical products, it would be interesting to find both the index
of average price (2.15) and the index of average price adjusted for
quality (2.18) and to compare the results. The index of average price
is used in the form

Table 7.8. Output of the Electrotechnical Industry by Product Group (Million of Rubles)

Product Group	1960	1965	1970	1975 Value	1975 Growth (1960=100)
Turbine Generators	44.9	79.5	68.7	106.1	236
Large Electrical Machines	119.7	221.4	274.8	306.5	256
Small Electrical Machines	50.9	96.5	175.6	235.8	463
Electric Motors, 100 Kilowatts and over	26.9	51.1	76.3	82.5	307
Electric Motors, under 100 Kilowatts	155.6	283.9	396.9	648.5	417
Transformers	101.8	204.4	351.1	719.2	706
High-Voltage Equipment	83.8	187.4	305.3	495.2	591
Low-Voltage Equipment	247.4	494.0	961.8	1,662.4	677
Electric Locomotives	74.8	136.3	122.1	176.9	236
Electric Welding Equipment	62.9	124.9	206.1	294.8	469
Electrothermal Equipment	23.9	62.5	122.1	237.8	987
Lighting Engineering Fittings	56.9	136.3	458.0	672.0	1,181
Cable Products	876.9	1,493.3	2,177.4	3,147.9	359
Electric Light Bulbs	65.8	147.6	335.9	542.3	824

Source: Tables 7.5 and 7.7.

$$\bar{I}_t = \frac{\sum p_{it}q_{it}}{\sum p_{io}q_{io}} \Big/ \frac{\sum q_{it}}{\sum q_{io}}, \tag{7.2}$$

and the index of average price adjusted for quality, in the form

$$\bar{I}_t^r = \frac{\sum p_{it}q_{it}}{\sum p_{io}q_{io}} \Big/ \frac{\sum r_{it}q_{it}}{\sum r_{io}q_{io}}, \tag{7.3}$$

where p_{it} and p_{io} = price of product i in year t and 0, respectively, q_{it} and q_{io} = quantity of product i manufactured in year t and 0, respectively; and r_{it} and r_{io} = parameter of quality for product i in year t and 0, respectively.

The information needed for formulas (7.2) and (7.3) is given by Tables 7.8 and 7.9, though it is in aggregate forms rather than for individual products. Those tables provide the results of summation in formulas (7.2) and (7.3). For simplicity, there is only one summation subscript in formulas (7.2) and (7.3), referring to product. The results of summation not having a product subscript consequently total the relevant indicators into one product group. If, however, there are more than one product group, as in our case, the variables under summation must have two subscripts, referring to product. With such a correction, the sums in formulas (7.2) and (7.3) actually have the following meaning: $\Sigma_i p_{ijt}q_{ijt}$ and $\Sigma_i p_{ijo}q_{ijo}$ = value of output of product group j in current year t and base year 0, respectively; $\Sigma_i r_{ijt}q_{ijt}$ and $\Sigma_i r_{ijo}q_{ijo}$ = output of product group j in units of quality in current year t and base year 0, respectively; and $\Sigma_i q_{ijt}$ and $\Sigma_i q_{ijo}$ = output of product j in physical units in current year t and base year 0, respectively.

On the basis of the information in Tables 7.8 and 7.9, the following indices can be computed:

1) the index of average price for large electrical machines, electric motors of 100 kilowatts and over, electric motors under 100 kilowatts, electric light bulbs, electric welding equipment and electric wire, and

2) the index of average price adjusted for quality for turbine generators, electric motors of 100 kilowatts and over, electric motors under 100 kilowatts, transformers and electric furnaces.

Table 7.9. Output of the Electrotechnical Products in Physical Units and Quality Parameters

Product	1960	1965	1970	1975
Turbine Generators, Millions of Kilowatts	7.9	14.4	10.6	17.1
Large Electrical Machines, Thousands	8.0	15.3	17.0	24.0
Electric Motors, 100 Kilowatts and over, Thousands	19.5	25.2	28.0	35.5
Millions of Kilowatts	4.1	5.3	5.5	7.0
Electric Motors, under 100 Kilowatts, Thousands	2,820.0	4,688.0	5,837.0	8,026.0
Millions of Kilowatts	13.5	21.6	27.8	34.7
Transformers, Millions of Kilowatt-Amperes	49.4	95.3	105.9	137.0
Electric Light Bulbs, Millions	638.1	983.0	1,627.0	2,050.0
Electric Furnaces, Thousands of Kilowatts	541.0	NA	NA	1,660.0
Electric Welding Equipment, Thousands	96.7	NA	NA	274.0
Porcelain Ware, Thousands of Tons	54.5	NA	NA	150.0
Electric Wire, Thousands of Tons	242.6	NA	NA	430.0

Sources: *Narkhoz SSSR* (1974, p.239 and 1982, p.162) and Astaf'ev, et al. (1975, p.20).

Each of the indices is computed for four time periods: 1960-65, 1965-70, 1970-75 and, overall, 1960-75. The following two examples illustrate how the information from Tables 7.8 and 7.9 is used in this computation:

1) The index of average price for large electrical machines for the 1960-65 period. From Table 7.8, $\Sigma p_{it} q_{it} = 221.4$ million rubles for 1965 and $\Sigma p_{io} q_{io} = 119.7$ million rubles for 1960. According to Table 7.9, $\Sigma q_{it} = 15.3$ thousand machines for 1965 and $\Sigma q_{io} = 8$ thousand machines for 1960. Therefore,

$$\bar{I}_{65/60} = \frac{221.4}{119.7} \Big/ \frac{15.3}{8.0} = 96.7,$$

which means that, in the time period of 1960-65, the average price of large electrical machines dropped by 3.3 percent.

2) The index of average price adjusted for quality for turbine generators for the 1965-70 period. According to Table 7.8, $\Sigma p_{it} q_{it} = 68.7$ million rubles for 1970 and $\Sigma p_{io} q_{io} = 79.5$ million rubles for 1965. From Table 7.9, $\Sigma r_{it} q_{it} = 10.6$ million kilowatts for 1970 and $\Sigma r_{io} q_{io} = 14.4$ million kilowatts for 1965. Then,

$$\bar{I}^r_{70/65} = \frac{68.7}{79.5} \Big/ \frac{10.6}{14.4} = 117.4,$$

i.e., in the 1965-70 period, the average price of turbine generators adjusted for quality change rose by 17.4 percent.

Computation of the two indices and the results are demonstrated for each of the time periods in Tables 7.10 through 7.13.

As can be seen from Table 7.10, the average price declined between 1960 and 1965 for the group of large electrical machines but rose for three other product groups, most significantly for electric motors of 100 kilowatts and over (47 percent) and electric light bulbs (45.6 percent). Translated into average annual tempos, the decline was 0.7 percent for large electrical machines, while the increase for

Table 7.10. Computation of the Index of Average Price and the Index of Average Price Adjusted for Quality for 1960-65

Product Group	Computation	Average Annual Percentage
I. Index of Average Price		
Large Electrical Machines	$\frac{221.4}{119.7} / \frac{15.3}{8.0} = 96.7$	-.7
Electric Motors, 100 Kilowatts and over	$\frac{51.1}{26.9} / \frac{25.2}{19.5} = 147.0$	8.0
Electric Motors, under 100 Kilowatts	$\frac{283.9}{155.6} / \frac{4688}{2820} = 109.8$	1.9
Electric Light Bulbs	$\frac{147.6}{65.8} / \frac{983.0}{638.1} = 145.6$	7.8
II. Index of Average Price Adjusted for Quality		
Turbine Generators	$\frac{79.5}{44.9} / \frac{14.4}{7.9} = 97.1$	-.6
Electric Motors, 100 Kilowatts and over	$\frac{51.1}{26.9} / \frac{5.3}{4.1} = 147.0$	8.0
Electric Motors, under 100 Kilowatts	$\frac{283.9}{21.6} / \frac{21.6}{13.5} = 114.0$	2.7
Transformers	$\frac{204.4}{101.8} / \frac{95.3}{49.4} = 104.1$	.8

Sources: Tables 7.8 and 7.9.

electric motors of 100 kilowatt and over was 8 percent. When measured by the index of average price adjusted for quality, the prices for turbine generators fell by 2.9 percent in that five-year period, or 0.6 percent per annum, and those of electric motors of 100 kilowatts and over rose by 47 percent, or 8 percent per annum.

The case of the two groups of electric motors presents an interesting opportunity for the comparison of growth in the product group's average prices and those same prices adjusted for quality. As a matter of fact, quality change did not affect the movement of prices for electric motors of 100 kilowatts and over. As Table 7.10 shows, the annual growth rate of the average price, both unadjusted and adjusted, equals 8 percent for this product group. For the second group of electric motors, those under 100 kilowatts, the average price adjusted for quality rose by 14 percent in the 1960-65 period, or 2.7 percent per annum, i.e. faster than the unadjusted average price (1.9 percent per annum). This result means that the quality change, measured by the electric motors' capacity, lagged behind their average price rise in that period.

The 1967 price reform brought about some corrections for the EI prices, but, in addition, they rose because of changes in product assortment, costs, technology and structural shifts. As Table 7.11 shows, the trend of declining prices for large electrical machines was reversed in the 1965-70 period, and the average price rose by 11.7 percent, or 2.2 percent a year. The prices of other product groups rose even faster, with the biggest increase for the average price of electric light bulbs – 37.5 percent, or 6.6 percent per annum. However, this increase is lower than the rise of the average price of electric light bulbs at the rate of 7.8 percent in the 1960-65 period. In general, the 1965-70 average price increase exceeded that of the 1960-65 period, with a smaller spread between the highest and the lowest annual rates.

Looking at average prices adjusted for quality, one notices that they began rising in the 1965-70 period for turbine generators at an average annual rate of 3.3 percent, rather than continuing the decline of the previous five-year period. Instead of the earlier moderate increase at an annual rate of 0.8 percent, the average price of transformers adjusted for quality change soared at an annual rate

Table 7.11. Computation of the Index of Average Price and the Index of Average Price Adjusted for Quality for 1965-70

Product Group	Computation	Average Annual Percentage
I. Index of Average Price		
Large Electrical Machines	$\dfrac{274.8}{221.4} / \dfrac{17.0}{15.3} = 111.7$	2.2
Electric Motors, 100 Kilowatts and over	$\dfrac{76.3}{51.1} / \dfrac{28.0}{25.2} = 134.4$	6.1
Electric Motors, under 100 Kilowatts	$\dfrac{396.9}{283.9} / \dfrac{5837}{4688} = 112.3$	2.3
Electric Light Bulbs	$\dfrac{335.9}{147.6} / \dfrac{1627}{983} = 137.5$	6.6
II. Index of Average Price Adjusted for Quality		
Turbine Generators	$\dfrac{68.7}{79.5} / \dfrac{10.6}{14.4} = 117.4$	3.3
Electric Motors, 100 Kilowatts and over	$\dfrac{76.3}{51.1} / \dfrac{5.5}{5.3} = 143.9$	7.6
Electric Motors, under 100 Kilowatts	$\dfrac{396.9}{283.9} / \dfrac{27.8}{21.6} = 108.6$	1.7
Transformers	$\dfrac{351.1}{204.4} / \dfrac{105.9}{95.3} = 154.6$	9.1

Sources: Tables 7.8 and 7.9.

of 9.1 percent in the 1965-70 period. As before, there was a close movement of both types of prices – average unadjusted and adjusted for quality – for electric motors (34.4 and 43.9 percent, respectively, for those of 100 kilowatts and over, and 12.3 and 8.6 percent, respectively, for smaller ones).

As Table 7.12 shows, there were more decreases of average prices in the third five-year period, 1970-75, than in the previous ten years. The sharpest decline of 21 percent, or 4.6 percent per annum, occurred for large electrical machines. Both types of prices – average unadjusted and adjusted for quality – for electric motors of 100 kilowatts and over dropped by the same percentage, at the annual rate of 3.1 percent. Average prices of electric motors under 100 kilowatts rose by 18.8 percent, i.e. 3.5 percent a year, and, when adjusted for quality, by 30.9 percent, or 5.5 percent a year. In this case, again, price growth surpassed that of quality. In general, the two groups of electric motors demonstrate much similarity in the movement of their average prices, both unadjusted and adjusted, in the three five-year periods, as one can see from Tables 7.10-7.12. This effect is possible if the average capacity of an electric motor remained relatively stable in the period under consideration, but individual motor prices rose.

The average price of electric light bulbs rose in the 1970-75 period at an annual rate of 5.1 percent, continuing the trend of decelerated inflation growth (compared with an annual 7.8 percent in the 1960-65 period and 6.6 percent in the 1965-70 period). As in the previous five years, the average price of transformers continued to rise, at a record high annual rate of 9.6 percent. The adjusted-for-quality prices of turbine generators, on the other hand, reversed the upward trend of the 1965-70 period, dropping by 4.3 percent, or 0.9 percent per annum. Taking into account the metal-intensive character of turbine generators and price increases for metal in that period, such a decline might be surprising, but one should realize that the adjusted-for-quality prices in this case measure the cost of a unit of capacity. If we possessed the information on average unadjusted prices for turbine generators, we might have seen an upward tendency. Since turbine generators had presumably become more powerful over time, their capacity growth surpassed the increases in their average price. Such

Table 7.12. Computation of the Index of Average Price and the Index of Average Price Adjusted for Quality for 1970-75

Product Group	Computation	Average Annual Percentage
I. Index of Average Price		
Large Electrical Machines	$\dfrac{306.5/24}{274.8/17} = 79.0$	-4.6
Electric Motors, 100 Kilowatts and over	$\dfrac{82.5/35.5}{76.3/28.0} = 85.3$	-3.1
Electric Motors, under 100 Kilowatts	$\dfrac{648.5/8026}{396.9/5837} = 118.8$	3.5
Electric Light Bulbs	$\dfrac{542.3/2050}{335.9/1627} = 128.1$	5.1
II. Index of Average Price Adjusted for Quality		
Turbine Generators	$\dfrac{106.1/17.1}{68.7/10.6} = 95.7$	- .9
Electric Motors, 100 Kilowatts and over	$\dfrac{82.5/7.0}{76.3/5.5} = 85.0$	-3.1
Electric Motors, under 100 Kilowatts	$\dfrac{648.5/34.7}{396.9/27.8} = 130.9$	5.5
Transformers	$\dfrac{719.2/137.0}{351.1/105.9} = 158.3$	9.6

Sources: Tables 7.8 and 7.9.

a result, when a hypothetical generator becomes more expensive but a unit of its capacity becomes cheaper to the user, corresponds to the planners' policy of setting new prices.

Table 7.13 summarizes the computation of the price indices for the whole fifteen-year period. Generally, the 1960-75 index can be found as a chain index which is equal to the product of three five-year indices found above, i.e.,

$$I_{75/60} = I_{75/70} \cdot I_{70/65} \cdot I_{65/60}.$$

For example, for large electrical machines, in decimals,

$$.853 = .790 \cdot 1.117 \cdot .967.$$

However, it is not possible to compute a chain index for all product groups in Table 7.13 since the table also contains the information for the three product groups not considered before – electric welding equipment, electric wire and electric furnaces. For this reason, the indices are found by the direct comparison of 1975 and 1960. Of the six product groups for which the index of average price is computed, only large electrical machines demonstrate a price decline of 1.1 percent per annum. The highest annual growth rate of 6.5 percent is recorded for electric light bulbs, with the second highest (6.4 percent) for the average price of transformers adjusted for quality. The average prices of the three new products rose at a rate compatible with most of the other product groups. Thus, the average price of electric wire doubled in 15 years, rising at an annual rate of 4.8 percent. For electric welding equipment it rose by 65.4 percent, or 3.4 percent per annum. The growth of the average price of electric furnaces was much more moderate – 23 percent in 15 years, or 1.4 percent a year.

As noted above, there are similarities in the movement of the average price, unadjusted and adjusted, for electric motors in the three five-year periods. Overall, the average price of electric motors of 100 kilowatts and over rose at an annual rate of 3.5 percent, and the adjusted price, at a rate of 4 percent. The corresponding percentages for small motors were 2.6 and 3.3 percent, respectively. Hence, in both cases the cost of a unit of capacity rose somewhat

Table 7.13. Computation of the Index of Average Price and the Index of Average Price Adjusted for Quality for 1960-75

Product Group	Computation	Average Annual Percentage
I. Index of Average Price		
Large Electrical Machines	$\frac{306.5}{119.7} / \frac{24}{8} = 85.4$	-1.1
Electric Motors, 100 Kilowatts and over	$\frac{82.5}{26.9} / \frac{35.5}{19.5} = 168.5$	3.5
Electric Motors, under 100 Kilowatts	$\frac{648.5}{155.6} / \frac{8026}{2820} = 146.4$	2.6
Electric Light Bulbs	$\frac{542.3}{65.8} / \frac{2050}{638.1} = 256.5$	6.5
Electric Welding Equipment	$\frac{294.8}{62.9} / \frac{274.0}{96.7} = 165.4$	3.4
Electric Wire	$\frac{3147.9}{876.9} / \frac{430.0}{242.6} = 202.5$	4.8
II. Index of Average Price Adjusted for Quality		
Turbine Generators	$\frac{106.1}{44.9} / \frac{17.1}{7.9} = 109.2$	.6
Electric Motors, 100 Kilowatts and over	$\frac{82.5}{26.9} / \frac{7.0}{4.1} = 179.6$	4.0
Electric Motors, under 100 Kilowatts	$\frac{648.5}{155.6} / \frac{34.7}{13.5} = 162.1$	3.3
Transformers	$\frac{719.2}{101.8} / \frac{137.0}{49.4} = 254.7$	6.4
Electric Furnances	$\frac{235.8}{62.5} / \frac{1660}{541} = 123.0$	1.4

Sources: Tables 7.8 and 7.9.

faster than the average price. The fact of a close movement of the two types of prices, if established, can generally be used in other cases when information on only one of the prices is available.

After the analysis of price changes by product group, the next step is to estimate the overall index of average price and the index of average price adjusted for quality for the part of EI represented by the product groups in Tables 7.10-7.13. The easiest way in this multiproduct case is to apply a weighting procedure, given the individual product group indices. The products' proportions of total value of output could be used as weights. Since there is a choice of different timing for the weights, we pick the current-year weights, in a belief that they may best serve the purpose of adjusting the indices to the end of the period. If, for example, the index is measured for the 1960-65 period, then

$$I_{65/60} = \Sigma I_{j,65/60} \cdot w_{j,65}, \qquad (7.4)$$

where $I_{65/60}$ and $I_{j,65/60}$ = price index for the 1960-65 period for the industry and for product group j, respectively; $w_{j,65}$ = the weight of product group j in the total output in 1965, i.e $w_{j,65} = Q_{j,65}/Q_{65}$. ($Q_{65}$ and $Q_{j,65}$ = value of output for the industry and product group j in 1965, respectively, $Q_{65} = \Sigma Q_{j,65}$.) Formula (7.4) is then used in the form

$$I_{65/60} = \frac{\Sigma I_{j,65/60} \cdot Q_{j,65}}{\Sigma Q_{j,65}}.$$

The output information for the computation of weights in the index of average price and in the index of average price adjusted for quality for the EI is from Table 7.8. For convenience, the necessary data are in Tables 7.14 and 7.15.

The computation of both indices – average unadjusted and adjusted for quality – is demonstrated in Table 7.16, along with average annual growth rates. Possible errors in the indices can be a result of the discrepancy between the theoretical definition of price growth and the method used for the computation, as discussed in Sections 2.2 and 2.3. Another problem arises from the errors and

Table 7.14. Outputs for the Computation of Weights in the Index of Average Price for Electrotechnical Industry

Product Group	Period of Computation			
	65/60	70/65	75/70	75/60
Large Electrical Machines	221.4	274.8	306.5	306.5
Electric Motors, 100 Kilowatts and over	51.1	76.3	82.5	82.5
Electric Motors, under 100 Kilowatts	283.9	396.9	648.5	648.5
Electric Light Bulbs	147.6	335.9	542.3	542.3
Electric Welding Equipment	–	–	–	294.8
Electric Wire	–	–	–	3,147.9
Total	704.0	1,083.9	1,579.8	5,022.5

Source: Table 7.8.

Table 7.15. Outputs for the Computation of Weights in the Index of Average Price Adjusted for Quality for Electrotechnical Industry

Product Group	Period of Computation			
	65/60	70/65	75/70	75/60
Turbine Generators	79.5	68.7	106.1	106.1
Electric Motors, 100 Kilowatts and over	51.1	76.3	82.5	82.5
Electric Motors, under 100 Kilowatts	283.9	396.9	648.5	648.5
Transformers	204.4	351.1	719.2	719.2
Electric Furnaces	–	–	–	235.8
Total	618.9	893.0	1,556.3	1,792.1

Source: Table 7.8.

inconsistencies in the information as those due to using several different sources. These are familiar problems in this type of research. An important question involves the extent to which the product groups in the Table 7.16 aggregates actually represent the EI. The product groups included in the computation of the indices – average unadjusted and adjusted for quality as shown in Table 7.13 – accounted for 52 percent of the EI value of output in 1977 and may be considered representative. We therefore view the results based on the product groups in Table 7.16 as reflecting the entire EI.

As one can see from Table 7.16, the EI weighted average price increased by 15.9 percent in the 1960-65 period. In the next five years, the price inflation accelerated to 21.5 percent, and, finally, decelerated to the level of 12.5 percent in the 1970-75 period. The 1960-75 composite index rose by 91.1 percent, at an annual rate of 4.4 percent. This is much higher than an increase of 58.4 percent that one would have obtained by multiplying the 1960-65, 1965-70, and 1970-75 indices. The difference is the result of taking into account two additional product groups for the overall 1960-75 computation that are not available by the five-year periods. Since we accept the 1960-75 index as the most comprehensive measure, it follows that the average price of an electrotechnical product grew at a rate of 4.4 percent per annum over that fifteen-year period.

We now examine the pattern of change in average prices adjusted for quality. As the comparison of the two parts of Table 7.16 shows, there is much similarity in the movement of the two indices, although the tendencies differ by the five-year periods. Unlike the unadjusted price, the adjusted average price exhibits an accelerated upward trend. After an increase of 11.3 percent in the 1960-65 period, it rose by 30.4 percent between 1965 and 1970 and by 38.7 percent in the 1970-75 period. As a result, every new unit of capacity of electrotechnical machines and equipment became consistently more expensive to the user. If, in the computation of the overall 1960-75 index, only the product groups used for each of the five-year periods were considered, the adjusted average price would increase by 101.3 percent, not 91.8 percent as in Table 7.16. In this case, the inclusion of a new product group does not alter the results as significantly as in the case of the index of unadjusted average prices.

Table 7.16. Computation of Price Indices for Electrotechnical Industry

Period	Computation	Average Annual Percentage
	Index of Average Price	
1960-65	$\dfrac{96.7(221.4) + 147.0(51.1) + 109.8(283.9) + 145.6(147.6)}{704.0} = 115.9$	3.0
1965-70	$\dfrac{111.7(274.8) + 134.4(76.3) + 112.3(396.9) + 137.5(335.9)}{1083.9} = 121.5$	4.0
1970-75	$\dfrac{79.0(306.5) + 85.3(82.5) + 118.8(648.5) + 128.1(542.3)}{1579.8} = 112.5$	2.4
1960-75	$\dfrac{84.5(306.5) + 168.5(82.5) + 146.4(648.5) + 256.5(542.3) + 165.4(294.8) + 202.5(3147.9)}{5022.5} = 191.1$	4.4
	Index of Average Price Adjusted for Quality	
1960-65	$\dfrac{97.1(79.5) + 147(51.1) + 114(283.9) + 104.1(204.4)}{618.9} = 111.3$	2.2
1965-70	$\dfrac{117.4(68.7) + 143.9(76.3) + 108.6(396.9) + 154.6(351.1)}{893.0} = 130.4$	5.5
1970-75	$\dfrac{95.7(106.1) + 85.2(82.5) + 130.9(648.5) + 158.3(719.2)}{1556.3} = 138.7$	6.8
1960-75	$\dfrac{109.2(106.1) + 179.6(82.5) + 162.1(648.5) + 254.7(719.2) + 123.0(235.8)}{1792.1} = 191.8$	4.4

Sources: Tables 7.10-7.15.

An important message of Table 7.16 is that, overall, both types of prices – unadjusted and adjusted for quality – moved closely together for the EI in the 1970-75 period. They increased by almost the same 91 to 92 percent, at an annual rate of 4.4 percent. As we discussed above, according to Soviet pricing philosophy, average prices may rise, but at a lower pace than product quality improvements. The "absolute" prices of new technologies are viewed as less important than the "relative" prices, i.e., prices per unit of productivity or capacity. To put it differently, a machine's price increase should be accompanied by an even higher productivity or capacity growth, so that a unit of productivity or capacity becomes cheaper to the user. According to Table 7.16, this did not occur for the EI. Moreover, if the two products that overlap in both indices – electric motors of 100 kilowatts and over and electric motors under 100 kilowatts – are considered, their averaged annual price increases, unadjusted and adjusted for quality change, were 2.8 percent and 3.5 percent, respectively, for the 1960-75 period. Hence, in this case, the cost of a unit of capacity even rose more rapidly than the cost of a unit of equipment as the average capacity of a motor declined. We conclude from the computation in Table 7.16 that the average of 4.4 percent reflects the annual inflation rate for electrotechnical products in the 1960-75 period.

The Soviet EI experienced exceptionally high growth over the 1960-75 period, after starting from a relatively low production level in the 1950s. Table 7.17 demonstrates the official growth indices for that period. The high growth rates in Table 7.17 should now be corrected on the basis of our analysis. Assuming that Table 7.17 reports the nominal growth rates, the real and inflationary components could be separated in a procedure similar to one used in Chapter 6. The data – the price indices and the nominal growth rates – are in Tables 7.16 and 7.17. The index of the average price adjusted for quality from the second part of Table 7.16 is used as a proxy for the price index. Rather than applying formula (6.9) to the annual growth rates, as we did in Chapter 6, a version of formula (6.9) is used which enables us to obtain the real growth index in percentage terms:

Table 7.17. Official Growth Indices for the Electrotechnical
Industry in the 1960-75 Period (Percent)

Period	Index	Average Annual Rate
1960-65	190	13.7
1965-70	159	9.7
1970-75	151	8.6
1960-75	456	10.6

Source: *Narkhoz SSSR* (1970, pp. 205-6 and 1975, pp. 255-6).

$$R = \left(1 + \frac{r^v - r^p}{1 + r^p}\right) 100.$$

The computation, along with the information used, is in Table 7.18.

It is clear from the results in Table 7.18 that the 1960-65 five-year period was the golden age for the Soviet EI. The officially reported growth for that period equals 90 percent. In our analysis, this growth is referred to as nominal, with the resultant real component amounting to 70.7 percent. Hence, adjustment for inflation does not significantly affect that period's growth figures, which still remain high. Translated into annual rates, the real average growth equals 11.3 percent, instead of a 13.7 percent equivalent for the official growth index. In the next two five-year periods, price increases accelerated, and that leads to a much greater discount of the official growth rates in Table 7.18. Thus, the official growth of 59 percent in the 1965-70 period, or 9.7 percent per annum, becomes a moderate 21.9 percent real growth, or 4 percent per annum. The most dramatic reduction though occurs in the 1970-75 period, when real growth should be only 8.9 percent, i.e. 1.7 percent per annum,

Table 7.18. Computation of Real Growth for the Electrotechnical Industry (Percent)

Period	Nominal Growth Index	Price Increase Index	Real Growth Index	Real Annual Growth Rate
1960–65	190	111.3	$(1 + \frac{.90 - .113}{1.113})100 = 170.7$	11.3
1965–70	159	130.4	$(1 + \frac{.59 - .304}{1.304})100 = 121.9$	4.0
1970–75	151	138.7	$(1 + \frac{.51 - .387}{1.387})100 = 108.9$	1.7
1960–75	456	191.8	$(1 + \frac{3.56 - .918}{1.918})100 = 237.7$	5.9

Sources: Tables 7.16 and 7.17.

rather than the 51 percent, or 8.6 percent per annum, that follows from the official data.

Finally, as shown in Table 7.17, Soviet statistics report an index of the EI production of 456 percent for the 1960-75 period, which means an impressive growth of 356 percent. Our calculation transforms this into a much more modest real growth of about 138 percent. (As noted above, the product of real growth indices for the three five-year periods is not exactly equal to the entire 1960-75 index because the product groups taken into account do not coincide.) As a result, the real annual growth rate turns out to be 5.9 percent, compared to an official rate of 10.6 percent. This is still a respectable performance by any standards. Comparing the estimated real average growth rate of 5.9 percent with the nominal rate of 10.6 percent $(4.56^{1/15}-1)$, we conclude that the EI's growth rates from 1960 to 1975 may be overstated by official Soviet statistics by as much as 80 percent.

Chapter 8
Estimating Growth of Energy and Power Machinery

8.1. The Reconstruction Process

Table 4.3 shows the value of output of energy and power machinery (EPM) as little more than one percent of total Soviet MBMW production in 1982. This does not, however, diminish the role of the industry. The importance attached to the EPM is that it shares the success of the Soviet electrification program with the electric power industry. The data in Table 4.3, computed on the basis of the input-output tables, show that the EPM declined from 1.4 to 1.1 percent of MBMW production over the 1972-82 period. This was generally true for all branches of heavy machinery and equipment. Examples are mining and metallurgical, hoist-transport, electrotechnical, pump, chemical and construction machinery and equipment. These industries are metal intensive, and their outputs are large in size and require long production periods. Consequently, their product turnover is rather slow, except in some product groups of the electrotechnical industry. This puts the heavy-machinery industries at a disadvantage compared to high-technology industries. Table 4.2 compares the official Soviet growth rates for the EPM with several branches representing a variety of MBMW products – eletrotechnical, machine tools, instruments, automobiles and agricultural machines – since 1970. All of those branches, as well as the entire MBMW sector, grew faster than the EPM.

The official growth rates, combined with the values of output for the EPM from the input-output tables, are used at the first stage of the data reconstruction process. The gross values of output are

245

Table 8.1. The Output of Soviet Energy and Power Machinery
(Millions of Rubles)

Year	Producers' Prices	Purchasers' Prices
1959	596	622
1966	1,441	1,486
1972	1,495	1,587
1982	2,227	2,365

Sources: Gallik, et al. (1975, pp. 53 and 71 and 1983, pp. 40 and
68) and Kostinsky (1976, pp. 13 and 69 and 1987).

available for 1959, 1966, 1972 and 1982; the data are in Table 8.1. As
the table shows, the difference between producers' and purchasers'
prices for the EPM was insignificant. That effect is predictable because the EPM has produced very few consumer goods. In our
further calculations, the output values are in producers' prices. The
official growth index for the Soviet EPM is reported in Table 8.2.
The values are combined in one time series on the basis of piece-
wise indices from 1960 to 1985. Looking at these indices by five-year
periods, the highest average growth rate for the EPM was in the
1961-65 period (12.3 percent) and the lowest, in the 1976-80 period
(4.5 percent). In the 11th five-year period (1981-85), an attempt
was made to reverse the declining growth of the EPM which led to
an increase of the average annual growth rate to 5.9 percent.

On the basis of the growth indices and the values of output from
the input-output tables, in principle it is possible to restore the entire time series of the EPM outputs for the 1959-85 period. The
problem, however, is that the official growth indices pertain to outputs in comparable prices. The input-output tables, on the other
hand, measure the outputs in current prices, since they are based on
the official Soviet input-output statistics. In our methodology, the
data in current prices should be used in order to capture the full extent of inflationary growth. For this reason, we use the four outputs

from Table 8.1 and correct the official growth rates accordingly. For example, the official growth index for the 1960-66 period, from Table 8.2, equals 223, and the index that follows from the input-output tables, from Table 8.1, equals 242 (i.e., 1441÷596). The coefficient by which we correct the official growth rates for the 1960-66 period is then found to be 1.15 (i.e., 142÷123). One should note that the growth rates, not the indices, are corrected in this procedure. Similar corrections are made for the 1967-72 and 1973-82 periods. The official growth rates are applied to the 1982-85 interval. The resultant output estimates are in Table 8.3.

Table 8.2. The Official Growth Index for Soviet Energy and Power Machinery in the 1960-85 Period (1959=100)

Year	Growth Index	Year	Growth Index
1960	113	1973	371
1961	127	1974	396
1962	142	1975	417
1963	154	1976	450
1964	174	1977	477
1965	201	1978	498
1966	223	1979	513
1967	243	1980	519
1968	259	1981	535
1969	283	1982	571
1970	302	1983	607
1971	323	1984	649
1972	347	1985	690

Sources: *Narkhoz SSSR* (1964, p.182, 1970, p.206, 1975, p.256, 1980, p.164, and 1985, p.129).

The physical outputs of the EPM three major product groups – turbines, steam boilers and diesels – are in Table 8.4. One product group – reactors – is omitted. Soviet sources do not provide specific information on production of reactors. The number of reactors could be estimated, but other equipment for nuclear power plants and the characteristics of equipment quality create a problem. Therefore, for reactors, we can only estimate the value of production as a residual, i.e., as the difference between the total EPM output and the values of output for turbines, steam boilers and diesels. For all three products in Table 8.4, the total annual power of manufactured equipment is given. The data for steam boiler production from 1961 to 1964 and from 1966 to 1968 are estimates. The reason is that, prior to 1969, the power of all steam boilers was reported, but since then only the power of steam boilers of over 10 metric tons of steam per hour was published. Since the relevant outputs are not available for the 1961-64 and 1966-68 periods, they are estimated on the basis of total production of steam boilers and the ratios of output of steam boilers of over 10 metric tons of steam per hour to their total output for 1960, 1965 and 1969.

Table 8.3.   The Estimated Output of Soviet Energy and Power Machinery (Millions of Rubles)

Year	Output	Year	Output
1959	596	1973	1,540
1960	685	1974	1,614
1961	781	1975	1,794
1962	882	1976	1,839
1963	966	1977	1,914
1964	1,103	1978	1,973
1965	1,293	1979	2,033
1966	1,441	1980	2,063
1967	1,450	1981	2,108
1968	1,458	1982	2,227
1969	1,469	1983	2,361
1970	1,478	1984	2,539
1971	1,487	1985	2,695
1972	1,495		

Sources: Tables 8.1 and 8.2.

Table 8.4. The Physical Production of Soviet Energy and Power Machinery in the 1960-85 Period

Product	1960	1961	1962	1963	1964	1965	1966	1967	1968	1969	1970	1971
Turbines, Thousands	0.5	0.4	0.3	0.4	0.4	0.3	0.3	0.3	0.3	0.3	0.3	0.3
Millions of Kilowatts	9.2	10.7	11.9	11.9	13.3	14.6	15.2	14.7	15.7	15.0	16.2	16.8
Steam Boilers, Thousands of Tons of Steam per Hour	34.0	38.8	44.1	46.8	51.3	53.2	57.1	58.2	56.4	56.2	48.3	44.2
Diesels, Millions of Horsepower	9.6	NA	NA	12.3	12.8	13.6	14.1	14.3	14.8	15.6	16.5	17.1

1972	1973	1974	1975	1976	1977	1978	1979	1980	1981	1982	1983	1984	1985
0.3	0.3	0.4	0.4	0.5	0.5	0.5	0.5	0.5	0.5	0.5	0.5	0.5	0.5
14.6	15.1	17.3	18.9	19.6	19.0	18.3	20.0	19.6	14.6	17.3	15.5	21.3	21.6
46.4	47.9	51.4	55.6	53.2	52.2	55.8	54.9	51.0	53.1	43.1	50.8	46.5	43.7
17.9	17.8	18.2	18.6	19.0	18.9	19.2	18.6	19.0	18.7	18.6	16.3	16.1	16.6

Sources: *Narkhoz SSSR* (1962. pp. 171-2, 1964, p.185, 1970, p.207, 1975, p.257, 1980, p.165, and 1985, p.130).

Table 8.5. Index of the Cost of a Unit of Equipment Power for
Soviet Energy and Power Machinery by Five-Year
Period (Previous Period=100)

Product Group	1971-75	1976-80	1981-85
Turbines	117	121	178
Steam Boilers	114	97	107
Diesels and Diesel-Generators	94	111	100

Sources: Fal'tsman (1987, p.138).

The central part of the reconstruction process is the estimation
of the value of output by product group and, consequently, the structural breakdown of the EPM. Along with physical outputs, information from several sources will be used. In the first, Fal'tsman (1987,
p.138) estimates the change of the cost of a unit of equipment power
for the EPM in the 1971-75, 1976-80 and 1981-85 periods. The index
of the cost of a unit of equipment power for the EPM is in Table
8.5. The data in that table are compiled on the basis of totals for
five-year periods, with the value of output in the numerator and the
sum of equipment power in the denominator.

The unit costs indices in Table 8.5, in combination with the data
on physical production, allow for the estimation of the growth indices
of the values of output by five-year period. To do so, we use the
formula of the index of the average price adjusted for quality (2.18)
in the following form:

$$\bar{I}_t^r = \frac{Q_t}{Q_o} / \frac{R_t}{R_o} \tag{8.1}$$

where $\bar{I}_t$ = the index of the average price adjusted for quality or,
in this case, the index of the cost of a unit of equipment power,
Q_o and Q_t = the value of output in the base and the current year,

Table 8.6. The Physical Output of Energy and Power Machinery by Five-Year Period

Product	1966-70	1971-75	1976-80	1981-85
Turbines, Millions of Kilowatts	76.8	82.7	96.5	90.3
Steam Boilers, Thousands of Tons of Steam per Hour	276.2	245.5	267.1	237.2
Diesels, Millions of Horsepower	75.3	89.6	94.7	86.3

Source: Table 8.4.

respectively, R_o and R_t = total power of equipment in the base 0 and the current year t, respectively.

Taking into account the type of information given in Tables 8.4 and 8.5, the knowns in formula (8.1) are $\bar{I}_t^r, R_o$, and R_t, and the unknowns are Q_o and Q_t. Transforming formula (8.1), we find

$$\frac{Q_t}{Q_o} = \bar{I}_t^r \frac{R_t}{R_o}. \tag{8.2}$$

Since there are two unknowns in formula (8.2), we cannot find the values of output from this formula, but we can estimate the growth indices by setting the base-year value Q_o equal to 100. Since the indices of the cost of a power unit in Table 8.5 are provided for three five-year periods, the physical production in power units is needed for four five-year periods (1966-70, 1971-75, 1976-80 and 1981-85). These physical outputs are in Table 8.6.

The growth indices for the three product groups of the Soviet EPM, computed with the use of formula (8.2), are in Table 8.7. As one can see from the table, the output of turbines surged from 1971 to 1985, at an average annual rate of 7.5 percent. Overall, there also was a modest gain in the production of diesels, while the production of steam boilers was virtually stabilized at the level of the 1966-70 period. One should, however, take into account that these are

Table 8.7. Computation of the Growth Indices for Product Groups of Soviet Energy and Power Machinery (Previous Period=100)

Product Group	1971-75	1976-80	1981-85
Turbines	$117\frac{82.7}{76.8} = 126$	$121\frac{96.5}{82.7} = 141$	$178\,\frac{90.3}{96.5} = 167$
Steam Boilers	$147\,\frac{245.5}{276.2} = 101$	$97\,\frac{267.1}{245.5} = 106$	$107\,\frac{237.2}{267.1} = 95$
Diesels	$94\,\frac{89.6}{75.3} = 112$	$111\,\frac{94.7}{89.6} = 117$	$100\,\frac{86.3}{94.7} = 91$

the nominal growth indices used below for splitting the real and inflationary components of growth.

The next logical step of the reconstruction process would be a switch from the growth indices for the three product groups to their values of output. But, to do so, such values for at least one of the time periods would be needed. One useful source of information for that purpose is provided by the Center for International Research of the U.S. Bureau of the Census which calculated the values of the EPM output by product group for 1975 (Tretyakova, Working Paper, 1978, pp. 23, 36, and 49). The source also gives the 1971-75 outputs for turbines and steam boilers. The information is in Table 8.8. The value of output of diesels for the 1971-75 period is estimated there as follows. First, the cost of a power unit of diesels in 1975 is found. It equals 52.5 rubles (976÷18.6). Second, this cost is multiplied by the total power of diesel equipment produced in the 1971-75 period, reported in Table 8.6 as 89.6 million horsepower. The resultant output of diesels is equal to 4,704 million rubles. The output of reactors is found as the difference between the total EPM output and the production of turbines, steam boilers, and diesels. Strictly speaking, that difference should not be treated as the output of reactors only. The reason is that, along with turbines, steam boilers, diesels and reactors, the EPM manufactures some other, less

Table 8.8. The Values of Output of Soviet Energy and Power
Machinery for the 1971-75 Period
(Millions of Rubles)

Product Group	1971-75	1975
Turbines	1,434	357
Steam Boilers	1,427	346
Diesels	4,704	976
Reactors and Miscellaneous	365	115
Total	7,930	1,794

Sources: Tretyakova (Working Paper, 1978, pp. 23, 36, and 49),
the estimates from this section, and Table 8.3.

"visible" items. There is also a statistical discrepancy that may make
the residual greater or smaller than the actual output of reactors.
We will, therefore, call the last product group category "Reactors
and Miscellaneous."

Applying the growth indices from Table 8.7 consecutively to the
1971-75 outputs from Table 8.8 yields the outputs by product group
for the 1966-70, 1976-80 and 1981-85 periods. The results are in
Table 8.9, with the 1971-75 outputs repeated for convenience. They
are used for estimating the inflationary growth of the EPM in Section
8.2. We estimate the EPM annual output by product group in Tables
8.10-8.13. For turbines, steam boilers and diesels, this is done by
dividing the total five-year values from Table 8.9 proportionally to
the annual physical outputs from Table 8.4. As noted above, the
annual output of reactors and miscellaneous products is estimated
as the difference between the total EPM production from Table 8.3
and the sum of the relevant outputs of turbines, steam boilers and
diesels from Tables 8.10-8.12.

Table 8.9. The Values of Output of Soviet Energy and Power
Machinery by Five-Year Period (Millions of Rubles)

Product Group	1966-70	1971-75	1976-80	1981-85
Turbines	1,138	1,434	2,022	3,377
Steam Boilers	1,413	1,427	1,513	1,437
Diesels	4,200	4,704	5,504	5,009
Reactors and Miscellaneous	545	365	783	2,107
Total	7,296	7,930	9,822	11,930

Sources: Tables 8.3, 8.7, and 8.8.

8.2. Real and Inflationary Growth of Energy and Power Machinery

How did the cost of a hypothetical unit of the EPM equipment
power change over time? We are in a position now to answer this
question since we have the information on the cost of a unit of power
and the values of output by product group. We compute a weighted
average price index which is a version of the index of average price
adjusted for quality. The indices of the cost of a unit of power are
from Table 8.5, and the values of output of turbines, steam boilers
and diesels are from Table 8.9. The resultant indices are as follows:
For the 1971-75 period,

$$\bar{I}^r_{75/70} = \frac{117(1434) + 114(1427) + 94(4704)}{7565} = 102,$$

with an average annual inflation rate of 0.4 percent.
For the 1976-80 period,

$$\bar{I}^r_{80/75} = \frac{121(2022) + 97(1513) + 111(5504)}{9039} = 111,$$

with an average annual inflation rate of 2.1 percent.

Table 8.10. The Estimated Output of Turbines (Millions of Rubles)

Period	Output	Year	Output
1966–70	1,138	1966	225
		1967	218
		1968	233
		1969	222
		1970	240
1971–75	1,434	1971	282
		1972	253
		1973	252
		1974	290
		1975	357
1976–80	2,022	1976	411
		1977	398
		1978	383
		1979	419
		1980	411
1981–85	3,377	1981	546
		1982	647
		1983	580
		1984	796
		1985	808

Sources: Tables 8.4 and 8.9.

Table 8.11. The Estimated Output of Steam Boilers
(Millions of Rubles)

Period	Output	Year	Output
1966-70	1,413	1966	292
		1967	298
		1968	289
		1969	287
		1970	247
1971-75	1,427	1971	252
		1972	264
		1973	272
		1974	293
		1975	346
1976-80	1,513	1976	301
		1977	296
		1978	316
		1979	311
		1980	289
1981-85	1,437	1981	322
		1982	261
		1983	308
		1984	281
		1985	265

Sources: Tables 8.4 and 8.9.

Table 8.12. The Estimated Output of Diesels (Millions of Rubles)

Period	Output	Year	Output
1966-70	4,200	1966	787
		1967	798
		1968	825
		1969	870
		1970	920
1971-75	4,704	1971	898
		1972	940
		1973	935
		1974	955
		1975	976
1976-80	5,504	1976	1,104
		1977	1,099
		1978	1,116
		1979	1,081
		1980	1,104
1981-85	5,009	1981	1,085
		1982	1,080
		1983	946
		1984	934
		1985	964

Sources: Tables 8.4 and 8.9.

For the 1981-85 period,

$$\bar{I}^r_{85/80} = \frac{178(3377) + 107(1437) + 100(5009)}{9823} = 128,$$

with an average annual inflation rate of 5.1 percent. If, in the 1971-75 period, the average inflationary rate was negligible 0.4 percent, it rose to 2.1 percent in the 1976-80 period, and, finally, to 5.1 percent in the 1981-85 period. A pattern of accelerated inflationary growth thus emerges from this computation. The index of inflationary growth for the entire 1971-85 period can be found as a chain index:

$$I = 102(1.11)(1.28) = 145,$$

which reflects an average annual rate of 2.5 percent.

Table 8.13. The Estimated Output of Reactors and Miscellaneous Products (Millions of Rubles)

Period	Output	Year	Output
1966	137	1976	23
1967	136	1977	121
1968	111	1978	158
1969	90	1979	222
1970	71	1980	249
1971	55	1981	153
1972	38	1982	239
1973	81	1983	527
1974	76	1984	528
1975	115	1985	658

Sources: Tables 8.3, 8.10, 8.11, and 8.12.

On the basis of these calculations, the real growth rates for the Soviet EPM are found in Table 8.14. To estimate the real growth rates, we use formula (6.9)

$$r^q = \frac{r^v - r^p}{1 + r^p},$$

where r^q, r^v, and r^p = the real and nominal growth rate and the inflation rate, respectively. Using the nominal growth and inflation rates from Table 8.14, the real growth rates are as follows:

For the 1971-75 period,

$$r^q = \frac{.017 - .004}{1 + .004} = .013, \text{ i.e., 1.3 percent.}$$

For the 1976-80 period,

$$r^q = \frac{.044 - .021}{1 + .021} = .023, \text{ i.e., 2.3 percent.}$$

For the 1981-85 period,

$$r^q = \frac{.039 - .051}{1 + .051} = -.011, \text{ i.e., } -1.1 \text{ percent.}$$

For the entire 1971-85 period,

$$r^q = \frac{.033 - .025}{1 + .025} = .008, \text{ i.e., 0.8 percent.}$$

These results show that the average real growth rate for the Soviet EPM is 1.3 percent for the 1971-75 period, 2.3 percent for the 1976-80 period, and negative 1.1 percent for the 1981-85 period. The entire 1971-85 period is characterized by a modest real growth rate of 0.8 percent; this is one fourth of the official growth rate. The difference would be even greater if the official indices (based on a series in comparable prices) from Table 8.2 were used. Thus the Soviet EPM is characterized by much higher inflation and, consequently, lower real growth than the automotive industry. The electrotechnical industry is in the intermediate position between the two. We have estimated the nominal growth rate for the output of the EPM in current prices to be equal to 3.3 percent, of which 2.5 percentage

Table 8.14. The Estimated Real Growth of Soviet Energy and Power Machinery (Percent)

Period	Output, Millions of Rubles	Five-Year Nominal Growth Index	Nominal Growth Rate				Inflation Rate				Real Growth Rate			
			1971-75	1976-80	1981-85	1971-85	1971-75	1976-80	1981-85	1971-85	1971-75	1976-80	1981-85	1971-85
1971-75	7,930	109	1.7				0.4				1.3			
1976-80	9,822	124		4.4				2.1				2.3		
1981-85	11,930	121			3.9	3.3			5.1	2.5			-1.1	0.8

Sources: Table 8.9 and the estimates from this section.

points is inflationary. Moreover, the industry experienced a pattern of inflation that sharply accelerated by five-year periods, from 1970 to 1985. As a result, in the 1981-85 period there even was negative real growth at an average annual rate of 1.1 percent.

In sum, inflation was discovered in all three MBMW branches we studied. The extent of it, however, is different: the real growth rates we obtained are the result of deflating the official growth rates by approximately 15 percent for the automotive industry, 45 percent for the electrotechnical industry, and 75 percent for energy and power machinery. The estimates reflect differences in the gap between the growth of the value of output and the product quality characteristics. Basing the quality index for the automotive industry on six characteristics of trucks and cars, while only one characteristic is used for the other two branches, may have affected the estimates. These findings are considered in Chapter 9 from a broader perspective of the analysis of alternative approaches to estimating Soviet real economic growth.

Chapter 9

A General Approach: Challenges to Soviet Official Statistics

9.1. The Methodology

In the last three chapters, we have estimated the real and inflationary growth of three Soviet industries – automotive, electrotechnical and energy and power machinery – representing the variety of different producers' and consumers' durables. In this chapter, we look at the relevance of these results to the overall growth of the Soviet MBMW sector and compare them with other available sources. But first we will interpret these findings in light of new evidence provided by Soviet writers critically assessing the meaning and value of Soviet official statistics.

Only several years ago, Soviet writers were not permitted to say what they meant. Obligated to support the official version of events, their writings had to pass four phases of censorship – self, the organization of the employer, the publisher and *Glavlit* (a notorious censorship division on the protection of state secrets in press). It might be fair to say that the rules by which Soviet economists had to play found their way to western Sovietology: To be accepted, one could not be too critical of the Soviet economy. Thanks to Gorbachev, much freer expression by Soviet economists may enrich their theory and methodology, assuming no dramatic political turmoil. It is difficult to overestimate the importance of this new development for western Sovietology. Benefiting not only from freer flows of information but, foremost, from a greater competition of ideas in Soviet publications, the field itself may become more competitive and challenging.

If this scenario comes true, we will be most indebted to Seliunin and Khanin for their 1987 publication in the Soviet literary and social journal *Novyi Mir*. That article sharply criticized Soviet official statistics and presented alternative estimates of Soviet economic growth. The methodology of the approach was developed by Khanin for a number of years and outlined in two of his earlier papers (1981 and 1984). The thrust of the methodology is discussed in this section. Although we point to both the pros and the cons of Khanin's methodology, we would like to stress its overall significance. There were economists in the U.S.S.R. who attempted to come up with their own estimates of Soviet economic growth (including the author of this study who tried to estimate the "true" growth of Soviet national income in the 1970s). But, to our knowledge, no one else combined his results into a consistent set of both the methodology and numbers and, moreover, tried to defend his results against the establishment. Fortunately, his time has come, and there is a need for alternative statistics at the upper echelon of power in the U.S.S.R. On the one hand, in his speeches Gorbachev has to lean upon the official data. On the other hand, he realizes that it is impossible to denounce the Stalinist economic model and the Brezhnev period of stagnation (*zastoi*) using the official statistics that paint a rosy picture of Soviet economic history. It is hard to say how far Gorbachev wants to go in reforming Soviet statistics, but people like Khanin could be of much help in this process.

Given the importance attached to the task of rebuilding Soviet statistics, the western readership would certainly benefit from knowledge of Khanin's methodology as well as other unorthodox approaches to the problem. However, it is difficult to comprehend Khanin's methods from the cryptic description of his earlier papers. To explain his methods in detail, Khanin would have needed numerical examples which were not permissible at that time. For this and other reasons, the methods are not clear. Our analysis is based in part on Khanin's words and in part on our interpretation of them. Central to Khanin's approach are six alternative methods for estimating industrial growth (1981, pp. 62-73). They are important not only because half of the Soviet national product is created in industries that produce raw materials, energy and manufactures, but also because most price inflation takes place there. Since Khanin realizes that each of the methods would have shortcomings, the essence of his approach is in using as many methods as possible, checking the consistency of the resultant estimates, and averaging them. Whenever building alternative indices, Khanin tries to avoid using prices or the value indicators that he believes are significantly affected by price increases.

In the first method, a representative sample of outputs in physical units is selected, and a growth index in a form reminding a conventional Laspeyres type is constructed. However, instead of the base-year prices used as weights in the Laspeyres quantity index, the coefficients of labor time required for the production of each good in the base period are used. As usual, the chief problem of building the index is in linking new goods which were not manufactured in the base period. It seems that Khanin manipulates the list of the new goods, and he considers only those for which substitutes had previously been available. The old good's labor coefficient in the base period is then used as a weight for each such pair. Even if an increase in the labor time for the new good can be justified, for instance, when there is a quality improvement, it is probably not taken into account. Hence, this index of Khanin is probably equivalent to the conventional Laspeyres index in which the base-year prices of new goods are always the same as the base-year prices of old goods.

In the second method, the growth index is measured as the product of a labor productivity index and an employment index. The estimation of labor productivity is the key part of the method. Measured by *Goskomstat* as an average product per worker, labor productivity can grow as a result of the increase of both real output and prices. As we understand it, in the absence of data on real output and not willing to use inflated output, Khanin substitutes industry's material expenditure (purchases from other firms) in the numerator of the labor productivity index. Actually, real, not total material expenditure should have been related to real output, but data on real expenditures are harder to find. In making this substitution, two underlying assumptions are required: first, that the material expenditure-to-output ratio is constant over time, and, second, that there is no significant price inflation of material inputs. However, the fact that material expenditure per ruble of industrial output officially fell by only five percentage points in the 1971-85 period suggests strong correlation between the two variables (*Narkhoz SSSR 1985*, p.127). Khanin probably excluded certain unspecified components of material expenditure (e.g., purchases of finished parts) in order to reduce the influence of price increases.

Given the two assumptions, the computation of the index of labor productivity is based on the fact that material expenditure is the difference between production costs and wages. Using the indices of cost, average wage per worker and the proportion of wages in cost, Khanin finds the index of labor productivity. Since the formula explaining this computation is the only one in Khanin's article, it deserves special attention. Unfortunately, the formula is erroneous, and we will derive a correct version of it. The expression which Khanin uses for finding the index of labor productivity is as follows:

$$IP_{ij} = \frac{IZ_{ij} \cdot KZ_{ij}}{IC_{ij}} \qquad (9.1)$$

where IP_{ij}, IC_{ij} and IZ_{ij} = percent of the growth of labor productivity, cost and average wage per worker, respectively, in the ith month of the jth year compared to the ith month of the $(j{-}1)$th year; KZ_{ij} = proportion of wages in cost in the ith month of the jth year.

Apparently, the meaning of the variables used by Khanin is incorrect since indices, not percentages are to be used in formula (9.1). Yet, even with such a correction, the formula is wrong for the following reasons. By definition, labor productivity rises with a rise in output for a given number of workers and/or a decline in the number of workers for a given level of output. According to the assumptions made by Khanin, the material expenditure-to-output ratio is constant, and there are no price increases for material inputs. Material expenditure, in turn, is the difference between cost and wages. Therefore, the greater the cost and the lower the proportion of wages in cost, the greater labor productivity. But formula (9.1) shows the relationship the other way around.

To derive an alternative version of formula (9.1), we will retain Khanin's notation with one simplification. Since the first index i is the same for both jth and $(j{-}1)$th years, it can be dropped. The following are the variables used:

Index of labor productivity

$$IP_j = \frac{Q_j}{L_j} / \frac{Q_{j-1}}{L_{j-1}}, \qquad (9.2)$$

where Q_j and Q_{j-1} = output in the jth and (j-1)th period, respectively; L_j and L_{j-1} = number of workers in the jth and (j-1)th period, respectively.

Index of average wage per worker

$$IZ_j = \frac{W_j}{L_j} / \frac{W_{j-1}}{L_{j-1}}, \qquad (9.3)$$

where W_j and W_{j-1} = wages in the jth and (j-1)th period, respectively.

Index of cost

$$IC_j = \frac{C_j}{C_{j-1}}, \qquad (9.4)$$

where C_j and C_{j-1} = production cost in the jth and (j-1)th period, respectively.

Index of employment

$$IL_j = \frac{L_j}{L_{j-1}}. \qquad (9.5)$$

In addition, $KZ_j = \frac{W_j}{C_j}$ = proportion of wages in production cost in the jth period, and M_j = material expenditure (purchases of material inputs) in the jth period.

Index of labor productivity (9.2) can be transformed using the assumption that the material expenditure-to-output ratio must be constant and the fact that the production cost is the sum of material expenditure and wages ($C_j = M_j + W_j$). Consequently,

$$IP_j = \frac{Q_j}{Q_{j-1}} \cdot \frac{L_{j-1}}{L_j} = \frac{M_j}{M_{j-1}} \cdot \frac{L_{j-1}}{L_j}$$

$$= \frac{C_j - W_j}{C_{j-1} - W_{j-1}} \cdot \frac{L_{j-1}}{L_j} = \frac{(1 - KZ_j)C_j}{(1 - KZ_{j-1})C_{j-1}} \cdot \frac{L_{j-1}}{L_j}$$

$$= \frac{1 - KZ_j}{1 - KZ_{j-1}} \cdot \frac{IC_j}{IL_j}. \tag{9.6}$$

To insert the index of average wage per worker in formula (9.6), it should first be transformed with the use of index of cost (9.4), index of employment (9.5), and the proportion of wages in production cost:

$$IZ_j = \frac{W_j}{W_{j-1}} \cdot \frac{L_{j-1}}{L_j} = \frac{W_j}{W_{j-1}} \cdot \frac{L_{j-1}}{L_j} \cdot \frac{C_j}{C_j} \cdot \frac{C_{j-1}}{C_{j-1}}$$

$$= \frac{KZ_j \cdot IC_j}{KZ_{j-1} \cdot IL_j}. \tag{9.7}$$

From this expression,

$$\frac{IC_j}{IL_j} = \frac{IZ_j \cdot KZ_{j-1}}{KZ_j}. \tag{9.8}$$

After substituting expression (9.8) for the ratio $\frac{IC_j}{IL_j}$ in formula (9.6), the index of labor productivity is

$$IP_j = \frac{(1 - KZ_j)IZ_j \cdot KZ_{j-1}}{(1 - KZ_{j-1})KZ_j}. \tag{9.9}$$

Several other versions of the index of labor productivity could also be derived on the basis of Khanin's assumptions. Index (9.9) has the advantage of using minimum information.

We have corrected formula (9.1) for two reasons. Firstly, we are going to apply it for the computation of the index of labor productivity, to illustrate the use of Khanin's method and to compare the results with the official indices. Secondly, if the formula is wrong, it should be corrected anyway. We do not, however, think that Khanin's methodology would be affected by this exercise. Since he obtained estimates consistent with those from other methods, it is unlikely he actually used the wrong formula. We therefore believe that his computation is correct from the standpoint of his methodology, but he failed to formalize it adequately in the text.

Table 9.1. Information for the Computation of the Production Index for Soviet Industry (Second Method)

Indicator	1970	1975	1980	1985
Proportion of Wages in Production Cost (Percent), KZ_j	16.1	14.6	14.8	14.1
Average Monthly Wage Per Worker (Rubles), W_j/Lj	133.3	162.2	185.4	210.6
Number of Workers in Industry (Thousands), L_j	31,593	34,054	36,891	38,103

Sources: *Narkhoz SSSR* (1970, p.174, 1975, p.230, 1980, p.153, 1985, pp. 126, 391, and 397).

Using the index of labor productivity IP_j from formula (9.9) and the index of employment IL_j, the index of production IQ_j is determined:

$$IQ_j = IP_j \cdot IL_j. \qquad (9.10)$$

Unlike Khanin's first method, this one does not require the use of a sample of goods; it is intended for the aggregate level of the Soviet industry. Taking into account that the information at this level is available, we do our own computation for the 1971-75, 1976-80, and 1981-85 periods. The data are in Table 9.1, and the computation is in Table 9.2. The index of labor productivity IP_j is found with the use of formula (9.9), where the proportion of wages in cost KZ_j is from Table 9.1 and the index of average wage per worker IZ_j is from Table 9.2. The index of real output is found with the use of formula (9.10), where both multiplicands are from Table 9.2.

As the computation in Table 9.2 illustrates, the idea of formula (9.9) is that, the greater the level of wages per worker and the lower the share of wages in production cost in the current compared to the base period, the greater the level of material expenditure. This in turns means that, under the assumption of material expenditure rising along with real output, average product per worker also rises. The index of real output from Table 9.2 is compared with the estimates from the two other methods, obtained below, and with the official Soviet indices in Table 9.7. The results are apparently close to the official indices. This could have been expected, because cost is affected by the same forces as the value of production. Khanin assumes that material expenditure is less subject to inflationary pressure than total output. If the assumption is correct, then the total output has to grow more slowly than its net value component, i.e., the sum of wages and profit. At the same time, the index of average wage per worker computed in from Table 9.2 was growing much less than the index of industrial production illustrated in Table 9.3. As for the profit component, only in the 1981-85 period did it grow more than industrial output. To generalize, there need not be a strong correlation between the economic growth of Soviet industry and the variables used in the example above (i.e., costs, wages and material expenditure). This implies that the data used by Khanin must differ from those in Table 9.1, but we do not know what discounting procedure, if any, he has applied. Using this and other examples, we thus find the essence of Khanin's approach in the combination of both a special methodology and a special treatment of the information; we may perceive the former, but not the latter.

While the material expenditure component is imputed in the second method, it is directly accounted for in the third method. The purpose of this third method is to estimate the index of material expenditure and to use it as a proxy for the index of real production. One recognizes here the need for the same assumptions as in the second method, i.e., that real output grows at the same rate as material expenditure and that material inputs are much less subject to price increases than the goods they help to produce. To justify the

Table 9.2. Computation of the Production Index for Soviet Industry (Second Method)

Indicator	1971-75	1976-80	1981-85
Index of Average Wage per Worker, IZ_j	$\dfrac{162.2}{133.3} = 1.22$	$\dfrac{185.4}{162.2} = 1.14$	$\dfrac{210.6}{185.4} = 1.14$
Index of Labor Productivity, IP_j	$\dfrac{(1-.146)1.22(.161)}{(1-.161)(.146)} = 1.37$	$\dfrac{(1-.148)1.14(.146)}{(1-.146)(.148)} = 1.12$	$\dfrac{(1-.141)1.14(.148)}{(1-.148)(.141)} = 1.21$
Index of Employment, IL_j	$\dfrac{34054}{31593} = 1.08$	$\dfrac{36891}{34054} = 1.08$	$\dfrac{38103}{36891} = 1.03$
Index of Real Output, IQ_j	$1.37(1.08) = 1.48$	$1.12(1.08) = 1.21$	$1.21(1.03) = 1.25$

Source: Table 9.1.

use of the index of material expenditure as an indicator of economic growth, Khanin (1981, p.67) appeals to the experience of developed capitalist countries. He asserts that the difference between their growth rates for outputs and material inputs, as a rule, does not exceed 0.2 to 0.3 percentage points.

However, if one looks at the U.S. statistics, one will find a variety of different relationships between the two variables. For instance, in the 1972-80 period the average growth rate of the cost of material inputs in U.S. manufacturing was 13.2 percent, and that of output (the sum of value added and the cost of material inputs) was 11.9 percent, with a difference of 1.3 percentage points (*Statistical Abstract*, 1986, p.723). In the 1980-84 period these rates were 4.2 and 5 percent, respectively, with output this time surpassing the cost of inputs by an average 0.8 points. Since the difference between these growth rates changed direction in the two consecutive periods, it narrowed for the entire 1972-84 period but still remained 0.6 percentage points. Even if the difference between the two rates for the U.S. had been within the narrow margin indicated by Khanin, there is no clear relevance for the Soviet economy.

As in the second method, the computation in the third method is performed at the aggregate level. We therefore do it for the 1971-75, 1976-80, and 1981-85 periods. Since the data on industrial material expenditure are not available, we estimate an implicit index of material expenditure in the following form:

$$IM_j = \frac{HM_j \cdot IQ_j}{HM_{j-1}}, \tag{9.11}$$

where HM_j and HM_{j-1} = the proportion of material expenditure in the output of the jth and $(j-1)$th period, respectively; IM_j and IQ_j = index of material expenditure and output in the jth period, respectively. One can verify that index (9.11) is equivalent to an explicit index in question $IM_j = M_j/M_{j-1}$, given the definitions $HM_j = M_j/Q_j$ and $IQ_j = Q_j/Q_{j-1}$. In essence, formula (9.11) uses the index of production to restore the index of material expenditure; the production index is then ignored, and the material expenditure index is identified with the index of real production. The data used in formula (9.11) are in Table 9.3, and the computation is illustrated in Table 9.4.

Table 9.3. Information for the Computation of the Index of
Material Expenditure for Soviet Industry
(Third Method)

Indicator	1970	1975	1980	1985
Proportion of Material Expenditure in Industrial Output (Percent)	64.1	65.2	63.4	61.8
Index of Industrial Production by Five-Year Period (Percent)	–	143	124	120

Source: *Narkhoz SSSR* (1985, pp. 99 and 127).

Table 9.4. Computation of the Index of Material Expenditure for
Soviet Industry (Third Method)

Year	Index
1975	$\dfrac{.652(1.43)}{.641} = 1.45$
1980	$\dfrac{.634(1.24)}{.652} = 1.21$
1985	$\dfrac{.618(1.20)}{.634} = 1.17$

Source: Table 9.3.

In Table 9.7, the estimated indices are compared with other results and with the official growth indices. As follows from the table, the estimates from the third method obtained in Table 9.4 are almost exactly the same as the official indices. Hence, this method, as well as the second one, does not dramatically reduce the official growth figures as it should have. As noted above, we may not replicate Khanin's results by following his methodology. However, in the case of the third method, he also indicates that he excludes from material expenditure the cost of purchased finished parts; this leaves the cost of raw materials and energy. It is not clear whether other discounting procedures were also applied.

If the second and the third methods implement the same idea but use different computational schemes, the fourth method is yet another version in which the index of labor productivity is used. It is assumed that there is a functional relationship between the growth of output per worker and the production consumption of electricity. It is also assumed that the ratio between the growth of output per worker and production consumption of electricity must be the same for the U.S. and Soviet economies. Under these assumptions, the data on the U.S. can be used to derive conclusions for Soviet industry. More specifically, the index of labor productivity for Soviet industry can be found on the basis of two indicators: the ratio of average product per worker to production consumption of electricity in U.S. industry and the index of electricity consumption per worker in Soviet industry.

For example, if in a given period the average product per worker in the U.S. industry quadrupled and electricity consumption per worker doubled, the ratio between the two indices would equal 2. Therefore, if Soviet electricity consumption per worker grew 1.5 times in that period, the labor productivity index must equal 3. Actually, since Khanin's procedure is equivalent to solving a proportion in which output in the numerator and electricity consumption in the denominator are divided on a per worker basis for both the Soviet and the U.S. economies, the number of workers cancels out. Probably Khanin performed such a division since there was readily available information on electricity consumption per Soviet worker in statistical yearbooks. To illustrate the fourth method, we use the simplified version in which there is no division by the number of workers:

$$IQ_{SU} = \frac{IQ}{IE}_{US} \cdot IE_{SU}, \tag{9.12}$$

where IQ and IE = index of real industrial production and electricity consumption for Soviet and U.S. industries, respectively. The information and the computation according to formula (9.12) are in Tables 9.5 and 9.6. (Since the information on Soviet electricity consumption is given per worker, the index of electricity consumption is found by multiplying the Soviet index of electricity consumption per worker and the index of employment in industry.)

In Table 9.7 the estimates from Table 9.6 are compared with the estimates from the two other methods considered above and the official growth indices. As one can see from Table 9.7, if the official and the two other indices demonstrate a similar pattern of decline, the fourth method, on the contrary, depicts a slightly accelerating growth. In particular, this growth is significantly higher than officially reported for the 1981-85 period. One of the reasons for this result may be that there is no evident relationship between the ratio of U.S. industrial output to production consumption of electricity and the Soviet labor productivity. But, although this explains why the resultant estimates may be unreliable, this does not explain why Khanin obtained different estimates. He probably should have used the same data on the U.S. economy. Of the three indices in Table 9.6, the only one pertaining to Soviet industry refers to the production consumption of electricity. Yet, even for this index, it is difficult to expect significant discrepancies since it is verifiable by means of comparison with the growth of Soviet electricity production in physical terms.

The intent of Khanin's fifth method is to establish the discrepancy between meeting plan targets in money terms and meeting the targets in physical terms and to use this discrepancy in building the index of industrial production. For that purpose, the index of meeting the physical production quota is computed for each good from a selected sample. Using the individual goods indices, a weighted average index is found, with labor time spent on the production of each good as a weight. If it then follows from the average index that the plan for physical output is surpassed by 2 percent, but the

Table 9.5.   Information for the Computation of the Production
Index for Soviet Industry (Fourth Method)

	1970	1975	1980	1985
U.S. Industrial Production Index for the Five-Year Period	-	1.08	1.28	1.15
U.S. Electric Utility Sales to Industry (Billions of Kilowatt-hours)	571	688	815	827
Soviet Index of Electricity Consumption per Industrial Worker	–	1.27	1.09	1.13
Soviet Index of Industrial Employment	–	1.08	1.08	1.03

Source: *Statistical Abstract* (1987, pp. 553 and 734), *Narkhoz
SSSR* (1985, p.78), and Table 9.2.

plan for the value of output is surpassed by 5 percent, the difference
is attributed to inflationary growth. Consequently, the difference is
not counted as real growth. Thus, if in this example the planned
growth rate for the value of production is 4 percent, the estimate of
the achieved real growth rate equals 6 percent (104·1.02-100). The
method, is, therefore, based on the distinction made between the
planned production values that do not foresee hidden price increases
and the production values reported afterwards that do incorporate
such increases. The purpose of the index of meeting the plan targets
in physical terms is to permit a correction of the ex post estimates.

The fifth method can be considered a modification of the first
method, even though the two methods may seem unrelated. The
only difference is that, in the first method, the physical outputs of
the current and base years are directly compared, whereas, in the
fifth method, an intermediate indicator of plan targets in value terms
is inserted. It is reasonable to expect that in both methods the same
set of physical goods is used, and the same weighting procedure is
applied. Under these conditions, if no price increases or decreases
are planned, the two methods should result in the same estimates.

In the sixth method, Khanin again returns to the index of labor

Table 9.6. Computation of the Production Index for Soviet Industry (Fourth Method)

Indicator	1975	1980	1985
U.S. Index of Electricity Consumption in Industry	$\frac{688}{571} = 1.20$	$\frac{815}{688} = 1.18$	$\frac{827}{815} = 1.01$
Soviet Index of Electricity Consumption in Industry	$1.27(1.08)=1.37$	$1.09(1.08)=1.18$	$1.13(1.03)=1.16$
Soviet Index of Industrial Production	$\frac{1.08}{1.20} \cdot 1.37 = 1.23$	$\frac{1.28}{1.18} \cdot 1.18 = 1.28$	$\frac{1.15}{1.01} \cdot 1.16 = 1.32$

Source: Table 9.5.

Table 9.7. Comparison of Different Indices of the Growth of Soviet Industry (Previous Period=100)

Year	Estimated Index (Second Method), (1)	Estimated Index (Third Method), (2)	Estimated Index (Fourth Method), (3)	Official Index, (4)
1975	148	145	123	143
1980	121	121	128	124
1985	125	117	132	120

Year	Ratio (2)÷(1)	Ratio (3)÷(1)	Ratio (1)÷(4)
1975	.98	.83	1.03
1980	1	1.06	.98
1985	.94	1.06	1.04

Sources: Tables 9.2, 9.4 and 9.6 and *Narkhoz SSSR* (1985, p.99).

productivity used in the second and fourth methods. This time, the index of the cost of industrial export is estimated. Probably, the cost of industrial export is related to total cost, and the latter to output. What is clear from the method's description is that a ratio of the change in export cost to the change in export proceeds is calculated, and then, given this ratio and the index of export proceeds, the index of the cost of export is found. Export proceeds are estimated in constant world prices, and the reliance on the true "constant" nature of those prices seems to be the rationale for the method. We view this method as the least justifiable from an analytical standpoint, not to mention the number and the nature of required assumptions.

9.2. Alternative Estimates of Economic Growth

The methods described above give an idea of Khanin's approach to deriving "alternative estimates" of Soviet economic growth by sector and as a whole. Khanin does not demonstrate his estimates for industry and other sectors of the Soviet economy, but Seliunin and Khanin (S-K) do so for national income. The growth percentages from the S-K article are compared to the official data in Table 9.8. As one can see from the table, S-K especially discount the official growth rates for the period from 1976 to 1985. Yet the most dramatic assertion made by S-K is that Soviet national income did not grow about 90 times in the 1928-85 period as officially claimed, but only six to seven times (Seliunin and Khanin, 1987, p.192). Although S-K pay attention to distortions in growth indices caused by a variety of factors including manipulated or fraudulent statistical reports (*pripiski*),[12] concealed price inflation is stressed in Khanin's methodology.

Is a higher pace of price inflation in the Soviet economy in the 1976-85 period responsible for such a difference between the official and the S-K estimates? Unfortunately, there are no grounds for conclusive answers. The critics of official Soviet growth figures in general prefer physical output as a characteristic of economic growth. Thus, Val'tukh and Lavrovskii (V-L) use the indicator of physical production capacity to characterize the efficiency of the Soviet economy and to eliminate the effect of the "price factor." For estimating economic growth, they also use physical output. Calculations were performed for industry and its three sectors – electric power, chemical

Table 9.8. The Comparison of the Growth of Soviet National
Income (Percent)

	Seliunin-Khanin		Official	
Period	Total Growth	Growth Rate	Total Growth	Growth Rate
1961-65	24	4.4	37	6.5
1966-70	22	4.1	45	7.7
1971-75	17	3.2	32	5.7
1976-80	5	1.0	23	4.2
1981-85	3	0.6	19	3.5

Sources: Seliunin and Khanin (1987, pp. 196-7) and *Narkhoz SSSR*
(1975, p.563 and 1985, p.39).

and MBMW – by five-year periods since 1950. What is interesting
about the V-L estimates is that, until the 1966-70 period, they exceeded the official growth indices for industry, and then they sharply
decelerated (Val'tukh and Lavrovskii, 1986, pp. 24 and 29). Even
though it is impossible to compare Khanin's results with the V-L
estimates for industry, we learn that they deviate from the official
indices in opposite directions until the late 1960s and in the same
direction thereafter.

It is, however, possible to compare the V-L and the S-K estimates for the MBMW sector. Although the S-K article does not
contain their indices for this sector, one can restore their approximate range from the information they give. Thus, according to
S-K calculations, in each of the five-year periods since 1965 hidden
inflation in the MBMW sector floated between 27 and 34 percent.
The growth in the 12th five-year plan (1986-90) is foreseen to be 43
percent, 30 percent of which, according to S-K, will constitute the inflationary component, i.e., growth "on paper" (Seliunin and Khanin,
1987, p.187). (Apparently, S-K consider the real growth rate as the
difference between the nominal and inflation rates, neglecting the
crossrate term.) The S-K estimates obtained by discounting the of-

ficial Soviet growth indices are compared with the V-L estimates in Table 9.9. As one can see from Table 9.9, the 1961-85 deceleration rate in the S-K estimates, from an average growth rate of 8.2 to 0.9 percent, is much lower than in the V-L estimates, from 10.7 to 0.3 percent.

Fal'tsman uses the maximum power of equipment as an indicator of growth for the MBMW sector. In particular he says that, while from 1970 to 1982 the average rate of output growth for 11 civilian MBMW ministries was about 8 percent in money terms, it was only 3 percent in equipment maximum power (Fal'tsman, 1987, p.72). The difference of 5 percent is interpreted as an inflationary component of growth. Fal'tsman's average growth rate of 3 percent turns out to lie in between the V-L and the S-K average estimates of 2.5 and 4.5 percent, respectively, for the same 1971-82 period. Falt'sman's estimates take into consideration not only the physical output of machines and equipment, but also their power. His approach, however, is only justified when power could be singled out as the most important characteristic of machines, as in the cases of the electrotechnical industry and energy and power machinery considered in Chapters 7 and 8. However, for the automotive industry in Chapter 6 it was impossible to find such a characteristic; multi-characteristic indices of car and truck quality were therefore defined and constructed.

The three industries we have considered were responsible for one fifth of the MBMW output in 1982, according to Table 4.3. They are also representative of the variety of Soviet machines and equipment. To compare our estimates for these industries with other ones available for the MBMW sector, they have to be aggregated. However, the relevant time periods for the growth rates for the three industries in Chapters 6 through 8 do not always coincide. The reasons are in the different sources of the information and methodology. One common period was from 1970 to 1975. For that period we can find average weighted inflation and growth rates. The data are in Table 9.10.

Using the 1975 outputs as weights, the weighted average growth rate equals

280

Table 9.9. Growth of the Soviet MBMW Sector by Five-Year Period
(Percent)

Year	Seliunin-Khanin		Val'tukh-Lavrovskii		Official	
	Growth	Growth Rate	Growth	Growth Rate	Growth	Growth Rate
1965	45-52	7.7-8.7	66	10.7	79	12.3
1970	40-47	7.0-8.0	33	5.9	74	11.7
1975	39-46	6.8-7.9	26	4.7	73	11.6
1980	14-21	2.7-3.9	6	1.2	48	8.2
1985	1-8	0.2-1.6	1^2	0.3	35	6.2
1990	13^1	2.5	NA	NA	43^1	7.4

Sources: *Narkhoz SSSR* (1970, p.137, 1975, p.197, and 1985, p.99), Seliunin
and Khanin (1987, p.187), and Val'tukh and Lavrovskii (1986, pp.
24 and 29).

[1]Projection.
[2]1983.

Table 9.10. The Information for the Computation of Average Weighted Indices
for Three Industries in the 1971-75 Period

Industry	1975 Output, Millions of Rubles	Average Nominal Growth Rate, Percent	Average Inflation Rate, Percent
Automotive	12,646	12.6	1.1
Electrotechnical	11,790	8.6	6.8
Energy and Power Machinery	1,794	1.7	0.4

Sources: Tables 6.3, 6.50, 7.7, 7.18, 8.3, and 8.14.

$$r^v = \frac{12.6(12646) + 8.6(11790) + 1.7(1794)}{26230} = 10.1,$$

and the weighted average inflation rate equals

$$r^p = \frac{1.1(12646) + 6.8(11790) + 0.4(1794)}{26230} = 3.6.$$

Applying formula (6.9)

$$r^q = \frac{r^v - r^p}{1 + r^p},$$

the average real growth rate is

$$r^q = \frac{.101 - .036}{1.036} = .063, \text{ or } 6.3 \text{ percent.}$$

This weighted average growth rate of 6.3 percent is higher than the V-L 4.7 percent for the MBMW sector in the same 1971-75 period but lower than the S-K range of 6.8 to 7.9 percent (Table 9.9). The relevant CIA estimate equals 7.9 percent (Converse, 1982), and the official Soviet rate is 11.6 percent.

Why such a variety of estimates? It is easy to understand this in the case of western analysts. Since western analysts have to reconstruct Soviet data, it is natural to expect they would use different methodologies and come up with different solutions. But, when it comes to Soviet economists, an undisputed presumption has been that they have access to the true information and would not therefore go through the reconstruction process. On this basis, their estimates should not have differed. However, as we see in the case of the estimates by S-K, V-L and Fal'tsman, they do. Here we observe an interesting phenomenon. Some of the Soviet writers feel a need to reestimate what has already been estimated officially. They also use different methodologies, and a part of each is the process of the reconstruction of the data. It is thus apparent that they do not accept either the official information or the methodology. In the period of *glasnost'* this is not surprising. To what extent can these different results be trusted? This will remain an open question unless we understand the reasons for the differences. We analyze these reasons in Section 9.3, but before that it would be interesting to examine how *glasnost'* has affected the views of those who support the official version of Soviet economic growth.

Speaking of the official version, we should be careful since there are more than one now. Thus, if we identify the official position with Gorbachev himself, it may be closer to that of the critics than the supporters of the official statistics; yet he is not specific on where he stands. By the official version we therefore mean the views of the planning and statistical bureaucracy and, in part, the academic and research establishment, especially in provincial regions. More accurately, these views could be described as orthodox. They have not remained unchanged, either; after all, everyone has to engage in self-improvement that is consistent with the new requirements (*perestraivat'sia*). These people are more concerned with the future than the past. They welcome the improvement of statistical methodology, mainly by introducing new indicators which would better describe different aspects of economic and social life in the Soviet Union. The existing indicators are called separate (*razroznennye*) or piece-wise (*kusochnye*), while they are supposed to provide a composite picture of the economy. These suggestions are both vague, and unrealistic; Soviet planners have tried in vain to find composite indicators for decades. Take, for example, the plan for technological change. Many research projects in the U.S.S.R. were devoted to development of an indicator characterizing an overall state of technology. The projects failed because there is no such indicator.

The views of the orthodox economists on the existing statistical indices could be summarized as follows: These indices are right to the extent that the information used in their building is right. Hence, they think there are problems with the information, not the statistical methodology *per se*. They believe that management at lower levels is interested in the fabrication of the data (*pripiski*). Because of that, the indices may be wrong. Therefore, if someone would figure out the true growth rates by eliminating *pripiski*, these people would welcome such estimates. For instance, they would accept the estimates by Fal'tsman or V-L that are pertinent to specific industries. But the S-K gloomy assessment of the entire Soviet economic period and their suggestion to scrap the official statistical methodology could only be taken as an assault. S-K sowed the wind and reaped the whirlwind.

Most responses to the S-K challenge are simply libels of S-K. One of the few attempting to discuss the substance was made by Adamov (1987, p.14). His purpose is to defend both the official statistical methodology and the indices it produces. Thus, he believes that a growth index based on the entire output, as in the Soviet Union, is more accurate than one based on a sample of goods, as in the U.S. Adamov demonstrates that, by manipulating a sample of goods, it is possible to obtain for the 1976-85 Soviet industrial output either a decline of 29 or a rise of more than 300 percent. This is done to prove that, by purposeful selection of an "appropriate" sample of industrial goods, S-K intended to discredit official growth figures. Two comments are appropriate. First, the S-K estimates are much less vulnerable from Adamov's criticism than, for example, are the V-L estimates. The reason is that the V-L estimates were built on the basis of a sample in physical terms; it is quite possible that the growth characterized by the sample for which V-L were able to obtain data is biased with respect to the entire output. The S-K estimates, on the other hand, are averaged over the indices computed by several different methods, only two of which depend on sample estimation. Second, whereas there are both cons and pros in increasing the size of a sample, the chief problem is in the method applied, not in the fact of using a sample. Thus, if the methodology of the U.S. Bureau of Labor Statistics were applied to exactly the same set of goods the Soviets use, the results would undoubtedly differ from the Soviet official indices. Conversely, if the Soviet methodology, whose idea was discussed in Sections 2.2 and 2.3, were applied to the entire industrial output and separately to a representative Soviet sample, the two results would probably not differ significantly.

Adamov asserts that when a switch to new comparable prices takes place, the last year's value of output is recalculated in new prices, to allow for the computation of a chain growth index. This is true. However, the recalculation is done only for the so-called comparable products (*sopostavimaia produktsiia*), i.e., those manufactured in both current and previous years. The prices of these goods seldom rise, and the washing out of cheap items and the introduction of new goods make the difference. Therefore, despite Adamov's assertion, the Soviet experience has proved that the mere fact of using the chain index does not ensure the smooth continuity of indices. While Khanin's criticism is directed toward both the methodology and the information, Adamov believes that the prime sources of erroneous results in statistics are the distortions in the initial information, i.e., the notorious *pripiski*, or the use of samples rather than the entire sets of goods.

Adamov makes several points concerning the S-K estimates. He notes that if Soviet national income rose 6 to 7 times in the 1928-85 period as S-K say, then in 1985 the ratio of Soviet national income to that of the U.S. would remain at the 1928 level, i.e., the Soviet version of 10 percent. Then how could the Soviets afford parity in military spending and still produce consumer goods? The argument clearly makes sense. However, Adamov believes in both the official growth of about 90 times from 1928 to 1985 and in the official ratio of Soviet-to-U.S. national income of 66 percent in 1985. That combination does not make sense. Indeed, if, according to Adamov, a 10 percent ratio of Soviet-to-U.S. national income follows from a 6 to 7 times growth in Soviet national income, then a 66 percent ratio would reflect a 6.6 times greater growth, i.e., one in the 40 to 46 times range. The latter still falls short of the official growth of under 90 times.

Several other of Adamov's numerical examples are aimed at disproving the S-K estimates and can in turn also be challenged. For example, following up the S-K approach to look at the proportions between technologically related industries in the U.S. and Soviet economies, Adamov uses the links between the metallurgy and MBMW sectors. He states that in the 1961-85 period the ratio of MBMW-to-metallurgy growth for the U.S. was equal to 3.3, with the indices of 3.07 and 0.93, respectively. By way of comparison, Adamov believes that a similar 2.7 ratio for the Soviet economy is reasonable. Yet, to find the growth index for the Soviet MBMW sector, S-K might have used the metallurgy growth index in physical, not in value terms. Using steel production as an indicator, the growth index for Soviet metallurgy in the 1961-85 period would be 2.4 (*Narkhoz SSSR* 1985, pp. 98 and 140). Since a similar index for the MBMW sector equals 10.9, one would obtain a 4.5 ratio (10.9÷2.4), rather than 2.7. (The ratio is important in the sense that, the lower its level, the more "reasonable" the official growth rates for the MBMW sector.)

Overall, Adamov's assessment of S-K findings coincides with the reaction of *Goskomstat* and academic statisticians to them as "deeply erroneous" (Korolev, 1987). The younger generation of Soviet intelligentsia, on the contrary, likes such findings as just another indication that something is rotten in the land of Soviets. As for the search for true growth rates, few Soviet citizens would care. Soviet people are in general indifferent to high or low growth figures, an attitude not common in the West. The Soviets know that higher growth rates lead to a greater production of steel, chemicals or machines but do not result in more consumer goods on the store shelves.

9.3. Is It Possible to Establish the Truth?

There is a consensus among Soviet economists and statisticians that there is a problem with statistical information. Their views are, however, sharply divided over the methodology. Looking at the information issue first, we can, of course, only speculate as to what extent it is serious. Every Soviet leader beginning with Stalin tried to prosecute fabrication (*pripiski*) and peddle eye wash (*ochkovtiratel'stvo*). At the same time, the leaders themselves initiated and encouraged the fraudulent Stakhanov movement and other forms of "socialist competition." But this type of fraud was considered innocent; it was authorized, and it did not affect overall production statistics. In the new campaign against statistical fraud, Gorbachev may be sending a signal that there will be no discriminatory treatment of *pripiski* and that none will be tolerated any more.

There has already been some evidence of Gorbachev's new broom sweeping *pripiski*. For example, according to the head of Moldavian *Goskomstat* Vorotilo, after the 1986 resolution of the Central Committee on statistical manipulation and fraud in Moldavia, Kirovograd province, and the Ministry of the Automotive Industry, more than 2,000 communists were charged with misdemeanors in Moldavia (Excerpts, 1987, p.45). Disciplinary punishments were given to 1,260 people, one third of whom were managers, and 111 of them were fired. For fraudulent data, 29 cities and districts were stripped of their positions as the winners in the socialist competition. But, as the official admits, cheating is still alive. (If it will be impossible to "create" winners any more, the future of the socialist competition becomes questionable.) Further, the head of Uzbek *Goskomstat* Sadukov indicates that, despite all the effort, one out of six enterprises in the republic still engages in *pripiski* (Excerpts, 1987, pp. 36-7).

This is not the place to analyze the distortions of statistical information at industrial firms where the bulk of it originates. Even though the recent disclosures illustrate the serious nature of the problem, we think it is premature to conclude that the level of distortion is indeed critical. The reason is that, in such a case, no one knows what comes out of the disclosures and what comes out of a campaign. There have always been indicators that are more trustworthy, such as physical outputs, and those that are untrustworthy, such as economic benefit from modernization projects. Planners are well aware of exaggerated volumes of excavation or freight traffic. But in the past those false volumes were quietly accepted as a means of paying workers decent wages and thus keeping them on the job. As another example, plant economists are required to submit information on the future economic benefit from a variety of projects, which is impossible to estimate. A part of the game has been that the data are fabricated. However, industrial production is a different story. Everyone knows that the data are easily verifiable. Distortions happen at the end of a period when plant management may report some unfinished goods as finished. Although this type of behavior was widespread in the past, it still was punishable. Moreover, sooner or later the goods should be delivered, and there is no cumulative effect. Overall, we think that the accusation of thousands of plant managers as engaging in the criminal activity of outright fabrication is unacceptable.

If microdata are false, so are the macrodata. But what about *pripiski* at the macrolevel, in situations when aggregate statistics do not look impressive or even move in undesirable directions? Whenever Soviet statistical reports are unbelievable, western analysts naturally suspect deliberate distortions. We personally did not come across the cases of such "primitive" distortion, in the sense of cooking up good numbers, especially those that are used in planning. The distortions practiced are more of *a priori* nature that may have nothing to do with falsification. They follow from the Soviet planning and statistical methodology or the changes in the methodology or accounting procedures which remain undisclosed. For example, the production of milk sharply increased in the early 1970s by lowering fat and increasing its water content; the meat consumption per capita was "raised" by including the estimated consumption of lard by collective farm households which was not included before. One could find numerous examples of deliberate lowering product quality in order to increase outputs. Yet what is important in all these cases is that the production, of whatever quality, would actually grow if it is reported so. Otherwise, the numbers would disappear from statistical yearbooks. Western analysts have pointed to new discrepancies in Soviet statistics, in particular conflicting measures for certain crucial indicators appearing in different and even in the same reports. However, since Gorbachev has required greater scrutiny from statisticians, it is hard to believe that someone in *Goskomstat* would take a chance of "beautifying" the statistics.

Soviet statistical methodology should be considered as a part of the planning methodology. This makes sense since serving the planning process has been the prime task of the statistical information, especially in the past. Consequently, if there are any changes in the methodology, they have to be accomplished in planning first. For example, statisticians have been criticized for using gross (*valovye*) value indicators of economic growth. According to the rules of the game, the *Goskomstat* officials have engaged in self-criticism calling for the introduction of "scientifically justified" (*nauchno-obosnovannye*) success indicators (Belov, 1986, pp. 3-7). However, little could be done since a major shift from value to net indicators in planning has still not been completed. (Even if it is completed, the results may turn out to be far from scientifically justified.)

To make economic plans work, Soviet planners have always preferred indicators in physical goods to those in money terms. The national economic plan is primarily built on balances of production and distribution of physical goods, and in many instances monetary aggregates are only used for accounting purposes. Thousands of material balances drawn in planning, to a large extent, insulate plan targets from price distortions. The primacy of planning in physical terms led to a "neglect" of monetary indicators. They did not play an active role in planning before 1965, yet their important political function was to demonstrate high rates of Soviet economic growth. Since the 1965 economic reform, inflating value indicators became much more alarming from the planners' perspective. The reason is that profit and average labor productivity were chosen, among others, as new success indicators. Since the rise of these monetary indicators could affect wages and bonuses, this created a new reality in the game between plant management and planners; managers intensified their effort to raise prices, and planners attempted to create barriers for unjustified price increases. Continuing price rises indicate that the planners' preventive barriers did not succeed. As a matter of fact, along with the prewar years, the 1976-85 period is one for which the S-K estimates reduce the official growth rates the most drastically.

To understand why Soviet price increases may be concealed and reported as economic growth, the peculiarities of Soviet statistical methodology discussed in Sections 2.2-2.3 could be useful. The Soviet methodology of building growth and price indices is based on using comparable prices (*sopostavimye tseny*). In industry, 1982 prices are now used as comparable ones, with 1983 prices in agriculture and 1984 prices in construction. Only at the moment of setting these prices do they resemble conventional constant prices. For a good introduced later, say, in 1988, the first approved price becomes its 1982 comparable price. Technically, this solves the problem of estimating the base period price for the new goods, and the Soviets do not have to worry about linking the old and the new specifications when building an index. But what it actually means is that the whole array of goods introduced in between the dates for setting comparable prices does not affect the price index one way or another; their base and current year prices are one and the same. Such a price index, therefore, only reflects the revisions of prices for the goods produced in the base year.

As S-K suggest, the Soviets should have used representative samples of goods in each product category, instead of entire outputs, and built indices for the samples. The rationale is simple: Data verification on the entire output is hardly possible. This certainly makes sense, except that the Soviets apply the same comparable-price principle to sample indices, too. Therefore, the mere change of the sample size will not ease the problem of concealed inflation. Why then not change the methodology and switch to a conventional western procedure that involves the computation of base year or current year weighted indices?

To answer this question, we should note that, at a closer glance, the Soviet methodology is not bad at all. The linking procedure usually involves a comparison, either direct or indirect, of a new good with the existing ones in the same product category. One would hardly comprehend exactly how the Bureau of Labor Statistics in the U.S. makes a judgement for goods other than automobiles. The Soviets possess an advantage in this respect, since such a comparison is required and is performed in the process of approving a new good's price. It is therefore logical to set the new good's price taking account of improvements in its characteristics. Hence, theoretically, price increases for new goods are allowed to the extent of their projected quality improvement. Yet, as the critics of Soviet statistics probably believe, these improvements mostly remain on paper, while price growth is quite real.

Suppose that, under these circumstances, the Soviet methodology of constructing indices is revised, and more conventional procedures for linking newly introduced goods to those in the market basket are adopted. The same considerations that are now used in pricing new goods would have to be used in quality and price comparisons by statisticians. Then, in the cases when the *Goskomtsen* experts find price increases justifiable, there is little chance that the statisticians constructing the price index would be able to add any new insights to the issue. In other words, the procedures for assigning the base year prices for new specifications will have to turn into something similar to what *Goskomtsen* does at present; if so, the results would not be much different from theirs.

Here we come to the key issue related to the product quality change and its measurement in the Soviet context. If the base and current year goods were identical, the problem of the reliability of Soviet indices would probably have not existed, despite the evidence of the distortions in the information discussed above. But, since goods characteristics change over time, there is a question of what these changes mean. Depending on whether they are identified with quality improvements, different estimates of Soviet economic growth could be obtained. Fundamental differences in opinions on these changes, in our view, explain the broad variety of growth rates we have considered.

Soviet critics of official statistics do not pay much attention to the problem of product quality change, even though S-K, for example, note its existence. This attitude reflects the facts of life. People in the Soviet Union usually give quality less consideration than quantity. This should not be understood to mean that quality is not important to them; on the contrary, seeking goods of an adequate quality consumes a substantial part of their lives. But they are hardly used to improvements in domestic manufactures and, for that reason, often disregard the factor of quality change. Persistent shortages play their role, too. As for the producer, he takes whatever the supply system is able to provide. Since there is no shopping around, the problem of quality becomes hypothetical in the producer's case.

Economists in general, either in the West or the East, are not particularly good on the issue of product quality. This is quite natural since the valuation of quality by the consumer is inherently subjective. But, in a free economy, consumers' market choices send a signal whether a change in the product characteristic is accepted or rejected. Thus, it has been shown at the level of a model that, if a consumer faces a choice between two possibilities (neither of which is ideal, given his taste structure) and if the prices are equal, the one which is closer to the preferred good will be purchased (Waterson, 1984, p.113). Moreover, assuming consumers demand the characteristics of a good rather than the good itself, the competitive market will implicitly reveal the function relating the price of the good to its various characteristics. Hence, under the conditions of competition and the availability of a variety of goods and market information, the consumer maximizes his utility by choosing both qualities and quantities. In response to consumers' behavior, the competitive market sets prices by equating the marginal worth of each good's characteristic with its marginal cost. In fact the market works because firms, in the hope of greater profit, try to develop new or improved products which consumers would prefer. Accordingly, for example, tire producers have developed all-weather tires, radial tires and performance tires. While it is possible to understand how the market mechanism works, it would be impossible to imagine it being formalized and, in such a form, used for actual price setting. In the case of product quality, this would be equivalent to formalizing the valuations by millions of consumers who themselves may not realize what rules they apply. But this is exactly what Soviet certification committees and *Goskomtsen* are obliged to do!

There are numerous complaints in the U.S.S.R. that *Goskomtsen* is unable to verify the justification of prices on the basis of goods' quality improvements, because of its inability to control so many prices. The point is misleading since it implies that, by better organizing the activities of *Goskomtsen*, it would be possible to improve the Soviet pricing process. However, the problems of understaffing or the lack of computers may have nothing to do with the problem facing *Goskomtsen*, which essentially is how to discriminate between a change in a product's characteristic that is an improvement from one that is not. In doing its job, *Goskomtsen* is helped by state certification committees which determine a quality category for most new goods. When the approach is formalized, in order to be generally applicable to a large variety of goods, *Goskomtsen* and the certification committees can only utilize such "objective" characteristics as power, capacity or durability. As a result, for example, when a tractor's horsepower rises, *Goskomtsen* considers this an improvement.

Who is right and who is wrong? Even in the case of this simple example, it is difficult to take sides. The critics clearly have a point, but, on the other hand, one cannot exclude a possibility that there is also a demand for a more powerful tractor. Moreover, when machines and equipment are distributed via the supply system, one in principle does not know what is in demand and what is not. Under the conditions of consumer sovereignty, a company can produce a new good which all the experts may declare a success. But if the market rejects it, the improvement does not count. The well-known examples include the cases of automobile market failures, most notably – the Ford model Edsel turned down by the consumer in the 1950s (Sobel, 1984, pp. 20 and 77). But who can predict this type of development? Thus, in the 1950s the conventional wisdom outside of the Xerox corporation was that the famous Xerox copier was destined to be a commercial failure because of its large size and great cost compared to the then available alternatives. On the other hand, many products which are technical successes become commercial failures (Greer, 1984, pp. 510-1). This consideration illustrates that consumer evaluation of product quality is the essential ingredient.

The reliability of Soviet statistical data depends on the issue of product quality change and on some other problems discussed in the Soviet literature. There is a consensus that the prices and value indicators are much more reliable for raw materials than for manufactures, since there is room for the fabrication of fictitious output of manufactures. Again, the explanation is given in terms of the dishonest producer, with better control implied as a cure. But, as indicated above, without the consumer freely choosing, it is simply impossible to discriminate among different changes in product characteristics, to determine which are in demand and which are not.

In our studies of real and inflationary growth (Chapters 6 through 8), the change in the essential characteristics of cars, trucks, electrotechnical products and energy and power machinery is treated as quality improvement. We believe that such an approach would take Soviet economic realities into account. While the western producer has to please the consumer, the Soviet producer has to please *Goskomtsen* and the certification committees. The requirements are set by the authorities, and, in order to get a better price, the producer must turn out more powerful or heavier trucks and tractors, as examples. To the extent that product characteristics change and production cost rises, price increases are viewed as justified and are therefore authorized. We thus look at the situation from the producers', rather than the consumers' standpoint. For the critics of Soviet statistics this is probably an unacceptable compromise.

To summarize, we believe that Soviet statistical problems stem from the inability of the Soviet economic model to substitute for the market mechanism of accepting or rejecting goods with new use and quality characteristics. All the attempts since 1965 to introduce such a mechanism failed, for the market has to be real, not simulated. It has hardly been the failure of *Goskomtsen, Gosplan,* or *Goskomstat.* One may like or dislike these bureaucracies, but the job they did in the past was probably adequate for the Stalinist centralized economic model. Therefore, by criticizing Soviet official statistics, S-K, in the first place, attack the Stalinist economic model. But, as long as this model remains intact, the statistical methodology will produce ambiguous results that are subject to interpretation. In particular, based on different measures of product quality, a broad interval of estimates for economic growth will be possible. Thus, without consumer sovereignty, the Soviet statistical debate may never be resolved.

Conclusion

This book is about the theory and practice of Soviet economic growth and inflation. When it comes to the estimation of Soviet economic growth, everyone immediately expresses doubts: "Do you have the data?" Indeed, the issue of the data is crucial, and, not long ago, the main obstacle would have been identified with the inaccessibility of Soviet data. However, as many things have been revised in the short period of *glasnost'*, the Soviets themselves do not know now what the true data are. One comes to such a conclusion not only because of critical writings of some Soviet economists, but also because Gorbachev and forces backing him in the Central Committee encourage these writings and call for a radical reform of Soviet statistics. Thanks to those developments, we now have a better idea of the complexity of measuring "true" rates of Soviet economic growth. This study consequently demonstrates that ambiguities are inevitable and that they are a combination of factors related to the theory, methodology and practices of Soviet planning and statistics.

The theoretical part of the book emphasizes the pattern of change in growth and price models and the methodology of computation used by Soviet planners and statisticians. For example, Soviet price models have been modified repeatedly over the last two decades in an attempt to incorporate the profit component adequately. The model used since 1982 divides the total value of targeted profit among different goods in proportion to their values added, thus redistributing profit in favor of labor intensive industries. Along with the theoretical difficulties of incorporating the profit component, there is a practical problem of finding reasonable levels of cost on which prices would be based. For that purpose, a normative approach which sets costs at the level considered "progressive", i.e., lower than the existing ones, has been used. For each good, the average branch-of-industry cost is computed. As a rule, only specialized firms are considered in the averaging procedure, and those with obsolescent technologies and greater costs are ignored.

The most extensive methodological regulation of price setting is provided for the machine-building and metalworking (MBMW) sector. Prices change primarily in response to cost reductions or input price increases. MBMW branches with rapid turnover of products, such as instrument making or electronics, have better opportunities for raising their profits than other branches. This happens because new goods prices are based on higher-than-average costs that subsequently decline with mastering the technological process. There is, however, no room for cost reduction in those MBMW branches which do not often change their product mix, and their prices depend heavily on input (especially metal) costs. Along with prices, changes in physical and value indicators affect the measurement of Soviet economic growth. Planners often alter the set of physical indicators, in particular for machines and equipment, to reflect productivity, capacity or other qualities that would provide a reliable basis for pricing new products.

Measurement of Soviet economic growth is also affected by the policies of stimulating technological change and product quality improvements. The relationship between product prices and quality improvements is crucial in this respect. The three types of policies generally used for stimulating quality change in new machines and equipment are associated with: 1) temporary prices that are higher than comparable permanent prices; 2) a higher-than-otherwise cost component incorporated in permanent prices and 3) a surcharge for quality improvements. The task of temporary prices is to reimburse the producer for high costs of the starting period of production and to insulate permanent prices from the effects of those high costs. To provide incentives for the producer, the prices of new machines with improved quality are based on the cost of the first year of production, a decision made in 1982. Such a policy has significantly raised the profit markup and, consequently, prices of new products. Another cause of rising prices for new machines has been the recent increase in the surcharge for quality awarded to goods certified as being in the high-quality category.

There may generally be three causes of price inflation in the state sector of the Soviet economy: official price revisions and reforms, introduction of new products and changes in product mix. First, official revisions can push prices in different directions. When prices rise for a specific product group, the rise is usually a result of a chain process of price hikes beginning with the metal and energy producing industries. This type of price change is the one reflected in Soviet price indices. Second, when new products are introduced, their prices are set higher than the prices of existing analogue products. But, to obtain a higher price, the producer has to justify it by the good's quality improvement. If such an improvement is exaggerated, there will be price inflation. This type of price inflation is hard to record, but its existence in the Soviet economy is widely discussed. Third, if prices do not change over time, but the weight of more expensive items in the bundle grows, it is usually an indicator of an increase in the consumer's well being. Yet, in Soviet markets, the authorities decide what to produce, and the buyer takes more expensive items if the cheap ones disappear. In this case changes in the product mix can and probably do affect the price level in the economy.

These and other Soviet realities discussed in the theoretical part of the book have been reflected in the methodology of its practical part. The following several premises summarize our approach. Firstly, since there are no constant prices in the Soviet economy, using base or current year weighted quantity indices would actually mean using prices pertaining to different time periods. Soviet comparable prices resemble conventional constant prices only at the moment when they are first set. For goods introduced later, the first approved price is automatically traced back to the base year. Secondly, Soviet growth indices, whose computation is based on the comparable-price principle, reflect only price changes for those goods that have already been established in production. Thirdly, the quality characteristics of new Soviet goods are taken into account in the process of certifying them and setting their prices. Justification of these characteristics is, therefore, required from the producer.

Consequently, the producer is under pressure, on the one hand, to present fairly the characteristics of new machines and equipment, but, on the other, to inflate them in order to receive a good price for the products. Fourthly, an adequate procedure for measuring Soviet economic growth should contrast the growth of the value of output with the growth of the quality of manufactured goods. For that purpose, we have built an index of the average price adjusted for quality. It compares the rise of the good's average price with its quality characteristics. The resultant estimate shows the growth of the value of output per unit of a good's indicator of quality which could be expressed by an index or a single characteristic.

This methodology was applied to three Soviet industries – automotive, electrotechnical and energy and power machinery. Their specifics were taken into account in building the index of average price adjusted for quality. For example, according to the standards applied by the Soviet pricing authorities, the capacity or power of equipment characterizes quality in the electrotechnical industry and energy and power machinery. For the automotive industry, the construction of a more complex index of quality was required since it is impossible to single out a characteristic of cars or trucks that would dominate or represent the others. For this reason, a quality index for passenger cars includes the following characteristics: the number of occupants, size, weight, engine volume, horsepower and fuel efficiency. A similar index for trucks includes the indicator of maximum load, instead of the number of occupants.

For passenger car production, inflationary growth was studied at both the wholesale and retail levels. An important conclusion is that inflation at the retail level of Soviet passenger car production was significantly higher than at the wholesale level in the 1970-82 period. As a matter of fact, the overall average inflation rate at the retail level was more than twice that at the wholesale level (3.8 and 1.6 percent, respectively). Other than the difference in magnitudes, however, there is similarity in the behavior of the inflationary component. At both levels inflation plays a much greater role in the first of the two six-year periods and tends to subside in the second.

Another conclusion is that the parallel analysis of the output growth in both wholesale and retail prices sheds some light on the important question of the driving force behind price increases in the Soviet economy. Our analysis demonstrates that the Soviet authorities limited wholesale price inflation for Soviet car production more than they limited retail price inflation. If the widespread belief that plant management introduces cosmetic alterations in product quality and, under that umbrella, inflates prices were the case, the wholesale prices would be the first to reflect such behavior. But this is hardly true for Soviet passenger autos whose retail prices are several times wholesale, so that any given cost increase would be a higher percentage of the wholesale price than of a retail price. We use a simple example to illustrate. Suppose that a good's production cost is 80 rubles, profit 20 rubles, and turnover tax 300 rubles. The wholesale price is then 100 rubles, and the retail price 400 rubles. Further suppose that the cost rises to 90 rubles, in which case the new wholesale price equals 110 rubles (a 10 percent increase) and the retail price 410 rubles (a 2.5 percent increase). Our analysis consequently shows a consistent rise in the ratio of retail to wholesale car prices from 2.5 in 1970 to 2.7 in 1976 and 3.2 in 1982. This accounts for greater retail than wholesale price inflation over the 1970-1982 period.

For Soviet truck production, we find the lowest inflationary rates. The overall inflation rate from 1970 to 1982 was only 0.6 percent, and the 1970-76 period even experienced a deflationary growth. The analysis shows that one of the reasons for that was a reported rise in the fuel efficiency of trucks in the first of the two periods. In the second period, quality improvements became less visible, and the resultant inflation rate rose to two percent. (Adjusting fuel efficiency to reflect load capacity could affect this conclusion.) As a combination of passenger car and truck production, the automotive industry was characterized by a modest annual inflation rate of 1.2 percent in the 1970-82 period. Although the inflation rates we found discount the official average growth indices for the Soviet automotive industry, they nevertheless support the fact of impressive growth, especially for cars (12.4 percent per annum).

For the electrotechnical industry, no quality change in terms of the capacity of machines and equipment was revealed. As a matter of fact, the index of average price, both adjusted and unadjusted for quality, rose at an average rate of 4.4 percent in the 1960-75 period. As a result, the real average growth rate appears to be 5.9, not the 10.6 percent officially reported. Soviet energy and power machinery is characterized by higher inflation and, consequently, lower real growth than the electrotechnical and, especially, automotive industries. We estimated the nominal growth rate for the output of this branch in current prices to be equal to 3.3 percent, of which three quarters, or 2.5 percentage points, was inflationary. Moreover, energy and power machinery experienced a pattern of sharply accelerated inflation, at the rates of 0.4, 2.1 and 5.1 percent by five-year period from 1970 to 1985. As a result, in the 1981-85 period there was negative real growth at an average annual rate of 1.1 percent.

Averaging the inflation and growth rates for the three industries, representative of the variety of Soviet machines and equipment, yields estimates for the entire MBMW sector. For example, the 1971-75 sector's growth rate is found to be 6.3 percent, which lies in between the estimates by Val'tukh-Lavrovskii and Seliunin-Khanin. The generalization of these and other results makes us aware of the limitations of measuring Soviet economic growth. The fact that the Soviet writers have obtained different estimates of the country's economic growth on the basis of the same information can be interpreted as that the "true" growth rates may never have been estimated.

There are intrinsic ambiguities in estimating growth in industries whose product characteristics constantly change. In a free-market economy, the consumer accepts some of these changes and rejects the others. In the Soviet economy, the authorities can only use such "objective" product characteristics as capacity, size and weight. Therefore, if we believe that the improvement of the "objective" characteristics reflects genuine quality improvement equivalent to price increases, there is a possibility that we will have to accept the official Soviet growth rates (8 percent for national income in the 1928-85 period). Yet if we see no quality change in the Soviet economy, we may end up with the growth rates estimated by Seliunin and Khanin (in the range of 3.3 percent for the same period) or by other critics of Soviet official statistics. Although a position in between the two extremes seems to be more realistic, there may be no way to justify it. As the Soviets now admit, without help from the market, their planned economy is inherently unable to answer the question of what to produce. The extent of damage, according to both the authorities and critics, is staggering. By not knowing consumer demand, the Soviet economy produces goods that are nominally counted as components of GNP but are actually stockpiled, abandoned or liquidated. By not knowing how the consumer values goods and services, they may change output characteristics in a way that, under the condition of consumer sovereignty, could be interpreted as deterioration. The problem of low reliability of Soviet statistics may therefore not rest with the mere distortions in the data or methodology. The same outcome could probably be expected if a Soviet-type model were used in the U.S. economy.

Not surprisingly, high expectations of the improvement in Soviet statistics are associated with the current economic reform. But that reform has yet to address the fundamental problems of the Soviet socioeconomic model. The self-sufficiency and self-investment provisions introduced so far are based on the use of arbitrary normatives and prices and may only aggravate the inefficient distribution of inputs in the Soviet economy. On the other hand, the new emphasis on individual, rather than collective economic liability in production can eventually pay off, but this would occur only if the current reform is viewed as the beginning of the process, not its final stage. A way of tying individual economic interests to the interests of "socialist enterprises" would be the introduction of worker equity ownership.[13] This would make workers more sensitive to input spending, outputs and product quality, so that other measures promoting market competition, freer pricing and greater consumer sovereignty could be easier to undertake. But there should be incentives outside of the factory, too. Thus, if people are encouraged to work better, money they earn must acquire real goods and services.

This is, of course, easier said than done. Many people would have a similar menu for the improvement of the Soviet economy in mind, but they would differ on implementation. There is an intense debate in both the Soviet and western literature on the support (or opposition) to such reform. From the economic standpoint, the debate does not make sense; it simply means that the reform's economic mechanism does not work. As usual, too much emphasis is placed on one's conscience, while the reform should appeal to one's pocket. People ask themselves if they are better off. Therefore, if the reform architects envision layoffs, higher prices and greater overall uncertainty, they should give people some improvements now, rather than offer only promises to be filled in an uncertain future. Realizing this, Gorbachev should have started with massive investment in the consumer goods sector, to achieve at least a temporary improvement with a psychological impact. Instead, he invested in a long-term modernization program, again in heavy industry. Even assuming dramatic improvements in machines and technology, the Soviet economy is not ready to utilize them efficiently. Moreover, the stumbling block in the way of the Soviet consumer goods sector is a shortage of high quality agricultural raw materials rather than a lack of machines.

In this book, we analyze a broad spectrum of theoretical and methodological issues related to measuring Soviet economic growth. We also demonstrate the techniques of estimating the growth of three Soviet industries producing machines and equipment and then generalize the findings for the MBMW sector. But when it comes to the economy as a whole, we stop short of drawing conclusions. It is clear that, depending on the assumptions concerning product quality change, an entire array of growth rates for the Soviet economy may be feasible. Therefore, though we prefer the critics' estimates to the official Soviet growth figures, we believe that, with consumers' valuations unknown, there are no grounds for any particular choice. In assessing Soviet economic growth, there are more questions than answers. People may come forward with new estimates and new claims, but it is doubtful that a consensus could ever be reached. It is clear that further debate on Soviet statistics, both inside and outside of the Soviet Union, will be helpful.

Notes

1. The reader can find these specifics in a comprehensive handbook by Glushkov, et al. (1985).
2. Multifactor productivity has been measured by the Bureau of Labor Statistics of the U.S. Department of Labor since 1983 (see Grossman, 1984).
3. The idea of the approach described here follows Kushnirsky (1985).
4. This is documented for Soviet machines. In a research paper of the National Foreign Assessment Center (1980), 245 Soviet machines and their U.S. analogues are compared. The U.S. machines are usually lighter, more productive, more versatile or more accurate.
5. In their report, Nolting and Feshbach (1981, p.44) estimated about one million researchers in the U.S.S.R. in 1979.
6. When a new organizational form is created, only advantages are often seen from the beginning. Some of these are discussed by Beliakov (1986, p.2).
7. Downward and upward revisions of the reported 1981-85 investment growth figures took place several times in 1986, and conflicting percentages were given in Ryzhkov's and Gorbachev's speeches.
8. Such concerns were expressed in discussions organized prior to the approval of the guidelines for the 12th five-year plan (1986-90). Interesting, for example, are comments by Palterovich (*Voprosy Ekonomiki* 1, 1986, p.66) and by Loginov (*Planovoe Khoziaistvo* 1, 1986, p.21). The fact of inviting scholars to express their views on the final draft of the plan in public has been unprecedented since the mid-1960s.
9. This information is from Nekrasov and Troitskii (1981, pp. 236-55), Neporozhnii (1977 and 1980) and Grigor'ev and Zorin (1980 and 1987).

10. Ibid.
11. We realize that this information, as noted in Section 6.2, may be adjusted for the purpose of balancing the input-output table or for other purposes. Still, it is the best source of information on the total output of the electrotechnical industry.
12. Grossman (1960) translates the term *"pripiska"* as a "write-up."
13. On the model of worker equity ownership, see Kushnirsky (1987, pp. 71-80).

References

V. Adamov, Chto stoit za indeksami, *Ekonomicheskaia Gazeta* 29, 1987.

S. N. Afriat, *The Price Index*, (Cambridge: Cambridge University Press, 1977).

T. K. Alferova and G. T. Kaleniuk, *Sovershenstvovanie optovykh tsen na produktsiiu mashinostroeniia*, (Kiev: Vyshcha Shkola, 1984).

V. E. Astaf'ev, et al., *Ekonomika electrotekhnicheskoi promyshlennosti*, (Moscow: Energiia, 1967).

V. E. Astaf'ev, et al., *Ekonomika electrotekhnicheskoi promyshlennosti*, (Moscow: Energiia, 1975).

V. E. Astaf'ev, et al., *Ekonomika electrotekhnicheskoi promyshlennosti*, (Moscow: Energiia, 1977).

R. A. Azamatov, et al., *Avtomobili KamAZ: tekhnicheskoe obsluzhivanie i remont*, (Moscow: Transport, 1984).

K. Bakis, Opredelenie i analiz ekonomicheskikh rezul'tatov vnedreniia novoi tekhniki na promyshlennom predpriiatii, *Planovoe Khoziaistvo* 1, 1975.

V. P. Beliakov, Na triokh kitakh, Interview, *Izvestiia*, Aug. 19, 1986.

N. Belov, Povyshat' uroven' analiticheskoi raboty, *Vestnik Statistiki* 11, 1986.

Abram Bergson, On Soviet Real Investment Growth, *Soviet Studies*, Vol. 39, No. 3 (Jul. 1987).

Igor Birman, The Financial Crisis in the USSR, *Soviet Studies*, Vol. 32, No. 1 (Jan. 1980).

T. Boldyreva, Kuda zhe zavezli nas Zhiguli?, *EKO* 5, 1985.

S. H. Cohn, A Comment on Alec Nove ..., *Soviet Studies*, Vol. 33, No. 2 (Apr. 1981).

R. Converse, Index of Industrial Production in the USSR: Measures of Economic Growth and Development, 1959-1980, (Washington, D.C.: *Joint Economic Committee*, U.S. Congress, Dec. 1982).

K. Cowling and J. Cubbin, Hedonic Price Indices for United Kingdom Cars, *The Economic Journal*, Sep. 1972.

S. F. Demikhovskii, et al., *Ustroistvo i ekspluatatsiia avtomobilei Zhiguli i Moskvich*, (Moscow: DOSAAF, 1985).

Padma Desai, Soviet Growth Retardation, in Papers and Proceedings of the Ninety-Eight Annual Meeting of the American Economic Association, *American Economic Review*, May 1986.

Dogovornye optovye tseny, *Ekonomicheskaia Gazeta* 5, 1988.

F. A. Dronov, ed., *Tsena i effektivnost' proizvodstva*, (Minsk: Nauka i Tekhnika, 1979).

L. A. Ermak, Sovershenstvovanie tsenoobrazovaniia v mashinostroenii v khode peresmotra optovykh tsen, *Teoriia i Praktika Tsenoobrazovaniia* 3, 1982.

Excerpts, Uluchstat' delo statistiki, Meeting of the Collegium of TsSU, *Vestnik Statistiki* 5, 1987.

V. K. Fal'tsman, *Potentsial investitsionnogo mashinostroeniia*, (Moscow: Nauka, 1981).

V. K. Fal'tsman, *Proizvodstvennyi potentsial SSSR: voprosy prognozirovaniia*, (Moscow: Ekonomika, 1987).

Irving Fisher, *The Making of Index Numbers. A Study of Their Varieties, Tests, and Reliability*, (Boston: Houghton Mifflin, 1927).

K. S. Fuchadzhi and N. N. Striuk, *Avtomobil' Zaporozhets*, (Moscow: Transport, 1984).

Dimitri M. Gallik, et al., *Conversion of Soviet Input-Output Tables to Producers' Prices: The 1959 Reconstructed Table*, (Washington, D.C., 1975).

Dimitri M. Gallik, et al., *Input-Output Structure of the Soviet Economy: 1972*, (Washington, D.C., 1983).

E. K. Gerasimova, Tsenoobrazovanie na sredstva proizvodstva, *Voprosy Tsenoobrazovaniia* 9, 1976.

N. T. Glushkov, Faktor uskoreniia tekhicheskogo progressa, *Ekonomicheskaia Gazeta* 6, 1983.

N. T. Glushkov, et al., *Spravochnik po tsenoobrazovaniiu*, (Moscow: Ekonomika, 1985).

Stanislaw Gomulka, Soviet Growth Slowdown: Duality, Maturity, and Innovation, in Papers and Proceedings of the Ninety-Eight Annual Meeting of the American Economic Association, *American Economic Review*, May 1986.

M. S. Gorbachev, Speech at the 27th party congress, *Pravda*, Feb. 26, 1986(A).

M. S. Gorbachev, Speech at the Plenum of the Central Committee, *Pravda*, June 17, 1986(B).

V. Ya. Gorfinkel', *Nauchno-tekhnicheskii progress i sebestoimost' produktsii mashinostroeniia*, (Leningrad: Mashinostroenie, 1981).

Douglas F. Greer, *Industrial Organization and Public Policy*, (New York: Macmillan, 1984).

V. A. Grigor'ev and V. M. Zorin, eds., *Teploenergetika i teplotekhnika, Spravochnik*, (Moscow: Energiia, 1980).

V. A. Grigor'ev and V. M. Zorin, eds., *Teploenergetika i teplotekhnika, Spravochnik*, (Moscow: Energiia, 1987).

Elliott S. Grossman, Productivity Measures, in F. J. Fabozzi and H. I. Greenfield, eds., *The Handbook on Economic and Financial Measures*, (Homewood, IL: Dow Jones-Irwin, 1984).

Gregory Grossman, *Soviet Statistics of Physical Output of Industrial Commodities. Their Compilation and Quality*, (Princeton, NJ: Princeton University Press, 1960).

Philip Hanson, Soviet Real Investment Growth: A Reply to Bergson, *Soviet Studies*, Vol. 39, No. 3 (Jul. 1987).

Iu. V. Iakovets, *Tseny v planovom khoziaistve*, (Moscow: Ekonomika, 1974).

Instruction, Opredelenie optovykh tsen na novuiu mashinostroitel'nuiu produktsiiu proizvodstvenno-tekhnicheskogo naznacheniia, *Ekonomicheskaia Gazeta* 51, 1987.

Instruction, Poriadok attestatsii promyshlennoi produktsii po dvum kategoriiam katchestva, *Ekonomicheskaia Gazeta* 13, 1984.

I. Isaev, Plan, standart, kachestvo, *Planovoe Khoziaistvo* 12, 1983.

The July 1985 Resolution of the Central Committee and Council of Ministers on New Economic Mechanisms and Their Impact on the Acceleration of Technological Change, *Ekonomicheskaia Gazeta* 32, 1985.

E. M. Karlik, *Ekonomika mashinostroeniia*, (Leningrad: Mashinostroenie, 1977).

G. I. Khanin, Al'ternativnye otsenki rezul'tatov khoziaistvennoi deiatel'nosti proizvodstvennykh iacheek promyshlennosti, *Izvestiia Akademii Nauk SSSR, Seriia Ekonomicheskaia* 6, 1981.

G. I. Khanin, Puti sovershenstvovaniia informatsionnogo obespecheniia svodnykh planovykh narodnokhoziaistvennykh raschetov, *Izvestiia Akademii Nauk SSSR, Seriia Ekonomicheskaia* 3, 1984.

S. Kheinman, Zadachi razvitiia mashinostroeniia, *Voprosy Ekonomiki* 8, 1981.

Vladimir Kontorovich, Soviet Growth Slowdown: Econometric vs. Direct Evidence, in Papers and Proceedings of the Ninety-Eight Annual Meeting of the American Economic Association, *American Economic Review*, May 1986.

M. Korolev, Zadachi perestroiki statistiki, *Vestnik Statistiki* 4, 1987.

A. A. Koshuta and L. I. Rozenova, *Kachestvo i tseny produktsii mashinostroeniia*, (Moscow: Mashinostroenie, 1976).

Barry L. Kostinsky, *The Reconstructed 1966 Soviet Input-Output Tables: Revised Purchasers' and Producers' Prices Tables*, (Washington, D.C., 1976).

Barry L. Kostinsky, Preliminary Estimates of the 1982 Soviet Input-Output Table, Working Paper, 1987.

R. Kozhevnikov, Ekonomicheskoe stimulirovanie nauchno-tekhnicheskogo progressa, *Planovoe Khoziaistvo* 3, 1986.

G. A. Kraiukhin, ed., *Ekonomika mashinostroitel'noi promyshlennosti*, (Moscow: Vysshaia Shkola, 1987).

Kratkii avtomobil'nyi spravochnik NIIAT, (Moscow: Transport, 1985).

P. Krylov and P. Kanunnikov, Ispol'zovanie sopostavimykh optovykh tsen v planirovanii, *Planovoe Khoziaistvo* 9, 1977.

R. B. Kuliev, Kovarstvo defitsita, *Ekonomicheskaia Gazeta* 3, 1986.

G. Ya. Kurbatova and V. M. Sokolov, *Opimizatsiia razvitiia i razmeshcheniia proizvodstva v mashinostroitel'noi promyshlennosti*, (Novosibirsk: Nauka, 1978).

Fyodor I. Kushnirsky, Inflation Soviet Style, *Problems of Communism*, Jan.-Feb. 1984.

Fyodor I. Kushnirsky, Methodological Aspects in Building Soviet Price Indices, *Soviet Studies*, No. 4 (Oct. 1985).

Fyodor I. Kushnirsky, Soviet Economic Reform: An Analysis and a Model, *Comparative Economic Studies*, No. 4, 1987.

R. E. Leggett, Measuring Inflation in the Soviet Machine Building Sector, 1960-1973, *Journal of Comparative Economics*, Vol. 5, Jun. 1981.

308

A. Leshchevskii, Strategiia mashinostroeniia, *Ekonomicheskaia Gazeta* 29, 1988.

Herbert S. Levine, Possible Causes of the Deterioration of Soviet Productivity Growth in the Period 1976-80, in *Soviet Economy in the 1980's: Problems and Prospects*, Part 1, (Washington, D.C.: Joint Economic Committee, Congress of the United States, 1982).

I. I. Lukinov, *Vosproizvodstvo i tseny*, (Moscow: Ekonomika, 1977).

A. Malygin, Obnovlenie osnovnykh proizvodstvennykh fondov, *Planovoe Khoziaistvo* 7, 1985.

National Foreign Assessment Center, USSR and the United States: Price Ratios for Machinery, 1967 Rubles–1972 Dollars, Volume II, (Washington, D.C., 1980).

A. M. Nekrasov and A. A. Troitskii, eds., *Energetika SSSR v 1981-1985 godakh*, (Moscow: Energoizdat, 1981).

I. E. Nelidov, *Ekonomika energomashinostroeniia*, (Moscow: Vysshaia Shkola, 1979).

P. S. Neporozhnii, ed., *Elektrifikatsiia SSSR*, (Moscow: Energiia, 1977).

P. S. Neporozhnii, ed., *60 let Leninskogo plana GOELRO*, (Moscow: Energiia, 1980).

Yu. Nikitin, Resursy otrasli i ikh ispol'zovanie, *Planovoe Khoziaistvo* 1, 1984.

L. E. Nolting and M. Feshbach, Statistics on Research and Development Employment in the U.S.S.R., (Washington, D.C., 1981).

Alec Nove, A Note on Growth, Investment and Price Indices, *Soviet Studies*, Vol. 33, No. 1 (Jan. 1981).

Alec Nove, Soviet Real Investment Growth: Are Investment Volume Statistics Overstated? A Reply to Bergson, *Soviet Studies*, Vol. 39, No. 3 (Jul. 1987).

Gur Ofer, Soviet Economic Growth: 1928-1985, *Journal of Economic Literature*, Dec. 1987.

Osnovnye napravleniia ekonomicheskogo i sotsial'nogo razvitiia SSSR na 1986-1990 gody i na period do 2000 goda, *Ekonomicheskaia Gazeta* 46, 1985.

D. M. Palterovich, Obnovlenie oborudovaniia i tekhnicheskoe perevooruzhenie proizvodstva, *Planovoe Khoziaistvo* 9, 1980.

S. F. Pokropivnyi, et al., *Ekonomika promyshlennogo proizvodstva*, (Kiev: Tekhnika, 1982).

A. A. Reut, Plan v usloviiakh samofinansirovaniia, Interview, *Ekonomicheskaia Gazeta* 1, 1988.

L. Rozenova, Tsena i effektivnost' produktsii mashinostroeniia, *Voprosy Ekonomiki* 2, 1984.

L. Rozenova, Tsena i kachestvo tekhniki, *Voprosy Ekonomiki* 2, 1986.

L. Rozenova, Tsena i kachestvo tekhniki, *Ekonomicheskaia Gazeta* 5, 1987.

Boris Rumer, Soviet Investment Policy: Unresolved Problems, *Problems of Communism*, Sep.-Oct. 1982.

N. I. Ryzhkov, Ob osnovnykh napravleniiakh ekonomicheskogo i sotsial'nogo razvitiia SSSR na 1986-1990 gody i na period do 2000 goda, *Ekonomicheskaia Gazeta* 11, 1986(A).

N. I. Ryzhkov, O gosudarstvennom plane ekonomicheskogo i sotsial'nogo razvitiia SSSR na 1986-1990 gody, *Ekonomicheskaia Gazeta* 26, 1986(B).

Vasilii Seliunin and Grigorii Khanin, Lukavaia tsifra, *Novyi Mir* 2, 1987.

V. Senchagov and V. Ostapenko, Znachenie amortizatsii v tekhnicheskoi rekonstruktsii, *Voprosy Ekonomiki* 1, 1981.

V. Shalimov, Uchet ekonomicheskogo effekta v pooshchritel'nykh nadbavkakh, *Voprosy Ekonomiki* 6, 1981(A).

V. E. Shalimov, *Khozraschetnyi mekhanizm upravleniia tekhnicheskim progressom na predpriiatii*, (Moscow: Ekonomika, 1981) (B).

Nikolai Shmelev, Avansy i dolgi, *Novyi Mir* 6, 1987.

L. M. Shugurov and V. P. Shirshov, Avtomobili strany Sovetov, (Moscow: DOSAAF, 1980).

L. M. Shugurov and V. P. Shirshov, Avtomobili strany Sovetov, (Moscow: DOSAAF, 1983).

Robert Sobel, *Car Wars*, (N. Y.: Dutton, 1984).

J. Steiner, Inflation in Soviet Industry and Machine Building and Metalworking, 1969-1975, (Washington, D.C., 1978).

A. Stepun, O ratsional'nom napravlenii kapital'nykh vlozhenii v 11i piatiletke, *Planovoe Khoziaistvo* 10, 1981.

Tsennik No. 42 dlia pereotsenki avtomobilei, avtobusov vsekh vidov, avtopritsepov, motorollerov, spetsializirovannogo avtogarazhnogo i avtoremontnogo oborudovaniia na l ianvaria 1973 goda, (Moscow: Transport, 1972).

Tsennik No. 110 dlia pereotsenki avtomobilei, avtobusov, avtopritsepov i motorollerov, (Moscow: Atomizdat, 1970).

R. P. Valevich, *Spros, predlozhenie i ikh uchet pri planirovanii tsen*, (Minsk: Nauka i Tekhnika, 1979).

K. K. Val'tukh and B. L. Lavrovskii, Proizvodstvennyi potentsial strany, *EKO* 2, 1986.

D. P. Velikanov, ed., *Razvitie avtomobil'nykh transportnykh sredstv*, (Moscow: Transport, 1984).

V. A. Vershigora, et al., *Avtomobili Zhiguli modelei VAZ-2101, 2102, 21011: ustroistvo i remont*, (Moscow: Transport, 1984).

B. V. Vlasov, et al., *Ekonomika avtomobil'noi promyshlennosti*, (Moscow: Vysshaia Shkola, 1973).

B. V. Vlasov, et al., *Ekonomika avtomobil'noi promyshlennosti i traktorostroeniia*, (Moscow: Vysshaia Shkola, 1978).

Michael Waterson, *Economic Theory of the Industry*, (Cambridge: Cambridge University Press, 1984).

Toli Welihozkiy, Automobiles and the Soviet Consumer, In *Soviet Economy in a Time of Change*, (Washington, D.C.: Joint Economic Committee, Congress of the U.S., 1979).

P. Wiles, Soviet Consumption and Investment Prices, and the Meaningfulness of Real Investment, *Soviet Studies*, Vol. 34, No. 2 (Apr. 1982).

Zakon o gosudarstvennom predpriiatii (ob'edinenii), *Ekonomicheskaia Gazeta* 28, 1987.

K. I. Zamaraev, MNTK: shagi stanovleniia, Interview, *Ekonomicheskaia Gazeta* 21, 1986.

A. G. Zav'ialkov, *Tseny i tsenoobrazovanie v SSSR*, (Minsk: Vysheishaia Shkola, 1981).

Index